LIFE
IN THE
KINGDOM
TODAY

by Harley M. Fiddler

Vabella Publishing

Vabella Publishing
P.O. Box 1052
Carrollton, Georgia 30112

13-digit ISBN 978-1-938230-01-1

Library of Congress Control Number: 2011945951

10 9 8 7 6 5 4 3 2 1

Dedicated To

Donna

The lovely lady who is my companion of fifty-six years and faithful dedicated co-laborer in the Gospel. Her wisdom and depth of spirituality has been a constant source of inspiration and encouragement to me, our family, and the many friends who have known her over the years.

Contents

Foreword

I met Harley Fiddler a number of years ago at a Crusade in Columbus, Ohio. From that day, we became friends and through the years that friendship became a true brotherly relationship. Since then we have traveled to several foreign countries together where I have seen him at his best, doing what he loves most, "Mission Work." Harley and his faithful wife Donna are dedicated servants of the Master. Their goal is to reach as much of the lost world as possible. It is an honor for me to write the foreword for this great book. Harley has had a passionate desire to write this for some time.

Harley is a true student of the Word of God and expresses such with each page of this volume. His understanding of faith, giving, especially Faith-Promise Giving, loving, living a life of faith and believing God for the impossible shines forth like a beacon from these pages.

Through the years his teaching on Faith Promise Giving has been an inspiration to many churches and leaders to expand their faith in giving to reach the multitudes of un-churched people-groups. In these meetings he encourages all to whom he speaks to never give up but to believe God for bigger and greater things. With his assistance, encouragement and enthusiasm they have been able to give many thousands of dollars to missions, fulfilling what Jesus said: "Go ye into all the world and preach the Gospel."

On these pages Harley reveals his compassion and love for God's creation - the human race. These are some of the most complete and sound teachings I have ever read. Presented as sound doctrine your faith will increase as you read and absorb these truths. Full of Scripture, these pages can become a great Bible Study Guide.

R. Richard Edgar

Acknowledgments

I will forever be indebted to the many instructors whose personal friendships and powerful ministries have poured eternal truth and blessings into my life. Much of the content in this book is the result of what I have gleaned from these servants of God, and found to be very practical in my own life and walk with Christ.

I am very grateful for the excellent work that Michele Harper did in critiquing the manuscript and for her correction and suggestions.

I want to acknowledge our grandson, Wesley, for his designing the cover page of the book. Wesley is an architect student in his junior year at Ohio State University.

I want to acknowledge the multiplied thousands of students that have been in my classes throughout the world, and have given me the opportunity to teach these lessons.

Most of all, I want to thank God and His faithfulness, for saving me and calling me into the ministry of preaching this glorious Gospel of the Kingdom that I have enjoyed for nearly the past sixty years. I want to thank Him for giving me my high school sweetheart, Donna, for her unceasing love and support for me and the call on my life, and our three beautiful children (The Fiddler's Three) Ron, Debbie, and Cheryl who have been a great blessing, inspiration and encouragement to me.

All that is good in here reflects that which comes from the Author of Life. All that falls short is from yours truly

Harley M. Fiddler

PART I

Introduction

Understanding Life in the Kingdom

Introduction

There are only two Kingdoms—God's and Satan's! God's Kingdom is the Kingdom of Light and Life. Satan's is the Kingdom of Darkness and Death. Jesus makes this clear distinction in John 10:10, *"The thief comes only in order to steal and kill and destroy. I came that they may have and enjoy life, and have it in abundance (to the full, till it overflows)"* (AMP).

Furthermore, the Apostle Paul makes the same distinction in Colossians 1: 12-13 *"Giving thanks to the Father, Who has qualified and made us fit to share the portion which is the inheritance of the saints (God's holy people) in the Light. [The Father] has delivered and drawn us to Himself out of the control and the dominion of darkness and has transferred us into the kingdom of the Son of His love"* (AMP).

In this study we will be focusing our attention upon God's Kingdom, and our living in that Kingdom now in this present time. Before we get into the specifics, however, it will be advantageous to look at some background about the Kingdom.

A general overview of the Kingdom

The subject of the Kingdom of God and the Kingdom of Heaven has for many years been one of much discussion, debate, and vast differences of opinion. It is not my intent to cloud the issues or muddy the waters worse than what they may appear to be. However, it is my desire to share some truths that have been made very real to me and have been a wonderful blessing in my life. I am convinced that if you will approach this study with a listening ear, open mind, and receptive heart, you too, will experience the reality and blessing of these truths.

In approaching this study, as with all studies of God's Word, it is important to remember that the rules of hermeneutics (*the science and principles of Biblical exegesis and interpretation*) must be carefully followed when giving interpretation to any Bible passage or doctrine. We simply cannot impose our preconceived ideas upon the meaning of the text. We must allow the Scriptures to speak for themselves— and they will!

One of the most important fundamental rules of interpretation is to gather from the Scriptures themselves the precise meaning the writers intended to convey. "In doing this, one must take the *Bible as literal when it is at all possible.* When a statement is found that cannot possibly be literal, as Jesus being a "door", or of a woman being clothed with the sun and standing on the moon and on her head a crown of twelve stars, or of land animals coming out of the sea, and other statements which are obviously not literal, then we know the language is figurative. In such cases we must get the literal truth conveyed by the figurative language, and the truth intended to be conveyed will be as literal as if it were expressed in literal language without the use of such figures." **1**

Adherence to this basic rule is especially important when explaining the Kingdom of Heaven and the Kingdom of God. I have seen this rule ignored by authors of numerous books written on this subject over the past several decades that have resulted in much confusion, doctrinal error and spiritual harm.

One such teaching about the Kingdom, for example—to show the danger of not adhering to the rules of interpretation—is that we the Church will establish the Kingdom on earth, and then the King will be able to return to rule in His Kingdom. This teaching asserts that Christians will take the positions of authority in politics, governments, economics, religion, etc. As a result, things will get better and better until everything is perfect for the King to come, and we then shall present Him the Kingdom. Doesn't that sound great? There is only one thing wrong with this interpretation. It is false! There can be no Kingdom without a King! When Jesus returns He will bring His Kingdom with Him from heaven. (Matt.25: 31-46; Rev. 11:15; 19: 11-20; Zech. 14; Isa. 9:6-7; Dan. 2:44-45; 7:13-27; Lk.1:32-33).

It is interesting to note, some of these books have been on the market twenty, thirty years or longer and things haven't been getting better and better as they teach, but rather world conditions are getting worse! In fact, Christians are not in the majority and authority in human governments and world economies, but rather a minority that suffers much persecution. Furthermore, I urge you to look at the signs of the times! Everything Jesus, the apostle Paul and other New Testaments writers said would transpire in the last days before our Lord's coming is happening before our very eyes.

The Scriptures reveal many signs to watch for but the following five signs are glaring indicators that the times are not getting better but worse as we watch them come to pass:

1. **Moral and Spiritual fall out:** Jesus said, *"But as the days of Noah were, so shall also the coming of the Son of man be"* (Matt. 24:37). There is a perfect parallel between the day of Noah and our day. Notice three particular parallels:

   a. Decadent, rebellious attitude of the people
   b. A spirit of apathy and unconcern for Godliness and righteousness
   c. A spirit of anarchy and lawlessness abounding

2. **Cosmic Unrest:** *"And you will hear of wars and rumors of wars. See that you are not troubled; for all these things must come to pass, but the end is not yet. For nation will rise against nation, and kingdom against kingdom. And there will be famines, pestilences, and earthquakes in various places. All these are the beginning (birth-pangs) of sorrow"* (Matt. 24:6, 7). Notice two important features here:

   a. The upheaval of nations- wars and rumors of war
   b. The upheaval of nature- famines, pestilences, and increased earthquakes in various places, as well as tornadoes and Tsunami's

3. **The Incredible Increase of Knowledge:** *"But you, Daniel shut up the words, and seal the book until the time of the end; many shall run to and fro, and knowledge shall increase"* (Daniel 12:4). None can deny we are the generation that has witnessed the phenomenal breakthrough, explosion, and advance in scientific knowledge and technology.

4. **Distress of Nations:** Jesus said, *"…for there shall be great distress in the land, and wrath upon this people"* (Luke 21:23-25). Nations are in great distress over world-wide poverty, defying debilitating diseases, and the world-wide economic crisis.

5. **Perilous Times and Perilous Men:** *"But know this, that in the last days perilous times will come:"* (2Tim. 3:1-5).

You can readily see that Jesus and the writers of the New Testament didn't teach things would get better but rather worse! Therefore, we must conclude that such teaching that Christians are going to make everything get better and better then Christ can come and rule His kingdom is not in keeping with the true law of enterpretation.

As we continue to pursue this subject please bear in mind the Kingdom of God is both a present possession and a future hope. The teaching of Jesus concerning the Kingdom has three aspects: (1) the Kingdom of Heaven in this present time (Matt. 3:2, 4:17, 5:3, 10, 19-20; 13:3-8, 18-23, 24-30, 47-50); (2) the Kingdom of God existing in the hearts of redeemed men (John 3:3,5; Rom.14: 17); (3) and the visible Kingdom of the Messiah that He will set up when He returns (Matt. 24:14, 25:31-34, Luke 19:12-27, Daniel 2:34-45).

The term *Kingdom of Heaven* is found 33 times in the writings of Matthew only. It is a *dispensational* term and refers to the Messiah's kingdom on the Earth. It was introduced by John the Baptist, preached by Jesus, and offered to the Jews. The Jews, however, rejected the kingdom and its further proclamation (Matt. 22:2-7; Acts 1:6-7; 3:19-26). "Thereafter the earthly realization of the kingdom was postponed, and is now in abeyance until the return of the King from glory (Acts 3:20; Rev. 19:11-21). The Kingdom of Heaven is not now the literal reign of Heaven over the Earth, but is the *sphere of profession*, or the professing Christian world. In the Millennium, the Kingdom of Heaven ceases to be the *sphere of profession* and becomes the real, literal kingdom of the Son of Man, which was rejected at the beginning of this age." **2**

The term *Kingdom of God* is used 72 times, and "means the sovereignty of God over the universe and includes and embraces the Kingdom of Heaven and all other realms in the whole universe. Anything said of the kingdom of heaven can also be said of the kingdom of God, because the former is only the earthly dispensational aspect of the latter. Because the kingdom of heaven is part of the kingdom of God some things could be said of both, but there are other things said of the kingdom of God that could not be spoken of the kingdom of heaven." **3**

Understanding the difference between the two Kingdoms will prevent confusion and erroneous interpretation of related Scriptures. Finnis Dake's list of contrasts can be very helpful in making the distinction between the two Kingdoms and giving proper interpretation:

THE KINGDOM OF HEAVEN	THE KINGDOM OF GOD
1. Messiah as <u>king</u> (Jn. 18: 37; Rev. 20: 6)	God as king (1Cor. 15: 28)
2. <u>From</u> heaven, *under* Heaven (Jn. 18: 36; Dan. 7: 13)	In heaven and earth (Ps. 103: 19)
3. <u>Upon</u> earth only (Jn. 18: 37; Rev. 5: 10)	In heaven-earth (1Cor. 15: 28)
4. Scope <u>limited</u> (Zech. 14: 9)	Scope unlimited (Rev. 4: 11; 5:11)
5. <u>Political</u> (Isa. 9:7; Dan.7: 14)	Moral and spiritual (Rom. 14: 17)
6. <u>Future</u> (Mt. 6: 10; 2Tim. 4: 1)	Past, present and future (Ps. 90: 2)
7. <u>Under</u> Christ (Ps. 2: 6; Lk. 1: 32-33)	God over all (Ps. 103: 19)
8. <u>Given</u> to Christ (Dan. 7: 13-14; Lk. 1: 32)	Not given (Ps. 10: 16)
9. <u>Begins</u> at second advent (Zech. 14; 2 Tim. 4: 1)	Is now (Ps. 90: 2)
10. <u>Under</u> heaven (Dan. 7:27; Rev. 11: 15)	Over all (Ps. 103: 19)
11. <u>Jewish</u>-earthly (Isa. 9: 7; Lk. 1: 33)	Angelic-heavenly (Rev. 5: 11)
12. <u>Local-planetary</u> (Rev. 11: 15)	Universal-inter-planetary (Rev. 5: 11)

13. Earthly capital (Isa. 2: 3; Zech. 14)	Heavenly capital (Heb. 12: 22)
14. Dispensational in purpose (1 Cor. 15: 24-28)	Eternal in purpose (Eph. 3: 11)
15. Has a beginning (2Tim. 4: 1; Mt. 6: 10)	Timeless-endless (Ps. 90: 2)
16. Tares in it now (Mt. 13: 38-50)	Only born again ones in it (Jn. 3: 5)
17. Comes with outward show (Mt. 24: 29-31; 25: 31-46; 2Th.1: 7-10; Jude 14; Zech.14 1-5; Dan. 7: 13-14; Rev. 19: 11-21)	Without show (Lk. 17: 20; Rom. 14: 17; 1Cor. 4: 20)
18. "Flesh and blood" inherits it, for resurrected,it is for earthly, natural people (Ps. 37: 11; Mt. 5: 5; 25: 34; Dan. 7: 18, 28; Ez. 43: 7)	Does not, for only glorified saints inherit all things (Rom. 8: 17; 1Cor. 15: 50-58; Rev. 21: 7) 4

In comparing this list with the list he shares in his book, *God's Plan For Man,* there is a contrast listed that is not in the list in his Bible notes. I think this is worth noting. It is,

Men are never told to seek the Kingdom of Heaven.	Whereas, Men are told to seek the kingdom of God: (Matt. 6:33; Lk. 13:31) 5

Jesus said it is the Father's good pleasure to give you the kingdom (Luke 12:32). The purpose of this study is to share what the Lord has made available to us concerning the reality of various laws and secrets of the Kingdom for victorious Christian living today. Jesus wants us to have "abundant life" (John 10:10) and it is my prayer that these Kingdom realities and all the inheritance the Lord has provided for us will be made real to you.

If this study enables you to discover these amazing realities of the Kingdom, then my labor shall not have been in vain, and I am humbly thankful.

Romans 14:17

"For the kingdom of God in not food and drink, but righteousness and peace and joy in the Holy Spirit."

Luke 12:32

"Do not fear, little flock, for it is your Father's good pleasure to give you the kingdom."

Luke 17:20-21

"Now when He was asked by the Pharisees when the kingdom of God would come, He answered them and said, "The kingdom of God does not come with observation; nor will they say, 'See here!' or 'See there!' For indeed, the kingdom of God is within you."

Luke 22:29-30

"And I bestow upon you a kingdom, just as MY Father bestowed one upon Me, that you may eat and drink at My table in My kingdom, and sit on thrones judging the twelve tribes of Israel."

Matthew 16:18-19

"And I say to you that you are Peter, and on this rock I will build My Church, and the gates of Hades shall not prevail against it.

And I will give you the keys of the kingdom of heaven, and whatever you bind on earth will be bound in heaven, and whatever you loose on earth will be loosed in heaven," (NKJV).

A close study of all the passages relating to the Kingdom of God will show that it is regarded both as a present possession and a future inheritance.
The more we explore the Kingdom of God, the more exciting discoveries we make. God's Kingdom is simply inexhaustible and unsearchable in all its riches, glorious truth and reality!

It is interesting to note that the word *"Kingdom"* is mentioned some 124 times in the Gospels, whereas the word *"Church"* is found only 3 times. Based on this ratio of difference we readily see where our emphasis must be placed in our teaching, preaching and Christian living—namely, the Kingdom of God!

Does this mean then the Church is inferior to the Kingdom or less important than the Kingdom? ABSOLUTELY NOT! Jesus said He was building HIS CHURCH (Matt.16:18), and Paul declared to the Ephesians, *"to Him be glory in the church by Jesus Christ throughout all ages, world without end"* (Ephesians 3:21).

When Jesus sat with His disciples on the Mount of Olives explaining the signs of the times and the end of the age, He declared *"this gospel of the kingdom will be preached in all the world as a witness to all the nations, and then the end will come"* (Matthew 24:14).

The logic here is, as this gospel of the Kingdom is being preached, believed, and received into the hearts of people, wherever that people group may be, the Church will be produced.

When we are "born again" (John 3:6) into God's Kingdom and that Kingdom is planted in our hearts by the Holy Spirit (Rom. 5:5) we then become members of the 'Body of Christ' which is His Church (1Cor. 12: 13-27; Eph. 5: 23-32). For that reason, we must have a through understanding of the Kingdom of God and its related dynamics to the Church. Therefore, we must consider such questions as:

> What is the kingdom of God?
>
> How is it different from the kingdom of Heaven?
>
> How do we enter the kingdom?
>
> How does the kingdom operate?
>
> What must one understand to properly function as a citizen of the kingdom?

We will be considering such questions as well as other related features about the concepts and dynamics of the kingdom of God as we pursue this study.

Jesus had much to say about the Kingdom of God and the Kingdom of Heaven during the period of His earthly ministry. He mentions both Kingdoms no less than 124 times in the four accounts of the gospel. When He spoke about the

Kingdom, He was referring to the Government and ruler-ship of God in our lives. The Greek word for kingdom is *basileia*, meaning a realm, or a region governed by a king. God's sovereignty establishes His ownership. And there can be no Lordship of Christ over our lives without His ownership of our lives. And there can be no divine ownership of our lives until first we are 'born again' into His kingdom, and we make a full and complete surrender of our lives to Him (Romans 12: 1, 2).

Government is ordained of God and every country in the world has its own particular form of government. Government is the exercise of authority over a state, district, organization, institution, etc. It is the process or means by which the people in each country are governed, managed and controlled for civil order.

Likewise, in the Kingdom of God, there is a rule of authority and a process by which we properly function and operate as proper citizens of that Kingdom. Although we live on planet earth, Paul clearly explains we are citizens of another world: *"For our citizenship is in heaven, from which we eagerly wait for the Savior, the Lord Jesus Christ"* (Phil. 3:20).

Therefore, since we are citizens of the Kingdom of God, it is critically important that we know THE KING and understand HIS KINGDOM, that we accept the SAVIOR and fully implement HIS SYSTEM of operation in our lives, and that we know the PLAN FOR THE KINGDOM, and understand the PROCESS by which it is carried out in His Kingdom.

To properly begin this study, we must first understand the foundation upon which the Kingdom of God is established In His eloquent *Sermon on the Mount*, recorded in Matthew chapters 5, 6, and 7 Jesus presents the basic foundational pillars upon which His Kingdom is established. Every member of the Kingdom must be thoroughly familiar with these three chapters, if he expects to function effectively in the working dynamics of the Kingdom.

Jesus begins in chapter five by presenting the foundational premise of the Kingdom in the following beatitudes:

> *"Blessed are the poor in spirit, for theirs is the kingdom of heaven* (Vs. 3).

> *Blessed are those who mourn, for they shall be comforted* (Vs. 4).
>
> *Blessed are the meek, for they shall inherit the earth* (Vs. 5).
>
> *Blessed are those who hunger and thirst for righteousness, they shall be filled* (Vs. 6).
>
> *Blessed are the merciful, for they shall obtain mercy* (Vs. 7).
>
> *Blessed are the pure in heart, for they shall see God* (Vs. 8).
>
> *Blessed are the peacemakers, for they shall be called the sons of God* (Vs. 9).
>
> *Blessed are those who are persecuted for righteousness' sake, for theirs is the kingdom of heaven* (Vs. 10).
>
> *Blessed are you when they revile and persecute you, and say all kinds of evil things against you falsely for My sake* (Vs. 11).
>
> *Rejoice and be exceedingly glad, for great is your reward in heaven, for so they persecuted the prophets who were before you"* (Vs. 12).

Then beginning with verse 13 to chapter 7 Verse 29 He follows this introduction to the kingdom by moving directly into discussing numerous practical concepts that cover a broad range of subjects for our everyday living in the kingdom.

One of the reasons some people find life in the church dull, boring, and uninteresting, is that they have never discovered by revelation and personal experience with the Holy Spirit, the reality of abundant life in the Kingdom. They are like Nicodemus, though a very religious man, yet ignorant and blind to the dynamic function and operation of the kingdom.

Notice what is said in John 3:1-7 concerning Nicodemus: *"There was a man of the Pharisees named Nicodemus, a ruler of the Jews. This man came to Jesus by night and said to Him, 'Rabbi, we know that You are a teacher come from God; for no one can do these signs that You do unless God is with him.' Jesus answered and said to him.* **'Most assuredly, I say to you, unless one is born again he cannot see the kingdom of God'** *(emphasis is mine). Nicodemus said to Him, 'How can a man* *be born when he is old? Can he enter a second time into his mother's womb and be born?' Jesus answered, 'Most assuredly, I say to you, unless one is born of water and the Spirit, he cannot enter the kingdom of God. 'That which is born of the flesh is flesh, and that which is born of the Spirit is spirit.* **Do not marvel that I said to you, 'You must be born again.'"** (My emphasis)

But I assure you, once people's eyes are spiritually open by the power of the Holy Spirit in this 'new birth', like Saul of Tarsus, who had this glorious rebirth on his journey to Damascus, (Acts 9) they too will forever be a changed person.

Jesus tells us that knowledge is the Key to the Kingdom (Luke 11:52) and the lack of knowledge is destruction (Hosea 4:6). These scriptures most definitely apply to our having an understanding of Kingdom living today! The following observations will show why it is important to have an understanding of the Kingdom and why it is necessary to put major emphasis upon it today.

First, It Is Biblical--

The message of the Kingdom was a major focus of Jesus during His earthly ministry. The following scriptures give us an overview of this theme from the beginning to the end of His earthly ministry.

In Matthew 4: 17 we notice the first recorded teaching of Jesus: *"From that time Jesus began to preach and to say, 'Repent, for the kingdom of heaven is at hand.'"*

In Matthew 4: 23 we see He Preached the Gospel of the Kingdom.
"Now Jesus went about all Galilee, teaching in their synagogues, preaching the gospel of the Kingdom, and healing all kinds of sickness and all kinds of disease among the people." This was stated again in Matt. 9:35.

In Matthew 10:5-15 Jesus Sent His Disciples out to preach the Kingdom message.
"These twelve Jesus sent out and commanded them, saying: "Do not go into the way of the Gentiles, and do not enter a city of the Samaritans. But go rather to the lost sheep of the house of Israel.
And as you go, preach, saying, The kingdom of heaven is at hand.

Heal the sick, cleanse the lepers, raise the dead, cast out demons. Freely you have received, freely give."

In Matthew chapter thirteen, He taught them many things about the Kingdom in Parables. The use of parables was a unique and effective style of pedagogy Jesus adopted. By its use, He could explain Kingdom realities to those who truly wanted to follow Him, and at the same time, thoroughly confuse the critics who sought always to find fault and means by which to accuse Him of false teaching.

In Matthew 24:14 as the time gets nearer to His crucifixion, Jesus presses the necessity of all disciples taking the message of the Gospel of the kingdom to all nations.

In Acts 1:1-3 for the continuation of all Jesus began both to do and teach, he showed that the content of the kingdom of God was to be the message of the Church (His Body) soon to be inaugurated and sent out following the coming of the Holy Spirit at Pentecost (Acts 2).

The Kingdom was of primary importance to Jesus. What was important to Jesus MUST be important to us and all followers of Jesus as well. It is crucial that we preach what Jesus preached! If we have the Mind of Christ we will focus on the things He focused on. His message will be our message. If the subject of the kingdom was so paramount to Jesus, it then behooves us to examine our preaching and teaching to see if we give it similar attention.

Secondly, It Is Historical—

It is easily noted the message of the Kingdom was the message of the Apostles and the Early Church. There are no less than 28 references made to the Kingdom from Acts to Revelation, showing the prominent place it held in the teaching of the Apostles and the early Church. The following are a few examples:

Acts 1:3:
"To whom He also presented Himself alive after His suffering by many infallible proofs, being seen by them during forty days and speaking of the things pertaining to the kingdom of God."

Acts 1:6: *"Therefore, when they had come together, they asked Him, saying, "Lord will You at this time restore the kingdom to Israel?"*

Acts 8:12:

"But when they believed Philip as he preached the kingdom of God and the name of Jesus Christ, both men and women were baptized."

Acts 14:22:

"...strengthening the souls of the disciples, exhorting them to continue in the faith, and saying, "We must through many tribulations enter the kingdom of God."

Acts 19:8:

"And he went into the synagogue and spoke boldly for three months, reasoning and persuading concerning the things of the kingdom of God."

Acts 20:25:

"And indeed, now I know that you all, among whom I have gone preaching the kingdom of God, will see my face no more."

Acts 28:23, 30, 31:

"So when they had appointed him a day, many came to him at his lodging, to whom he explained and solemnly testified of the kingdom of God, persuading them concerning Jesus from both the Law of Moses and the Prophets, from morning till evening."   "Then Paul dwelt two whole years in his own rented house, and received all who came to him, preaching the kingdom of God and teaching the things which concern the Lord Jesus Christ with all confidence, no one forbidding him."

Rom. 14: 17:

"For the kingdom of God is not meat and drink; but righteousness, and peace, and joy in the Holy Ghost."

1Cor. 4: 20:

"For the kingdom of God is not in word, but in power."

1 Cor. 15: 24:

" Then cometh the end, when he shall have delivered up the kingdom to God, even the Father; when he shall have put down all rule and all authority and power."

1Cor. 15: 50:

"Now this I say, brethren, that flesh and blood cannot inherit the kingdom of God; neither doth corruption inherit incorruption."

Col 1: 13:

"Who hath delivered us from the power of darkness, and hath translated into the kingdom of his dear Son."

1Thess. 2: 12:

"That ye would walk worthy of God, who hath called you unto his kingdom and glory."

Heb.1:8

"But unto the Son he saith, Thy throne, O God, is forever and ever: a scepter of righteousness is the scepter of thy kingdom."

Heb. 12: 28:

"Wherefore we receiving a kingdom which cannot be moved, let us have grace, whereby we may serve God acceptably with reverence and godly fear."

Jas. 2: 5:

"Hearken, my beloved brethren, Hath not God chosen the poor of this world rich in faith, and heirs of the kingdom which he hath promised to them that love him?"

2Pet. 1: 11:

"For so an entrance shall be ministered unto you abundantly into the everlasting kingdom of our Lord and Savior Jesus Christ."

Rev. 1:9:

"I John, who also am your brother and companion in tribulation, and in the kingdom and patience of Jesus Christ, was in the isle that is called Patmos, for the word of God, and for the testimony of Jesus Christ."

Rev. 12: 10:

"And I heard a loud saying in heaven, Now is come salvation, and strength, and the kingdom of our God, and the power of his Christ: for the accuser of our brethren is cast down, which accused them before our God day and night."

Thirdly, It Is Personal—

Jesus is making a personal application to His statement when He said in Matt. 6: 33, *"But seek ye first the kingdom of God, and his righteousness, and all these things shall be added unto you."* In context here, Jesus was addressing the subject of worry. "Take no thought", that is, don't be fretful or over-anxious about what you will eat, drink, or clothes you will wear. Then He gives these words of comfort and assurance, *"For your heavenly Father knoweth that ye have need of all these things. BUT SEEK YE FIRST THE KINGDOM OF GOD, AND HIS RIGHTEOUSNESS; AND ALL THESE THINGS SHALL BE ADDED UNTO YOU."* (Emphasis mine)

Now let me ask you a question: If God says something is to be first, how smart is it to make it second, or last? Correct, not very smart! Too often we want to tamper and meddle with the process in the kingdom, only to make a mess of things. We must learn not to tamper or meddle with the process of divine order in the kingdom. For instance, we must not put question marks (?) where God puts periods (.)! Anytime we attempt to **adapt** the Word of God to our particular situation, we get ourselves into trouble. We must not adapt the Word to fit our particular convenience, but always be quick to **adopt** the Word! Obey it! How true the lines of the old hymn, *"Trust and obey, for there is no other way, to be happy in Jesus, but to trust and obey."* The greatest *'word of wisdom'* was given by Mary, the mother of Jesus, to the servants when she said, *"Whatever He says to you, do it"* (John 2:5).

One reason so many Christians fail to receive the benefits of the kingdom is because they have changed the process in God's divine order. We see this, for example, in the failure of some to get answers to prayer. In what we normally refer to as *The Lord's Prayer*, which actually is the *Disciples Prayer*, we note that the prayer begins with adoration: *"Our Father in heaven, Hallowed be Your name"* (Matt. 6:9-13). Then it moves to petition, and the very first petition is, *"Your kingdom come"*. But all too often we change the process! We begin prayer with our petitions and fail to make worship and praise the first and foremost aspect of praying. We tend to come to God with our hands out to receive rather than reaching up to present our offering of thanksgiving and praise which is a true spiritual sacrifice (Heb.13:15). Furthermore, we seem to pray for everything except the kingdom and then wonder why we do not get any answers.

A natural example of this would be seen in the arena of sports. What would you think if you went to see a football game and one team played the game by basketball rules and the other team by soccer rules? There would be nothing but chaos and confusion on the field. "What makes any difference, it's all sports", you say! Yes, but there are different *kinds* of sports and each sport has a different set of rules to play the game correctly. Likewise, with prayer—"It's all prayer"—you say. But we must understand there are different *kinds of prayer* as the apostle Paul clearly points out in Ephesians 6:18. There is, for example, the *prayer of faith*, the *prayer of consecration*, and the *prayer of intercession* to name a few. If we are going to get results with our prayers, we must pray according to the rule of each particular kind of prayer. We must learn the process and stay with it! Likewise, with God's Kingdom—we must stay with the process!

Fourthly, It Is Practical—

When the Holy Spirit gives us understanding of the 'word' of the Kingdom, it positions us to receive the blessings of the Kingdom. Without that understanding we are robbed of those blessings.

Jesus faithfully taught the *Word of the Kingdom*. It is so vividly portrayed in the Parable of the Sower in Matthew 13: 18-23: *"Therefore hear the parable of the sower: When anyone hears THE WORD OF THE KINGDOM, and does not understand it, then the wicked one comes and snatches away what was sown in his heart..."* (Emphasis mine).

The crucial point in this parable is the condition of the soils. The sower and the seed were okay and remained the same, but the soils were different. One was rocky, another was shallow, and a third was infested with thorns. Only one of the four was good soil, prepared to receive the seed and produce an abundant crop.

Our lives are much like these various soils. Satan is always there attempting to steal away the seed of God's word from our hearts. He is a thief that steals, kills, and destroys, Jesus said (John 10:10).

Some people have very *hard hearts* for one reason or another, and though they hear the word they do not receive it. They are unwilling to obey and submit to God. And thus the word does not take root and is totally lost from their lives.

Some have hearts like the *stony* ground. They receive the word but do not give proper attention to nurturing and cultivating the precious seed of the word and thereby lose out.

Then, there are those who gladly and quickly receive the word, but allow themselves to be encumbered with all the cares of life and the desire for the riches of this world choke out the life of the seed. The seed is smothered by the vanity of materialism and persecution.

The fourth hearer truly hears the word, absorbs and nurtures it through disciplined prayer and mediation, Bible reading, faithful study, worship and fellowship with others of 'like precious faith'. This one matures in Christian discipleship and becomes very fruitful and effective in the Kingdom.

To understand the "word of the kingdom" we must continually pray the prayer of Paul as recorded in Ephesians 1:15-23, *"Therefore I also, after I heard of your faith in the Lord Jesus and your love for all the saints, do not cease to give thanks for you, making mention of you in my prayers (praying) that the God of our Lord Jesus Christ, the Father of glory, may give you the spirit of wisdom and revelation in the knowledge of Him, (praying) the eyes of your understanding being enlightened; that you may know what is the hope of His calling, what are the riches of the glory of His inheritance in the saints, and what is the exceeding greatness of His power toward us who believe, according to the working of His mighty power which He worked in Christ when He raised Him from the dead and seated Him at His right hand in the heavenly places, far above all principality and power and might and dominion, and every name that is named, not only in this age but also in that which is to come. And He put all things under His feet, and gave Him to be head over all to the church, which is His body, the fullness of Him who fills all in all."*

Not until God's Word is quickened in us by the Holy Spirit will we understand the mysteries of the kingdom and mature in Christ-like character and conduct. There is nothing to compare to what He offers us in this *"word of the kingdom"*.

Far too many Christians see only the eternal aspect of the Kingdom. That is, they think of the kingdom in the sense that one day we will die and go to heaven to be with Jesus, and all the while Satan has robbed them of the glorious benefits and blessings of what the "word of the Kingdom" offers them now! Let's look at one example.

We are told in Hebrews 13:8 that *"Jesus Christ is the same yesterday, today and forever."* In these three dimensions of time Jesus Christ FILLS THE PAST, MAKES FRUITFUL THE PRESENT, AND FULFILLS THE FUTURE. His life and ministry touches each of these eras—past, present and future time.

The Bible clearly reveals three major appearances of Christ fulfilling past, present and future time in relation to His ministry to man and His fulfillment of God's total plan of redemption. However, many Christians are lacking in a complete understanding of this marvelous truth and are thereby robbed of heaven's blessings!

THE FIRST APPEARANCE OF JESUS IN THE *PAST* WAS TO PUT AWAY SIN. We read in 2Cor. 5:21, *"For He made Him who knew no sin to be sin for us, that we might become the righteousness of God in Him."*

In Col. 1:13, 14, Paul declares, *"Who delivered us out of the authority of darkness And translated us into the Kingdom of the Son of his love; in Whom we have our redemption, the remission of our sins."*

Thus you will note that from the garden gate of Genesis to the golden gate of Revelation, the Scriptures are voluminous in describing this particular aspect of redemption.

HIS SECOND APPEARANCE IS NOW SEATED IN THE PRESENCE OF GOD AT THE FATHER'S RIGHT HAND FOR US. Notice Ephesians 1:3, *"Blessed be the God and Father of our Lord Jesus Christ, who has blessed us with every spiritual blessing in the heavenly places in Christ."*

Paul elaborates on this truth in numerous scriptures:

Col. 3:1: *"If you then be risen with Christ, seek those things which are above, where Christ sitteth on the right hand of God."*

Heb. 7:25: *"Wherefore he is able also to save them to the uttermost that come unto God by him, seeing he ever liveth to make intercession for them."*

Heb. 9:24: *"For Christ has not entered the holy places made with hands, which are copies of the true but into heaven itself, now to appear in the presence of God for us."*

The Lord Jesus Christ is presently sitting at the right hand of the Throne of the Father in heaven. It could not be more clear than what Ephesians 1:20 states, *"which He worked in Christ when He raised Him from the dead and seated Him at His right hand in the heavenly places."* It is from this exalted position, *"far above all principality and power and might and dominion, not only in this age but also in that which is to come"* v. 21, that Christ faithfully carries out His high priestly ministry as mediator, intercessor, advocate and surety to all those who trust in Him.

THE THRID APPEARANCE OF JESUS IS TO COME THE SECOND TIME WITHOUT SIN UNTO SALVATION. We read in Hebrews 9: 28, *"So Christ was once offered to bear the sins of many, and unto them that look for him shall he appear the second time without sins unto salvation."*

It is in His second appearance seated in the heavenly places at the right hand of God the Father that unveils His present ministry. Where Jesus is now and what He is doing now for us is the glorious *"word of the Kingdom"*!

Tragically, however, so many Christians have little or no understanding where Christ is now, and what He is prepared to do for them presently! They do not know He is at the Father's right hand and lives for us there in as much reality as when He died for us.

First, He is there as our High Priest, *"Wherefore it behooved him in all things to be made like unto his brethren, that he might become a merciful and faithful high priest in things pertaining to God, to make propitiation for the sins of the people"* (Hebrews 2:17). Notice the beautiful way it is recorded in the Life Application Bible, *"We all know he did not come as an angel but as a human being— yes, a Jew. And it was necessary for Jesus to be like us, his brothers, so that he could be our merciful and faithful High Priest before God, a Priest who would be both merciful to us and faithful to God in dealing with the sins of the people."*

Then the authors share this wonderful note of explanation on these two verses (16, 17) in the following footnote:

> In the Old Testament, the High Priest was the mediator between God and his people. His job was to regularly offer animal sacrifices according to the law and to intercede before God for the people's sins. Jesus Christ is now our High Priest. He has *once* and for *all* paid the penalty for all our sins by his own sacrificial death, and he continually intercedes on our behalf before God. We are released from sin's domination over us when we commit ourselves fully to Christ, trusting completely in what he has done for us." **1**

In chapter four, verse 14 they offer further explanation which shows the reality and beauty of where Christ is now and what He is presently doing for us.

> To the Jews, the High Priest was the highest religious authority in the land. He alone entered the Holy of Holies once a year to make atonement for the sins of the whole nation (Leviticus 16). Like the High Priest, Jesus mediates between God and us. As man's representative, he intercedes for us before God. As God's representative, he assures us of God's forgiveness. Jesus has more authority than the Jewish High Priest because he is truly God and truly man. Unlike the High Priest who could go before God only once a year, Christ is always at God's right hand, interceding for us. **2**

Dear friend, He is no longer the lowly man of Galilee. He's not simply the Son made sin for us, BUT HE IS LORD! He is conqueror over Satan, sin, sickness, disease, demons, poverty and death. HE POSSESSES ALL AUTHORITY IN HEAVEN AND EARTH and His desire is that we too share in the benefits of all that authority (Matt. 28:18). From heaven He currently performs a High Priestly ministry, and one day He will rule in His Kingly ministry, and we shall also reign with Him as kings and priests in the ultimate or eternal Kingdom of God (Rev. 5:10, 20:6).

Meanwhile, we today can act fearlessly upon His word and receive the benefits of our glorious inheritance (see Psalm 103: 1-5; 2 Cor.1:20; Eph. 1: 3; Ps. 34:9-10, Ps. 84: 11; Matt. 21:22; Mark 11: 22-24; Jn.14:12-15, Jn.15:7, 16).

Notice what He provides for us now in His present High Priestly ministry:

JESUS IS OUR MEDIATOR

"For there is one God, one mediator also between God and men, the man Christ Jesus, who gave himself a ransom for all" (1Tim. 2:5).

By the power of His sinless blood He offered to God upon His ascension to heaven, Jesus Christ satisfied the claims of divine justice. As the only qualified mediator He stands between God the OFFENDED and sinful man the OFFENDER to effect reconciliation. In this connection we find numerous scriptures, (Jn.14:6; 16:23; 16:26, 27, 17:11, 24; Rom. 8:34; Eph. 3:12; Col. 3:17; Heb. 7:25, 9:15, 24; 12:24, 1Jn. 2:1).

Man is unrighteous, spiritually dead, and thus cannot on his own merit approach God. But Christ has redeemed us from the curse (Gal. 3:13) and thus we can now approach God and stand in His presence. Think of it! We now have entrance, access to God's throne of grace and mercy without any sense of guilt, condemnation, subjugation, fear, or sin consciousness (Rom. 5: 1, 2; 8: 1). *"Therefore, brethren, having boldness to enter the Holiest by the blood of Jesus"* (Heb.10:19).

We are further admonished in Heb. 4:14-16, *"Seeing then that we have a great High Priest who has passed through the heavens, Jesus the Son of God, let us hold fast our confession. For we do not have a High Priest who cannot sympathize with our weaknesses, but was in all points tempted as we are, yet without sin. Let us therefore come boldly to the throne of grace that we may obtain mercy and find grace to help in time of need."*

JESUS IS OUR INTERCESSOR:

As a Mediator Jesus introduces unsaved mankind to God and effects reconciliation. As soon as a sinner accepts Christ as his/her personal Savior, they become a child of God. *"As many as received Him, to them He gave the right to become children of God, even to those who believe in His name"* (Jn.1:12). THEN THE INTERCESSORY MINISTRY OF JESUS BEGINS ON THEIR BEHALF TO MAINTAIN THEIR FELLOWSHIP WITH GOD. *"Therefore He is also able to save to the uttermost those who come to God through Him, since He ever lives to make intercession for them"* (Heb. 7:25).

We need our Lord's ministry of intercession because of our human weaknesses, frailties and demon persecution. If we slip, fail, or sin, and don't understand there is an Intercessor, we could fall by the wayside. Sin breaks fellowship with God but *"if we confess our sins, He is faithful and just to forgive us our sins and to cleanse us from all unrighteousness"* (1Jn. 1:9).

JESUS IS OUR ADVOCATE

An advocate is one who pleads the cause of another as in the case of an attorney representing his client in a civil court of law. There are many Christians living in broken fellowship with God because they don't understand they have an advocate. The advocate stands in our place to plead our case as a lawyer or defender before the Father's throne. Christ is both our defender and defense. He is always there as a faithful and merciful High Priest. The apostle John instructs the believer,

"My little children, these things I write to you, that you may not sin, And if anyone sins, we have an Advocate with the Father, Jesus Christ the righteous" (1Jn.2.1). *"If we confess our sins, He is faithful and just to forgive us our sins and to cleanse us from all unrighteousness"* (1Jn.1:9).

Now He is unable to act as our advocate if we fail to confess our sins. No Christian should ever remain in broken fellowship any longer than it takes to ask the Father's forgiveness.

JESUS IS OUR LORD

"Therefore God also has highly exalted Him and given Him the name which is above every name, that at the name of Jesus every knee should bow, of these in heaven, and of those on earth, and of those under the earth, and that every tongue should confess that Jesus Christ is Lord, to the glory of God the Father" (Phil. 2:9-11).

Notice Col. 2:6-7, *"As you have therefore received Christ Jesus the Lord, so walk in Him, rooted and built up in Him and established in the faith, as you have been taught, abounding in it with thanksgiving."*

God wants us to be rooted and established in the reality of the Lordship of Jesus Christ! As Lord, He is our Bread-provider, Shield, and Protector. As such we can live in the serenity and quiet peacefulness of spirit knowing all is well for He is Jehovah our Shepherd and we do not want (Ps.23: 1).

JESUS IS OUR SURETY

"For on the one hand there is an annulling of the former commandment because of its weakness and unprofitableness, for the law made nothing perfect; on the other hand, there is the bringing in of a better hope, through which we draw near to God.......by so much more Jesus has become a surety of a better covenant" (Hebrews 7:18-22). Standing behind this New Covenant, what we call the New Testament, we have Jesus as its Surety! From Matthew 1 to Revelation 22, Jesus and His throne are back of every word to make it good. His blood is the red seal upon the document of this Covenant. On the ground of the integrity of that indissoluble covenant, you and I can build a Faith that cannot be shaken. THUS OUR POSITION BEFORE THE FATHER IS ABSOLUTELY PERFECT, SOUND, AND SECURE.

WE ARE SAFE! *"After that you believed, you were sealed with The Holy Spirit of promise"* (Eph. 1:13).

THINK OF It! WE ARE SEALED! The seal signifies in Biblical symbolism three vital features:

> a. *A Finished Transaction.* "It is finished" (Jn.17:4, 19:30) It is never again, do, do, do—but DONE! DONE! DONE!—FINISHED!
>
> b. *Ownership*
>
> *"Nevertheless the solid foundations of God stands, having this seal: "The Lord knows those who are His,"* and, *"Let everyone who names the name of Christ depart from iniquity"* (2Tim. 2:19; Jere.32: 11, 12). We are the redeemed, purchased property of God! We belong to Jesus! Hallelujah!
>
> c. *Security*
>
> *"And grieve not the Holy Spirit of God whereby you are sealed unto the day of redemption"* (Eph. 4:30). See Esther. 8:8; Dan. 6:17, Matt. 27:64). 3

Finally, It Is Prophetic—

John describes a beautiful scene he witnessed when taken up into heaven in Revelation 11: 15, *"And the seventh angel sounded; and there were great voices in heaven, saying, The kingdoms of this world are become the kingdoms of our Lord, and of his Christ; and he shall reign forever and ever."*

Oh, what a day that will be when Christ's Kingdom will rule and reign! The whole creation is groaning for that day! That day of millennial peace when the lion shall lie down with the wolf and men shall beat their swords into plowshares (Isa. 2:4; 11: 6-9)!

Meanwhile, we must occupy until He comes! The instructions of the Master are very clear, *"Go ye into all the world and preach the Gospel to every creature"* (Mk. 16:16) .

"And this gospel of the kingdom will be preached in all world as a witness to all the

nations, and then the end shall come" (Matt. 24:14).

This is the Master's Commission and THE GREAT COMMISSION OF CHRIST IS THE SUPREME BUSINESS OF THE CHURCH. As we faithfully preach this message of the Kingdom, God will plant and establish His Church in every people group on planet earth. What a message of good news, glad tidings to all men. This is Missions— and Missions is the heartbeat of God, and must be ours as well! Charles Wesley expresses it well in his hymn, *The Everliving Christ*:

> Ye servants of God, your Master proclaim, And publish abroad His wonderful Name: The Name all victorious of Jesus extol; His kingdom is glorious and rules over all.
> God ruleth on high, almighty to save; And still He is nigh, His presence we have: The great congregation His triumph shall sing, Ascribing salvation to Jesus our King.
> "Salvation to God, who sits on the throne!" Let all cry aloud, and honor the Son: The praise of Jesus the angels proclaim, Fall down on their faces and worship the Lamb.
> Then let us adore, and give Him His right, All glory and power, all wisdom and might, All honor and blessing, with angels above, And thanks never ceasing for infinite love. **4**

PART II

KINGDOM LAWS

The Law of the Spirit of Life

The Law of Confession

The Law of Obedience

The Law of Faith

The Law of Frustration

The Law of Love

The Law of Giving

Chapter One

The Law of the Spirit of Life REVIVES Me

"Do not fear, little flock, for it is your Father's good pleasure to give you the kingdom" (Luke 12:32).

The Kingdom of God is a spiritual reality and operates in accordance with Divine law and order. The laws of the Kingdom (of the Spirit) are no less exact and dependable than any physical law we exercise and enjoy.

We understand that we cannot function independently of natural laws. Our very existence and survival depends upon our understanding and proper use of these laws. For example, consider the law of "seed time and harvest." If we do not plant the seed in our gardens in the springtime, we will not see any food come harvest time in the fall. That is a fact, and because this law is immutable (unchanging) and dependable, we are neither afraid nor ashamed to operate it for our benefit.

Likewise, we should not fear to use the spiritual laws or principles of the Kingdom for our benefit. In order to discover how to fit, to function, and to flow in the purposes of God for our lives, it is necessary that we gain understanding of these important principles, and how to enact them for our growth and development in Christian character and victorious Christian living.

There are many of these laws or principles outlined for us in Scripture, but for the purpose of this study, I want to focus on seven particular laws or principles of the kingdom, and show how they affect and impact our lives today. I am convinced, if we understand and flow in obedience to these seven laws or principles, we will live in the fullness and abundance of victorious living God promises to each of us.

It must be stressed and understood these laws or principles are governed or controlled by a law of motion, known as the *Law of Reciprocity*. That is, for every action there is a re-action! This is often refered to as the principle of 'cause and effect'—for every action, there is a reciprocal action— it works for every natural law, just so, the same principle holds true in the operation of the spiritual laws of the Kingdom.

Our study will cover the following seven laws or principles and how the principle of "cause and effect" is related to each spiritual law:

CAUSE	EFFECT
1. The Law of the "Spirit of Life" --	REVIVES ME
2. The Law of "Confession" ---------	RULES ME
3. The Law of "Obedience" ---------	RENEWS ME
4. The Law of "Faith" ---------------	REWARDS ME
5. The Law of "Frustration" --------	REPRODUCES ME
6. The Law of "Love" ---------------	REFINES ME
7. The Law of "Giving" -------------	REPLENISHES ME

As we study each law or spiritual principle, it will become evident from the Scriptures the mighty impact they have upon our lives.

First, let us notice,

The Law Of The Spirit Of Life REVIVES Me.

Man in his natural state is spiritually dead! His physical being (Body) and emotional being, (Soul—mind, will and emotions) are alive, but his spiritual being is dead. He was born this way! The Bible says, *"Behold, I was shapen in iniquity; and in sin did my mother conceive me"* (Psa. 51: 5).

Paul makes the case clear in Eph. 2: 1-3, *"And you He made alive, who were dead in trespasses and sins, in which you once walked according to the course of this world, according to the prince of the power of the air, the spirit who now works in the sons of disobedience, among whom also we all once conducted ourselves in the lusts of our flesh, fulfilling the desires of the flesh and of the mind, and were by nature children of wrath, just as the others."*
This natural man needs to be quickened or "made alive", and that is precisely what the Law of the Spirit of Life does! That is why there must be a "new birth" as Jesus explained to Nicodemus in John chapter three. Please notice,

"It is the Spirit who gives life; the flesh profits nothing. The words I speak to you are spirit, and they are life" (John 6:63).

"There is therefore now no condemnation to those who are in Christ Jesus, who do not walk according to the flesh, but according to the Spirit.
For the law of the Spirit of life in Christ Jesus has made me free from the law of sin and death.
For what the law could not do in that it was weak through the flesh, God did by sending His own Son in the likeness of sinful flesh, on account of sin: He condemned sin in the flesh that the righteous requirement of the law might be fulfilled in us who do not walk according to the flesh but according to the Spirit" (Romans 8:1-4).

The Law of the New Covenant is a perfect contrast to the Law of the Old Covenant--For example:

OLD COVENANT	NEW COVENANT
"Law of sin & death"	"Law of spirit of life"
"Bondage"	"Freedom"
"Legalism"	"Grace"
"Sins are covered"	"Sins are cleansed"
"Hate"	"Love"
"Old nature"	"New nature"
"Condemnation"	"Liberty"
"Sealed with blood of bulls"	"Sealed with blood of Christ"

Both sin and death come from Satan the Adversary. Under the Old Covenant man's nature was controlled by Satan—he lived in Satan's realm. He was a hopeless slave living in defeat and despair.

Jesus, however, inaugurated the New Covenant. A covenant that offers life, light, love, liberty and freedom from all sin, guilt, condemnation and eternal shame!

The heart of the New Covenant Law is seen in John 13:34, 35: *"A new commandment I give to you, that you love one another; as I have loved you, that you also love one another. By this shall all men know you are my disciples, if you have love for one another."*

The books of Leviticus, Numbers, and Deuteronomy give exposition of the Old Law. In the Pauline Epistles, we have the revelation and exposition of the New Law.

The New Covenant Law is not for people outside of Christ, because the natural man cannot understand the things of the Spirit, *"for the carnal mind is enmity against God; for it is not subject to the law of God, nor indeed can be"* (Romans 8:7).

The New Covenant law is the law of love, and since love is the fulfilling of all law, the old law (*ceremonial*) is no longer necessary. Always remember, the law of love will never violate any law (*moral*) of the old covenant that was instituted to curb sin.

The best the old law could do, however, was act as a correcting rod for man's behavior. It could never bring men to Christ, only the Holy Spirit can do that! When people are brought to Christ by the Holy Spirit they become new creatures in Christ. (2Cor. 5:17) They receive a completely new nature: *"Whereby are given unto us exceeding great and precious promises: that by these ye might be partakers of the divine nature, having escaped the corruption that is in the world through lust"* (2Pet. 1: 4). Consequently, they are no longer Jew, Gentile, bond, free, black, white, male, female, but one new man in Christ Jesus (Gal. 3:26-29; Eph. 2:15).

It is God's wonderful law of the Sprit of Life that quickens and revives us; and we are transformed from 'death to life'; from the 'power of Satan to the power of God'; from the 'kingdom of darkness to the kingdom of light' (Acts 26:18; Col. 1:13; 1Jn. 3: 14).

"And you He made alive, who were dead in trespasses and sins, in which you once walked according to the course of this world, according to the prince of the power of the air, the spirit who now works in the sons of disobedience" (Eph. 2: 1, 2).

When we become a "new creature" in Christ Jesus some exciting and vital things transpire:

First, there is the Removal of all condemnation

Notice Romans 8:1, *"There is therefore now no condemnation to those who are in Christ Jesus, who do not walk according to the flesh, but according to the Spirit"* (NKJV).

Romans 5: 1, *"Therefore, having been justified by faith, we have peace with God through our Lord Jesus Christ"* (NKJV).

In this new creation we have been given a glorious freedom. We are no longer in servitude and bondage to Satan and the works of darkness. We no longer have his nature. We have a new nature, praise God! We are free!

This freedom, like a coin, has two sides of truth, a *legal* side and a *vital* side. Please notice,

The Legal Side of Redemption and Freedom

We are legally adopted into the family of God. John 1:12 states, *"But as many as received Him, to them He gave the power (right) to become children of God, even to those who believe in His name."*

The key word here is "power". In this verse and context this power comes from the Greek word, *exousia*, meaning right or authority to be the Sons of God.

We are God's children legally! *"For you did not receive the spirit of bondage again to fear, but you received the Spirit of adoption by whom we cry out, "Abba, Father"* (Romans 8:15). Satan no longer has any claim to our lives.

We should meditate long on this thought of adoption. Adoption in natural law is a very serious and strong transaction. Actually, when one is adopted into a family naturally, he holds a position stronger than the natural children in that family. The parents can disown their natural children, but they cannot disown their adopted children.

Secondly, there is the Restoration of Righteousness

Righteousness is the Vital Side of Redemption

Paul declares we have been made the righteousness of God in Christ Jesus. In 2 Cor. 5:21 we read, *"For He made Him who knew no sin to be sin for us, that we might become the righteousness of God in Him."*

"For we are His workmanship, created in Christ Jesus for good works, which God prepared beforehand that we should walk in them" (Eph. 2:10).

'But of Him you are in Christ Jesus, who became for us wisdom from God---and righteousness and sanctification and redemption--" (1Cor. 1; 30).

Righteousness is having "rightness with God." Spiros Zodhiates gives a more in-depth explanation of the term 'righteousness':

The Greek word for righteousness is *"Dikaiosune,* from *dikaios,* righteous, and *dike,* justice or righteousness. It is the essence of *to dikaion,* that which is just, or *dikaios,* of him we are just or righteous. Righteousness fulfills the claims of *dike,* which in the case of the believer is God's claims; and in the case of the nonbeliever, the claim of that higher authority which a person adopts as his own standard. *Dikaiosune,* righteousness, is thus conformity with the claims of higher authority and stands in opp. to *anomia,* lawlessness. In both the O.T. and N.T., righteousness is the state commanded by God and standing the test of His judgment (II Cor. 3:9; 6:14; Eph. 4:24). It is conformity to all that He commands or appoints. Since God Himself is the standard of the believers, the righteousness of God means the righteousness which belongs to God or to oneself for God, or God-like righteousness (Mt. 6:33; Js. 1:20). Thus righteousness in general is God's uprightness or standard, without reference to any particular form of its embodiment, to which man is expected to conform. The righteousness of God is the right which God has upon man. In order for man to recognize and fully submit to that right of God upon his life, he must receive God as He offers Himself or His righteousness to him as a gift (Rom. 5:17). The recognition and acceptance of God's right upon man realized through faith stands in opp. to the righteousness which is of the law (Rom. 10:5; Gal. 3:21) which is man's acceptance of the claims of the law upon his life. Man in his natural state, fallen condition tends rather to accept his own set of standards, creating his own righteousness (Rom. 10:3; Phil. 3:6). Such, however, is not really righteousness (Rom. 10: 5, 3; Gal. 3:21) and does not satisfy God. God's righteousness is imputed and imparted as a gift to man and not earned. It results in God's act of justification by faith through Christ. Man can only accept the claims of God upon his life as he repents of his sin and receives Christ as His Saviour by faith, and thus becomes a child of God, realizing God's claims upon him by the miraculous regenerating action of the Holy Spirit (Jn. 1: 12; Rom. 4: 11-13; 5: 21; 6: 16; 8: 10; 9: 30; 10: 6; II Cor. 6: 7, 14; Eph. 4: 24; 6: 14; II Pet. 1:1)." 1

It is interesting that at the root of all the religions in the world is the desire to be righteous. It is the quest of every religious pilgrim. Sadly, however, no religion can make a person righteous. They all fail miserably!

It is at this point Christianity part's company with all other religions in the world. Christianity is not a religion per se, that is, a man-made system of rules, regulations and legalistic rituals and customs; but a dynamic living relationship with Jesus Christ, who proved He is God when He was resurrected from the dead! Only Jesus Christ can save and make one righteous and acceptable to God! Paul declares in Rom. 5: 17, *"But not as the offense, so also is the free gift. For if through the offense of one many be dead, much more the grace of God, and the gift by grace, which is by one man, Jesus Christ, hath abounded unto many."*

This is why the Apostle declared so boldly in Romans 1:16, 17, *"For I am not ashamed of the gospel of Christ: for it is the power of God unto salvation to everyone that believeth; to the Jew first, and also to the Greek.*
For therein is the RIGHTEOUSNESS OF GOD revealed from faith to faith:" (My emphasis)

True righteousness restores to mankind all that was lost in the fall of Adam, the representative man, plus a new relationship with God as sons with privileges.

This is the vital side of redemption and righteousness!

Now in connection with this vital side of righteousness we are given another kind of power— *dunamis* power (Acts 1:8). *Dunamis* power is the dynamic ability *"to be"* and *"to do"*. We derive our English word, *dynamite* from this word *dunamis*. Also from the same root comes the word *dynamo* which describes the ability 'to be.' This kind of power gives us the dynamic ability to witness to Him and to serve Him. This is why the early believers waited for the promise of the Father (Luke 24: 49; Acts 1: 4).

In the restoration of this righteousness several things happen:

- **Our Standing With God Is Restored**

We have been given the right of access to God without any sense of fear, shame, guilt, condemnation, sin consciousness, or any sense of inferiority—Think of it!

We can come boldly to the throne of Grace at anytime from anyplace. We can do at anytime what the High Priest of the Old Testament could only do once a year. The Hebrew writer said, *"Let us therefore come boldly unto the throne grace, that we may obtain mercy, and find grace to help in time of need"* (Heb. 4:16).

We can act in the same fearlessness of Jesus in the face of sin, Satan, sickness, death and demons. What a standing we have with God, not because we merit or deserve it, but because of God's amazing grace and mercy. It is His free gift! What a standing we have in Him!

In his introduction to the first Corinthian letter, Paul describes our standing with God:

> Vs. 2- We are the *Church of God.*
> Vs. 2- We are *sanctified* in Christ Jesus.
> Vs. 2- We are *called to be saints.*
> Vs. 2- We *call* upon the name of Jesus Christ our Lord.
> Vs. 4- We have been *given the grace* of God.
> Vs. 5- In *everything we are enriched* by him, in all utterance, and in all knowledge.
> Vs. 6- We *have the testimony* of Christ confirmed in us.
> Vs. 7- We *come behind* in no gift.
> Vs. 7- We are *waiting for the coming* (revelation) of our Lord Jesus Christ.
> Vs. 8- We are *confirmed* unto the end, blameless.

What a glorious position every child of God occupies! Unfortunately, however, so many Christians do not understand their position in Christ. Consequently, the contemporary Church has the same problem the Corinthian believers had. Notice 1Cor. 3: 1-7, *"And I, brethren, could not speak unto you as unto spiritual, but as unto carnal, even as unto babes in Christ. I have fed you with milk, and not with meat: for hitherto ye were not able to bear it, neither yet now are ye able. For ye are yet carnal: for whereas there is among you envying, and strife, and divisions, are ye not carnal, and walk as man? For while one saith, I am of Paul; and another, I am of Apollos; are ye not carnal? Who then is Paul, and who is Apollos, but ministers by whom ye believed, even as the Lord gave to every man? I have planted, Apollos watered; but God gave the increase. So then neither is he that planted anything, neither he that watereth, but God that giveth the increase."*

The problem of the Corinthian Christians was their PRACTICE of Christian living was not on the same level as their POSITION in Christ. It is when Christians bring their *'state or practice of living'* to the same level as their *'standing or position'* in Christ, that the maturity God requires is achieved, and we impact the world with our victorious living.

- **Our Fellowship With God Is Restored**

We have been given the ability to commune and walk with God without any sense of guilt or condemnation. John declares, *"But if we walk in the light as He is in the light, we have fellowship with one another, and the blood of Jesus Christ His Son cleanses us from all sin"* (1John 1; 7).

Like Adam before the fall, we can walk and talk with God continually. Fellowship is an interesting thing. It has been described as "two fellows in the same ship." Fellowship with God is described by Jesus as abiding in the vine. *"If you abide in Me and My words abide in you, you will ask what you desire, and it shall be done for you"* (John 15:7).

Fellowship with God is a combination of "union" and "communion", a two-way relationship. Paul stated it this way, *"In Him we live and move and have our being"* (Acts 17:28).

The word "communion" neatly describes this restored fellowship; it is the contraction of two Anglo-Saxon words: *"common"*, and *"union"*. Contracted together we have "communion". Our communion with God is a common-union with God. Understanding this gives us a glorious insight into the Holy Communion or Lord's Supper.

The celebration of the Lord's Supper should never be a dull ritualistic church ceremony. God forbid! It is the revelation of a precious union and continual communion with the Father because of the precious blood and sacrifice of Jesus on the Cross.

What a fellowship, what a joy divine!

- **Our Faith Is Restored**

"For I say, through the grace given to me, to everyone who is among you, not to think of himself more highly than he ought to think, but to think soberly, as God has dealt to each one a measure of faith" (Rom. 12: 3).

This glorious faith is a gift from God. *"For by grace are ye saved through faith; and that not of yourselves: it is the gift of God:"* It gives us the ability to come to God, to believe God, and to receive from God. Hebrews 11:1, 6, *"Now faith is the substance of things hoped for, the evidence of things not seen. But without faith it is impossible to please him; for he that cometh to God must believe that he is, and that he is a rewarder of them that diligently seek him."*

This beautiful grace of faith enables us to LIVE BY FAITH and not sight (2 Cor. 5:7); to fight the good fight of faith (1Tim. 6: 12); and overcome the world by faith (1Jn. 5:4).

- **Our Peace Is Restored**

Isaiah says there is no peace for the wicked (Isa. 48:22), but for all those who have become new creatures in Christ there is PEACE!   Peace WITH God and the peace OF God.

"Therefore, having been justified by faith, we have peace with God through our Lord Jesus Christ" (Rom. 5:1).

"And the peace of God, which surpasses all understanding, will guard your hearts and minds through Christ Jesus" (Phil.4:7).

- **Our Son-ship is Restored**

"For as many as are led by the Spirit of God, these are sons of God" (Rom. 8:14).

This is so beautifully illustrated by our Lord in the story of the Prodigal son (Luke 15: 11-32) who took his inheritance, went into a far country, and wasted his substance with riotous living. It is a powerful illustration of God's love, acceptance and forgiveness to all man-kind. In this story of degradation and sinful, rebellious living, the young man hit rock bottom of despair and want. It took this shock to awaken him, and he realized how far he had gone from his father's love and care. But, he came to himself! He made the decision to return to his father, no longer as a son, but a hired servant so he could survive. What a shock and surprise he had waiting for him. The father, who patiently waited and watched each day for his son's return, saw him in the far distance returning home. Rather than wait for the son to arrive, humble himself and beg for mercy, the father rushes to him, hugging and kissing his wayward, lost son, crying *"For this my son was dead, and is alive again; he was lost, and is found."*

His son is restored, not to be a hired servant, but with all the rights and privileges of son-ship. This is illustrated in the three prominent gifts the father bestowed upon him: the best **robe**, symbolic of the robe of righteousness (Isa. 61: 10); **ring** on his hand, indicative of reconciliation (2Cor. 5: 18, 19) and **shoes** on his feet (Ruth 4: 7) symbolic of authority and service. Thus, we see the great rejoicing and festive celebration. Likewise, there is rejoicing in heaven over one sinner that repents of his sins and is restored to son-ship!

Thirdly, we are Re-leased from 'The Law of Sin and Death'

God replaces the negative with the positive. He takes out the old nature and replaces with the new nature, the nature of Christ. We are now 'new creation realities'!

"For what the law could not do in that it was weak, through the flesh (sarx, senses) God sending his own Son in the likeness of sinful flesh (senses) and for sin, condemned sin in the flesh (senses)" (Rom. 8:3).

God has called us to a life of victory, joy, and triumphant! We are daily over-comers of the flesh, the world, and the devil as we seek earnestly to operate this *Law of Life* by continually renewing our minds daily by:

> **G**OING TO GOD IN PRAYER

> **R**EADING AND MEDITATING IN THE WORD OF GOD

> **O**BEYING HIS WORD

> **W**ORSHIPPING AND WITNESSING

As we are faithful to do these four simple disciplines, we will *"GROW in the grace and knowledge of our Lord and Savior Jesus Christ. To Him be glory both now and forever. Amen"* (2 Peter 3:18). (My emphasis)

Chapter Two

The Law of Confession RULES Me

"But seek first the kingdom of God and His righteousness, and all these things shall be added to you" (Matt. 6:33).

"Therefore, holy brethren, partakers of the heavenly calling, consider the Apostle and High Priest of our confession, Christ Jesus" (Hebrews 3:1).

"Seeing then that we have a great High Priest who has passed through the heavens, Jesus the Son of God, let us hold fast our confession" (Hebrews 4:14).

"So Jesus answered and said to them, "Have faith in God. For assuredly, I say to you, whoever says to this mountain, 'Be removed and be cast into the sea,' and does not doubt in his heart, but believes that those things he says will come to pass, he will have whatever he says.
Therefore I say to you, whatever things you ask when you pray, believe that you receive them, and you will have them" (Mark 11:22-24).

I was amazed when the Holy Spirit made me realize the power of the tongue, and how our words play such a vitally important role in determining the outcome and destiny of what we choose to speak. The wise man, Solomon said, *"Death and life are in the power of the tongue: and they that love it shall eat the fruit thereof"* (Prov. 18: 21). A greater than Solomon said, *"For by thy words thou shalt be justified, and by thy words thou shalt be condemned"* (Matt. 12: 37). Our words will determine whether we live in victory or defeat.

Though unseen, the Kingdom of God is not unreal! Though invisible it is not impotent! The invisible world is very real! In fact, it is more real than the physical world in which we live and operate each day. The visible world is transitory, temporal at best, and is decaying and will perish. But not so with the invisible world- It is eternal!

The reality of the invisible world is beautifully portrayed in the case with the prophet Elisha and his servant when they were being surrounded by the army of Syria. *"And when the servant of the man of God arose early and went out, there was an army, surrounding the city with horses and chariots. And his servant said to him, "Alas, my master! What shall we do?'*

So he answered, "Do not fear, for those who are with us are more than those who are with them." And Elisha prayed, and said, "Lord, I pray, open his eyes that he may see." Then the Lord opened the eyes of the young man, and he saw. And behold, the mountain was full of horses and chariots of fire all a round Elisha" (2 Kings 6:15-17).

The New Birth opens our eyes to see the Law of the Spirit of Life operate. We are able to see from the visible which is finite, into the realm of the invisible which is infinite. We are able to look from a world filled with impossibilities into a world filled with possibilities.

The word, "seek" in Matthew 6:33 means "to hunt earnestly". We must make pursuing the Kingdom of God our number one priority in order to enter the realm of the invisible. Then we must press into the things of the invisible world. Jesus said in Luke 16:16, *"The law and the prophets were until John. Since that time the kingdom of God has been preached and everyone is pressing into it."*

Although we are surrounded by an unlimited world, a world of inexhaustible supply in the unsearchable riches of Christ, still we fail, struggle, suffer lack, and remain limited because we have tried to operate by the systems of this world and not by the laws of the Kingdom of God.

In the previous lesson we saw how we are "made alive" by the law of the Sprit of life. Now in this lesson **let's look closely at the *Law of Confession* and see how our words rule us.**

The one feature that distinguishes man from all other living creatures in creation is SPEECH! God created man with the ability to express what he thinks and feels with words, with language. Here is where man excels above all other living creatures

When God said, *"Let us make man in our image"* (Gen. 1: 26), he also gave him the ability to speak. God does speak and there is mighty power in His speech. No less than 15 times we read, *"God said or spoke"* in the history of creation in Genesis chapter one. Look at the following verses: v.3, 5, 6, 7, 8, 9, 10, 11, 14, 20, 22, 24, 26, 28, and 29.

In the historical account of the virgin birth of our Lord, the angel said to Mary, *"For with God nothing shall be impossible"* (Luke 1:37). The meaning of that is, "With God NO WORD shall be VOID or empty of power, which translates, "every Word of God contains in it the power for its own fulfillment."

Your words definitely have power. Jesus said, *"For by your words you will be justified, and by your words you will be condemned"* (Matt. 12:37).

You can be "hung by your tongue." Your words can either bless you or blast you; either curse you or cure you; either heal you or hurt you; either release you or bind you; they can give you victory or defeat!

Your words are like floats or weights (Bobs or Sinkers). They will either hold you up or pull you down. The wisdom writer said, *"Thou art snared with the words of thy mouth, and that art taken captive with the words of thy lips"* (Prov. 6:2). And again he states in 18:21, *"Death and life are in the power of the tongue."*

Man's greatest challenge lies with his tongue. *"Even so the tongue is a little member and boasts great things. See how great a forest a little fire kindles"* (James 3:5). NKJV In verse 3, James says, *"For we all stumble in many things. If anyone does not stumble in word, he is a perfect (mature) man, able also to bridle the whole body."* Therefore, we must carefully guard our words, because we can trip on our lips.

> CLEARLY, GOD PROMISES POWER THROUGH THE WORDS OF THE REDEEMED:

We read in Job 22:28, *"Thou shalt also decree a thing and it shall be established unto thee."*

This form of decree does not mean that we command God. It is however, an expression of the HIGHEST LEVEL OF RELATIONSHIP AND COMMUNION WITH GOD. It does not mean we have any right or authority to "boss God" nor to "play God." But as faithful and obedient servants of God, we can trust God to work miracles as we believe and speak His word over the need or situation at hand.

When Moses pleaded with Pharaoh to let the people go and he refused, God sent numerous plagues in judgment upon Pharaoh and his people. Then Pharaoh pleaded with Moses to implore God to remove the plague by promising to let the people go, but did not keep his word. You will note in the following example where we see this demonstrated—there was a vital and close relationship and communion between Moses and God:

Moses spoke to various plagues that had come upon the Egyptians, and they ceased: In Exodus 8: 13 we read, *"And the Lord did according to **the word** of Moses; and the frogs died out of the houses, out of the villages, and out of the fields."* Pharaoh further hardened his heart and God sent a plague of flies upon Pharaoh, his servants, and his people. He promised Moses he would allow them to go if he would have God remove the plague. We read in 8: 31, *"And the Lord did according to the word of Moses; and he removed the swarms of flies form Pharaoh, from his servants, and from his people; there remained not one."*

In one of the major battles Joshua fought in conquering the promised land from their enemies, we read in Joshua 10: 12-13, *"Then spake Joshua to the Lord in the day when the Lord delivered up the Amorites before the children of Israel, **and he said** in the sight of Israel, Sun, stand thou still upon Gibeon; and thou, Moon, in the valley of Ajalon. And the sun stood still, and the moon stayed, until the people had avenged themselves upon their enemies, Is not this written in the book of Jasher? So the sun stood still in the midst of heaven, and hasted not to go down about a whole day."* (Emphasis mine) Modern science substantiates this glorious miracle!

There are many cases of the power of the spoken word in the ministry of Jesus: In Mark 4: 39, *"and **He said** unto the sea, Peace, be still. And the wind ceased, and there was a great calm."* The Master **said** in Mark 11: 14 to the fig tree, *"No man eat fruit of thee hereafter forever."* The disciples heard Jesus say this, and on the following morning they saw the fig tree and Peter said, *"Master, behold, the fig tree which **thou cursedst** is withered away."* When Jesus and his disciples came to the Gadara, (Mark 5: 1-20) He encountered the man possessed with 2000 demons, and **Jesus said** in verse 8, *"Come out of the man, unclean spirit!"* and we read in verse 13, *"...Then the unclean spirits went out and entered the swine (there were about two thousand)."* (Emphasis mine)

Likewise, the early Church had numerous examples of healing and deliverances by the power of the spoken word. In Acts 9: 34 Peter spoke to Aeneas who had been bedridden for eight years and was paralyzed, *"And **Peter said** to him, 'Aeneas, Jesus the Christ heals you. Arise and make your bed.' Then he arose immediately."*

Paul encountered Elymas the sorcerer **and said**, *"O full of all deceit and fraud, you son of the devil, you enemy of all righteousness, will you not cease perverting the straight ways of the Lord? And now, indeed, the hand of the Lord is upon you, and you shall be blind, not seeing the sun for a time."* And immediately a *dark mist fell on him, and he went around seeking someone to lead him by the hand"* (Acts 13: 9-11).

In Acts 16: 16-24 we have the record of Paul speaking to the spirit of divination in the slave girl, *"I **command you** in the name of Jesus Christ to come out of her. And he came out that very hour."*

The power of speaking was not confined to Jesus and the Apostles, but among ordinary people we see the power of words or confessions, as noted in the following examples:

The woman with the issue of blood for twelve years, followed behind Jesus **and said,** *"If I may touch his garment, I shall be whole. And Jesus turned him about, and when he saw her, he said, 'Daughter, be of good comfort; thy faith hath made thee whole. And the woman was made whole from that hour"* (Matt. 9: 20-22).

The Syrophenician woman ***"kept asking** Jesus to cast the demon out of her daughter. But Jesus said to her, 'Let the children be filled first, for it's not good to take the children's bread and throw it to the little dogs.' And she answered and **said to Him**, 'Yes, Lord, yet even the little dogs under the table eat from the children's crumbs.' Then He said to her, 'For **this saying** go your way; the demon has gone out of your daughter.' And when she had come to her house, she found the demon gone out, and her daughter lying on the bed"* (Mark. 7: 25-30). (Emphasis mine)

Thus, we see if we are faithful to the Word of God, the God of the Word will be faithful to us and our confessions.

THREE IMPORTANT KINDS of CONFESSIONS IN GOD'S WORD:

1. The Confession of Sin

> *"But if we walk in the light as He is in the light, we have fellowship with one another, and the blood of Jesus Christ His Son cleanses us from all sin.*
> *If we say that we have no sin, we deceive ourselves, and the truth is not in us.*
> *If we confess our sins, He is faithful and just to forgive us our sins and to cleanse us from all unrighteousness"* (1 John 1: 7, 8, 9).

We must remember these verses were written to Christians not non-believers.

It is not God's will Christians sin, however, due to the weakness of the flesh, temptations, etc, Christians sometimes do sin.

I well remember as a young teen-ager, some months after I had received Christ as my personal Savior, I became angry and spoke a word of profanity. I felt so condemned! Immediately the devil began to accuse me—telling me I had lost my salvation and I was hopelessly lost! In agony, I cried out to God to forgive me and I immediately sensed His presence, His love and forgiveness!

I learned a vital lesson that day about confession. To maintain our fellowship and communion with God, it is necessary to confess sin the moment it is committed. Don't carry the baggage of sin. You should not hold on to your sin any longer than it takes to say, "Father forgive me". This is how we stay in Victory!

There is nothing in this world like sweet fellowship and communion with God. Satan hates that and relentlessly attempts to destroy that relationship. We should hate sin like God hates it, because it breaks our fellowship with God. Thank God for confession! If we will properly judge ourselves and confess our sin(s) to the Father, He immediately restores our fellowship and communion.

There is a tremendous power in this Confession, *"Whosoever covereth his sins shall not prosper, But whoever confesses and forsakes them will have mercy"* (Prov. 28:13).

2. The Confession of Jesus Christ as Lord

> *"But what does it say? 'The word is near you, even in your mouth and in your heart; (that is, the word of faith which we preach):*
> *That if you confess with your mouth the Lord Jesus and believe in your heart that God has raised Him from the dead, you will be saved.*
> *For with the heart one believes to righteousness, and with the mouth confession is made to salvation"* (Romans 10: 8, 9, 10).

This confession is for the unbeliever. Before an individual can ever be a Christian, as a sinner, he/she must be willing to repent of his/her sins and confess Jesus Christ as his/her personal Lord and Savior.

Jesus must be crowned the Lord of ones life! As the great Scottish missionary, John R Mott said: "He must be Lord OF All or He will not be Lord AT all". As long as we are going to run our lives, do-our-thing, depend on ourselves, go our own way, and be what we want to be, we will never be a Christian. VICTORY over the devil, the world, the flesh will never come until one confesses Jesus Christ as Savior and Lord! There is no other way to salvation (John 14:6; Acts 4:12).

3. The Confession of the Word.

"......the words I speak to you are spirit, and they are life" (John 6:63).

"For indeed the gospel was preached to us as well as to them; but the word which they heard did not profit them, not being mixed with faith in those who heard it."

"For the word of God is living and powerful, and sharper than any two-edged sword, piercing even to the division of soul and spirit, and of the joints and marrow, and is a discerner of the thoughts and intents of the heart" (Hebrews 4: 2, 12).

THERE IS NOTHING AS POWERFUL AS GOD'S WORD! Hebrews 1:3 states *"He upholds all things by the word of His power."*

Jesus said, *"Heaven and earth shall pass away, but My words by no means pass away"* (Matt. 24:35).

Peter said, *"But the word of the Lord endures forever"* (1Peter 1:25).

The Psalmist said, *"Forever, O Lord, Your word is settled in heaven"* (Psalm 119:89).

In Jeremiah 1:12, God said, *"I will hasten my word to perform it"* Literally, God is watching over His Word to see it come to pass—He is ready to perform His Word!

Through the prophet Isaiah God said, *"So shall my word be that goeth forth out of my mouth; it shall not return unto me void, but it shall accomplish that which I please, and it shall prosper in the thing whereto I sent it"* (Isa. 55: 11).

However, with Israel His word did not profit them, because it was not mixed with faith (Heb. 4: 2). **How do we mix the word with faith?** With our confession!

With our words! *"For assuredly, I say to you, whoever says to this mountain, 'Be removed and be cast into the sea,' and does not doubt in his heart, but believes that those things he says will come to pass, he will have whatever he says"* (Mark 11:23).

Please note that the word **"says"** is used three times and the word **"believe"** is used once. It takes three times as much "saying" or "speaking the word" as it does believing the word!

There is great power when we confess the Word! There is no greater example of speaking the Word than Jesus himself.

> "He taught them as one with authority" (Matt. 7:29).
> "He spoke to the sea to be calm" (Mark 4:39).
> "He spoke to two blind men to see" (Matt. 9:27-29).
> "He spoke to a fig tree to die" (Mark 11:14).
> "He spoke to the demons to come out" (Mark 5:8).

Jesus used Peter's boat for a pulpit to teach the multitudes. When He had finished, he instructed Peter to *"launch out into the deep and let down your nets for a catch."* Peter responded, "Master, we have toiled all night and caught nothing: **NEVERTHELESS AT YOUR WORD** I will let down the net. And when they had done this, they caught a great number of fish, and their net was breaking." (Luke 5: 1-10). (Emphasis mine)

We must keep focused on the Word, because ONLY the Word gives faith. *"So then faith comes by hearing, and hearing by the word of God"* (Romans 10:17).
We must confidently speak the word for results! *"When Jesus entered Capernaum, a centurion came to Him, pleading with Him, saying, 'Lord, my servant is laying at home paralyzed, dreadfully tormented.' And Jesus said to him, 'I will come and heal him.' The centurion answered and said, 'Lord I am not worthy that You should come under my roof. But **speak a word only**, and my servant will be healed.' 'And his servant was healed in the selfsame hour"* (Matt. 8:5-13). (Emphasis mine)

Faith is like a muscle, the more you work it the stronger it gets. We strengthen our faith when we speak God's Word. The devil wants you to speak fear, doubt, defeat and negativism. But the Bible says, *"give no place to the devil"* (Eph. 4:27). RATHER SPEAK GOD'S WORD!

The word "confession" is most usually thought of in the context of acknowledging our sin, or confession of sin to a priest, etc. However, it is important to remember that confession, in the positive sense, means "to say the same thing". It simply means AGREEING WITH GOD'S WORD! We refuse to believe what we feel or what others say, but believe and say what God says about our need or situation.

WE NEVER RISE ABOVE THE LEVEL OF OUR CONFESSION. That is why the Apostle Paul urges us to "make a good confession" (1Tim. 6:12). The natural, human tendency is to speak negatively. It is easier to complain, criticize or condemn than to praise. It seems always easier to say, "I can't", than to say "I can". The Israelites are an excellent example. They continually said, *"Can God?"* rather than *"God Can."* *"Yea, they spake against God; **they said**, Can God furnish a table in the wilderness? ...can He give bread also? Can he provide flesh for his people? Therefore the Lord heard this, and was wroth: so fire was kindled against Jacob, and anger also came up against Israel; Because they believed not in God, and trusted not in his salvation"* (Ps. 78: 19-22). (Emphasis mine)

Oh, how important it is that we guard our tongues and the words we speak:

> ➢ When you said "I have no faith"...doubt came in and robbed you of victory.
>
> ➢ When you said "I am a failure"...discouragement took over.
>
> ➢ When you talked Fear, it rose up like a giant to paralyze you.

If you think about it, we all have seen and felt the power of speaking negative words. To develop healthy relationships with our spouse, children, and others, we must carefully watch our words. *"A soft answer turneth away wrath; but grievous words stir up anger"* (Prov. 15: 1). It is amazing how the right words, spoken in the right manner, can diffuse a very volatile situation and create a completely new atmosphere.

To maintain a consistent walk in victory, WE MUST LIFT THE LEVEL OF OUR CONFESSION TO THE LEVEL OF GOD'S WORD! Say what He says!

*"When men are cast down, then **THOU SHALT SAY** THERE IS A LIFTING UP"* (Job. 22:39).

*"Let **the weak SAY**, "I AM STRONG"* (Joel 3:10).

We are not talking here about "mind over matter." We are not suggesting the circumstances aren't real, because pain is real, etc. But we are saying, you must decide which you will agree with—your situation of pain, etc., or God's Word!

*"Whoso offereth praise glorifieth Me and to him that **ordereth his conversation aright** will I show the salvation of God"* (Ps. 50:23). (Emphasis mine)

We see an excellent example of this is in the life of Abraham. *"He staggered not at the promise of God through unbelief, but was strong in faith **GIVING PRAISE TO GOD"*** (Romans 4:20). Against all odds—his age, the age of his wife, and the long period of twenty-five years he waited, but he was faithful to God! The circumstances said it was impossible! He, however, did not consider the circumstances, but considered God's Word instead! He chose to agree with God's promise and not the prevailing circumstances. (Emphasis mine)

THE WORD OF PRAISE GLORIFIES THE LORD AND GIVES THE VICTORY. Therefore, I DETERMINE TO BE A BOLD PRAISER:

'I WILL BLESS THE LORD AT ALL TIMES; His praise shall continually be in my MOUTH" (Ps. 34:1) (Emphasis mine)

*"I will sing of the mercies of the Lord forever; **With my mouth** will I make know Your faithfulness to all generations. **For I have said,** "Mercy shall be built up forever"* (Ps. 89.1, 2). (Emphasis mine)

WORDS SPOKEN IN HARMONY WITH GOD'S WORD WILL ALWAYS WORK WONDERS. That is why *"no corrupt words shall proceed out of my mouth"* (Eph. 4:29). THEREFORE,

> ➢ I will speak "SWEET WORDS"
> ➢ I will speak "SEASONED WORDS"
> ➢ I will speak "SUITABLE WORDS"
> ➢ I will speak "SOUND WORDS"

Our confession always precedes our possession. Whether positive or negative, we will have what we say! *"Your are snared by the words of your own mouth; You are taken by the words of your mouth"* (Prov. 6:2).

THEREFORE DON'T TALK:

> Don't talk SICKNESS, when the Bible says, *'With His stripes we are healed'* (Isa. 53:5).

> Don't talk WEAKNESS, when the Bible says, *"The Lord is the strength of my life'* (Ps. 27:1).

> Don't talk DEFEAT, when the Bible says, "We are more than conquerors through Christ" (Rom. 8:37).

> Don't talk LACK, when the Bible says, *"My God shall supply all my need"* (Phil. 4:19).

> Don't talk BONDAGE, when the Bible says, *"The Son has made me free"*(John 8:36).

> Don't talk FEAR, when the Bible says, *"For God has not given us a spirit of fear, but of power of love and of a sound mind"* (2Tim. 1:7).

> Don't talk DISCOURAGEMENT, when the Bible says, *"Being confident of this very thing, that He who has begun a good work in you will complete it until the day of Jesus Christ"* (Phil. 1:6).

> Don't talk WORRY, when the Bible says, *"Do not worry"* (See Matt. 6:31-34).

> Don't talk GUILT AND CONDEMNATION, when the Bible says, *"There is therefore now no condemnation to those who are in Christ Jesus, who do not walk according to the flesh, but according to the Spirit"* (Rom. 8:1).

"WITH THE MOUTH CONFESSION IS MADE **UNTO**" (Romans 10:10). This includes "unto healing", "unto deliverance", "unto every spiritual and physical blessing" provided for in Christ. Because as Jesus said, *"If ye abide in Me, and my* *words abide in you, ye shall ask what ye will, and it shall be done unto you"* (John 15: 7*). (Emphasis mine)

THE LAW OF CONFESSION RULES ME: THEREFORE, I CHOOSE TO SPEAK WORDS THAT WORK WONDERS.

Chapter Three

The Law of Obedience RENEWS Me

"Behold, I set before you today a blessing and a curse: the blessing if you obey the commandments of the Lord your God which I command you today; and a curse if you do not obey the commandments of the Lord your God, but turn aside from the way which I command you today, to go after other gods which you have not known" (Duet. 11:26-28).

"Come now, and let us reason together," Says the Lord, "Though your sins are like scarlet, They shall be as white as snow; Though they are red like crimson, They shall be as wool.
If you are willing and obedient, You shall eat the good of the land; But if you refuse and rebel, You shall be devoured by the sword"; For the mouth of the Lord has spoken" (Isa. 1:18-20).

"He who has My commandments and keeps them, it is he who loves Me. And he who loves Me will be love by My Father and I will love him and manifest Myself to him" (John 14:21).

"Not everyone who says to Me, 'Lord, Lord,' shall enter the kingdom of heaven, but he who does the will of My Father in heaven" (Matt. 7:21).

"His mother said to the servants, 'Whatever He says to you, do it'"
(John 2:5).

As we explore the *Law of Obedience* in this lesson, it will become very apparent that our renewal or lack thereof hinges entirely on our obedience or disobedience to all God commands in His word.

The Law of Obedience is the GATEWAY, the HIGHWAY and the ONLY WAY to receive the blessings and favor of God in our lives! It only takes a brief survey of the Scriptures from Genesis to Revelation to see how predominant this law is.

In the twenty eight chapter of Deuteronomy God set forth to Israel the wonderful blessings of obedience: *"Now it shall come to pass, if you diligently obey the voice of the Lord your God, to observe carefully all His commandments which I command you today, that the Lord your God will set you high above all nations of the earth."*

"*All these blessings shall come upon you and overtake you, because you obey the voice of the Lord your God"* (Deut. 28:1, 2). In verses 1-14 we see the menu of blessings God promised them for simple obedience:

➢ The LORD God will set you on high above all nations of the earth and all these blessings shall come on you and overtake you (v 1-2).
➢ You will be blessed in the city (v 3).
➢ You will be blessed in the field.
➢ You will have many children (v 4).
➢ You will have abundant crops.
➢ You will have large flocks and herds.
➢ Your baskets and storehouses will have abundance (v 6, 8).
➢ You will have blessings when you come in (v 6).
➢ You will have blessings when you go out.
➢ The LORD will defeat you enemies (v 7).
➢ Your land will be abundantly fertile and productive.
➢ The LORD shall change you into a holy people dedicated to himself (v9).
➢ You will be a witness and example to all people on earth (v 10)
➢ All nations will stand in awe of you.
➢ You will be prosperous in goods, in children, in stock, and in crops in all the land (v 11).
➢ The LORD will open to you all His good treasure (v 12).
➢ The heavens will give you rain in due season in all your land.
➢ The Lord will bless all the work of your hands.
➢ You shall lend to many nations but you shall not borrow from them.
➢ The LORD shall make you the head and not the tail (v13).
➢ You shall be above all men and never beneath them, having the upper hand.

I have heard people testify, "All the promises in the Book (Bible) are mine." Quite frankly, I don't lay claim to such a statement. I don't want all the promises in the Book! If you will carefully read chapter 27: 14-26 and chapter 28: 15-68, you will see God's incredible list of judgments or curses for disobedience. These "curses" are just as much a promise of God as are the blessings!

In the opening chapter of the Bible we see the beautiful scene of a garden called PARADISE. We read, *"And the Lord commanded the man"* (Gen. 2:16).

Then in chapter three verse eleven, *"He said to the man, "Hast thou eaten of the tree whereof I commanded thee that thou shouldest not eat?"*

THEN TURN FROM GENESIS and go to the CLOSE of the BIBLE and read in Revelation 22:14, *"Blessed are those who do His commandments , that they may have the right to the tree of life, and may enter through the gates into the city."*

From the beginning to the end of the Bible, from Paradise Lost to Paradise Re-gained, *the Law of Obedience is unchangeable!* It is only through *OBEDIENCE* that we are given access to the tree of life and the favor of God!

What is interesting is that Mid-way between the beginning and the end...stands THE CROSS OF CHRIST!

We read, *"through the OBEDIENCE of One shall many be made righteous"* (Ro. 5:19).

"He became OBEDIENT unto death, therefore God hath highly exalted Him" (Phil. 2:8).

"'He learned OBDEIENCE by the things which He suffered...and became the author of eternal salvation unto all them that OBEY HIM" (Heb. 5:8, 9). (Emphasis mine)

(Beginning)	(Middle)	(End)
PARADISE...................CALVARY................HEAVEN		

Think about it! Paradise, Calvary, Heaven—ALL PROCLAIM WITH ONE ACCORD, the first and last thing God asks is simple, universal, and unchanging obedience.

What is further interesting: WE want MANIFESTATIONS, GOD wants OBEDIENCE; WE want POWER, GOD wants PURITY! However, it is only as we align ourselves with God's Word, and desire what He desires, will we ever see the glorious manifestations and power of God demonstrated!

THE BIBLE ABOUNDS WITH ILLUSTRATIONS AND EXAMPLES OF THOSE WHO KEPT THE LAW OF OBEDIENCE

1. NOAH: *"According to all that God commanded Noah so did he."* This is stated 4 times in Genesis 6: 22; 7: 5, 9, 16.

2. ABRAHAM: *"By faith Abraham OBEYED and went out...God said, "Blessing I will bless thee...because thou hast OBEYED my voice"* (Gen. 22:17-18).

3. MOSES: at Mount Sinai, God gave him the message to the people: *"If you will OBEY my voice indeed, ye shall be a peculiar treasure to Me above all people"* (Ex. 19:5).

4. IN THE BUILDING OF SANCTURARY in which God was to dwell. In the last three chapters of the book of Exodus you have the expression 19 times, *"According to all the Lord commanded Moses, so did* he and then the glory of the Lord filled the tabernacle."

5. ISRAEL: (THE NATION) As long as they walked in OBEDIENCE *"there was not one feeble person among them"* (Psalm 105:27). However, when they got into disobedience, *" God sent leanness into their souls."* (Psalm 106:15). (Emphasis mine)

The Israelites were always winding up at "WIT'S END CORNER"— struggling with their enemies, facing poverty, shame, defeat and captivity because of their DISOBEDIENCE. Because they were a stubborn and rebellious people and unwilling to obey God they discovered, *"The way of the transgressor is hard"* (Proverbs 13:15).

We can learn much from their example today (See Rom. 15:4; and 1Cor. 10:11). GOD WILL ALWAYS HONOR THE PERSON, THE CHURCH, OR NATION THAT WILL OBEY HIM. The prophet Samuel said: *"To OBEY is better than sacrifice"* (1Samuel 15:22). (Emphasis mine)

An expert dog trainer says: "Obedience is the foundation of all training. An obedient dog actually enjoys life far more than a disobedient dog." What a lesson we can learn from this!

OBEDIENCE IS HEALTHY

We can attain to a healthy state of spirit, soul, and body as we obediently get in line with the Word, and then let the Word work for us. Many Christians, however, make the unfortunate mistake of setting their interest primarily in "getting a blessing" only without much concern for total obedience. We are not to go around looking FOR A BLESSING. Rather, we are to OBEY AND BE BLESSED! God has already provided "all spiritual blessings in the heavenlies" for His children (Eph. 1:3).

According to Strong's Exhaustive Concordance, the word 'commandment' in the singular is used 56 times, in the plural 32 times, a total of 88 times in the New Testament and it's estimated there are over 1,000 commandments in these 27 books of the Bible.

For instance, THE WORD SAYS:

> ➤ "Walk by faith and not by sight" (2Cor.5:7).
> ➤ "Be ye filled with the Spirit" (Eph. 5:18).
> ➤ "Walk in the Spirit" (Gal.5:16).
> ➤ "Be led by the Spirit" (Rom. 8:14).
> ➤ "Seek those things which are above" (Col.3:1).
> ➤ "Wives submit yourselves to your own husbands- Husbands, love your wife's- Children obey your parents- Fathers provoke not your children to wrath" (Eph. 5:21-6:6).
> ➤ "Put on the whole armor of God" (Eph. 6:11).
> ➤ "Praying always in the Spirit" (Eph. 6:18).
> ➤ "Produce the fruit of the Spirit" (Gal. 5:22).
> ➤ "Speak evil of no man" (Titus 3:2).
> ➤ "Pray for those in charge" (1Tim. 2:1-2).
> ➤ "Forgive others" (Matt. 6:14).
>   "Have the God kind of Faith" (Mk. 11:22).
> ➤ "Don't do your alms to be seen of men" (Matt.6:1).
> ➤ "Judge not" (Matt. 7:1).
> ➤ "Seek first the kingdom of God" (Matt. 6:33).
> ➤ "Be not unequally yoked together w/ unbelievers (2Cor 6:14).
> ➤ "Love one another" (John 15:12).

If we want to receive the benefit and blessing of these commands, and all other commands and promises, we must humbly walk in total obedience to God and His Word.

Over the many years of serving Christ, I have learned the best kind of obedience is the INSTANT kind! We should always follow the example of Samuel, when as a lad he said: *"Speak, Lord, for your servant hears"* (1Sam. 3:9).

One of the ways we train our human spirit to hear the voice of God is by the continual practice of obedience. That is why in the *"School of the Spirit"* obedience is a required course.

Now allow me to point your attention to some important observations about obedience:

OBEDIENCE IS REQUIRED FOR PROSPERITY AND SUCCESS

"This Book of the Law shall not depart from your mouth, but you shall meditate in it day and night, that you may observe to do according to all that is written in it. For then you will make your way prosperous, and then you will have good success" (Joshua 1:8). (Emphasis mine)

OBEDIENCE IS THE KEY TO FELLOWSHIP AND ABIDING IN CHRIST

"Jesus answered and said to him, 'If anyone loves Me, he will keep My word; and My Father will love him, and We will come to him and make Our home with him" (John 14:23).

"If you abide in Me, and My words abide in you, you will ask what you desire, and it shall be done for you" (John 15:7).

"But if we walk in the light as He is in the light, we have fellowship with one another, and the blood of Jesus Christ His Son cleanses us from all sin" (1John 1:7).

OBEDIENCE IS THE KEY TO KNOWING TRUTH AND THE WILL OF GOD

"If anyone wants to do His will, he shall know concerning the doctrine, whether it is from God or whether I speak on My own authority" (John 7:17).

"And do not be conformed to this world but be transformed by the renewing of your mind, that you may prove what is that good and acceptable and perfect will of God" (Rom. 12:2).

OBEDIENCE IS THE KEY TO THE POWER OF GOD

"Behold, I send the Promise of My Father upon you; but tarry in the city of Jerusalem until you are endued with power from on high" (Luke 24:49).

"But you shall receive power when the Holy Spirit has come upon you; and you shall be witness to Me in Jerusalem, and in all Judea and Samaria, and to the ends of the earth" (Acts 1: 8).

"And we are His witness of these things; and so also is the Holy Spirit, whom God has given to those who obey Him" (Acts 5:32).

It is important to see that of the Five hundred (500) people that heard the command of Jesus to go to Jerusalem and wait for the promise of the Father, only one hundred twenty (120) obeyed. That means 76% were disobedient for one reason or another, while 24% obeyed and received the blessing of Pentecost. (See Acts 1, 2)

WITHOUT OBEDIENCE THE KINGDOM OF HEAVEN IS CLOSED TO US

"Not everyone who says to Me, 'Lord, Lord,' shall enter the kingdom of heaven, but he who does the will of My Father in heaven" (Matt. 7:21).

"But be ye doers of the word, and not hearers only, deceiving your own selves" (James 1: 22).

"I am the way, the truth, and the life: no man cometh unto the Father, but by me" (Jn. 14: 6).

"If ye keep my commandments, ye shall abide in my love; even as I have kept my Father's commandments, and abide in his love" (Jn. 15: 10).

The Bible offers many blessings and rewards for obedience. The following are a few examples:

1. LONG LIFE

"My son, do not forget my law, But let your heart keep my commands; For length of days and long life And peace they will add to you" (Prov. 3:1, 2).

The longer I live the more I can do for God. We have only a life time to serve Him. If I cannot serve the Lord, I don't need a long life. I don't need to be here.

2. KEEP YOU FROM EVIL

"Whoso keepeth the commandment shall feel no evil thing" (Ecc 8:5).

It is the Devil's business to hassle, harass and pester God's children. Through deception, seduction, and a host of other tactics he tries to steal, kill, and destroy (Jn.10:10).

But God says: *"No weapon formed against you shall prosper"* (Isaiah 54:17). We have a Divine Protection Plan!

3. GREAT PEACE

"Great peace have those who love Your law, And nothing causes them to stumble" (Ps. 119:165).

We can live without offense. This was the Apostle Paul's testimony, *"This being so, I myself always strive to have a conscience without offense toward God and men"* (Acts 24:6).

4. GREAT GLADNESS

King David said, *"I was glad when they said to me, 'Let us go into the house of the Lord'"* (Ps. 122:1). (See Neh. 8: 13-17)

There are 31 references to being glad in the book of Psalms alone. God's obedient people are blessed with gladness and joy!

5. BLESSED ASSURANCE

"Now he who keeps His commandments abides in Him, and He in him. And by this we know that He abides in us, by the Spirit whom He has given us" (1John 3:24).

The blessed Holy Spirit makes us conscious of His abiding presence.

"Now this is the confidence that we have in Him, that if we ask anything according to His will, He hears us" (1John 5:14).

6. ANSWERED PRAYER:

> *"And whatever we ask we receive from Him, because we keep His Commandments and do those things that are pleasing in His sight"* (1John 3:22).

7. THE LORD WILL LOVE AND MANIFEST HIMSELF TO US

> *"He who has My commandments and keeps them, it is he who loves Me. And he who loves Me will be loved by My Father, and I will love him and manifest Myself to him"* (John 14:21).

What glorious moments when you are alone and communing with the Lord, and suddenly, the room, the car, or where ever you are the area fills up with His presence! It is obedience that brings these moments to pass. If I am willing and obedient to do, to go, to say, He will come to me! And He will come to you also.

My friend, you have no need that God cannot meet when you obey Him. We have nothing to fear in this day of global foment and unrest. One famous astronomer said it well, "I cannot be afraid of the darkness here, I've lived too long with the stars."

We have lived too long with the Bright and Morning Star to be afraid of the darkness of the age. Well can we sing, *"Trust and obey, for there is no other way, to be happy in Jesus, than to trust and obey."*

The Law of Obedience RENEWS ME!

Chapter Four

The Law of Faith REWARDS Me

"Now faith is the substance of things hoped for, the evidence of things not seen. For by it the elders obtained a good testimony.
By faith we understand that the worlds were framed by the word of God,
By faith Abel offered to God a more excellent sacrifice than Cain, through which he obtained witness that he was righteous, God testifying of his gifts; and through it he being dead still speaks.
By faith Enoch was translated so that he did not see death, and was not found because God had translated him', for before his translation he had this testimony, that he pleased God.
*But without faith it is impossible to please Him, for he who comes to God must believe that He is, and that He is a **rewarder** of those who diligently seek Him"* (Heb. 11:1-6). (Emphasis mine)

One of the outstanding graces or virtues of the Christian life is FAITH. Without it, we simply cannot please God, nor receive from God! Faith is a vital condition to Salvation. *"Therefore, having been justified by faith we have peace with God through our Lord Jesus Christ"* (Rom. 5:1).
(See Romans 3:21-28)

The Bible has much to say about the PLACING OF OUR CONFIDENCE AND FAITH:

WE CAN:

WALK BY FAITH (2Cor. 5:7)
PRAY IN FAITH (James 5: 15)
ADD TO OUR FAITH (2Pet. 1:5)
CONTINUE IN THE FAITH (1Tim. 1:19; Acts 14:22)
OVERCOME BY FAITH (1Jn. 5:4)
PREACH THE FAITH (Gal. 1: 23)
LIVE BY FAITH (Gal. 2: 20)
FIGHT THE GOOD FIGHT OF FAITH (1Tim. 6: 12)

FAITH:

> SEES THE INVISIBLE
> TRIES THE IMPOSSIBLE
> BEARS THE INTOLERABLE

FAITH:

> MAKES HEAVEN REAL
> THE PRESENCE OF GOD SURE, AND
> THE PROMISES OF GOD DEFINTE AND SPECIFIC.

The principles of faith never change with the ensuing dispensations of time. It took Faith for Noah to trust God, and build the Ark when it had never rained, nor had ever such a ship been built before.

It was by faith Abraham left the Ur of the Chaldees, to go to a land of promise not knowing where he was going.

It was by faith that Moses refused to be called the son of Pharoah's daughter, forsook Egypt, kept the Passover, and delivered the children of Israel.

It was by faith David, as a young teen-age boy, challenged and defeated the giant Goliath.

There are many marvelous descriptions of faith recorded in the eleventh chapter of the book of Hebrews. These heroes were rewarded because of their faith. That has not changed! The law of faith works and we are rewarded because of our faith. We are not rewarded because of our feelings, our fame, our fortunes or fortune-tellers—but because of our faith!

We see the vital importance of faith when our Lord spoke to Peter: *"Simon, Simon! Indeed, Satan has asked for you, that he may sift you as wheat. But I have prayed for you, that **your faith should not fail**; and when you have returned to Me, strengthen your brethren."* (Luke 22:31) (Emphasis mine)

Notice that the Hebrew writer said in chapter 11verse 6, *"Without faith it is impossible to please Him, for he who comes to God must believe that He is, and that He is a rewarder of those who diligently seek Him."*

God is concerned about the Faith of His People. Jesus said: *"When the Son of man cometh, shall He find faith on the earth"* (Luke 18:8).

Faith is a golden Gem-- Peter calls its PRECIOUS FAITH,

"To those who have obtained like precious faith with us by the righteousness of our God and Savior Jesus Christ" (2Pet 1:1).

As we turn our spotlight upon this glorious gem of faith, we will obviously see several important aspects about faith:

First, let us notice THE MEANING (OR DEFINITION) OF FAITH

As to what is faith I suppose faith, like love, almost defies categorical definition. It means different things to different people, and you can get a variation of definitions from almost everyone you talk to.

> "Poetically speaking, faith has been called the eye that sees the invisible, the ear that hearts the inaudible, the hand that feels the intangible and the power that works the impossible." **1**

Faith is more easily described than defined. In fact, in Hebrews 11 there are no less than ten beautiful descriptions of faith, as we will see later in this lesson.

This chapter, (Hebrews 11), also gives us the most accurate definition of faith to be found anywhere. Notice, *"Now faith is the substance of things hoped for, the evidence of things not seen"* (Heb. 11:1). Note some other translations:

"Now faith is assurance of (things) hope for, a conviction of things not seen" (ASV).

"What is faith? It is the confident assurance that something we want is going to happen. It is the certainty that what we hope for is waiting for us, even though we cannot see it up ahead" (TLB).

"NOW FAITH is the assurance (the confirmation, the title deed) of things (we) hope for, being the proof of things (we) do not see and the conviction of

their reality (faith perceiving as real fact what is not revealed to the senses)"
(AMP).

It is important to understand there are many different kinds of faith: religious faith, natural faith, believing faith, but everyone, saved and unsaved alike, has a natural, human faith. We eat, sleep, drive a car, fly in a plane, sit down on a chair without examining, and do many other things by an act of natural or human faith.

These scriptures above; however, are talking about a supernatural faith, the God kind of faith—a faith that believes with the heart rather than believing what our natural physical senses may tell us. As my dear friend the late Dr. Kenneth Hagin would often say, when teaching on this grand subject, "FAITH IS GRASPING THE UNREALITIES OF HOPE AND BRINGING THEM INTO THE REALM OF REALITY." Such faith grows out of the Word of God.

For the believer, to seek or ask for faith is incorrect and unscriptural. Often times we hear believers say, "Oh, if only I had faith, I would get healed, if only I had enough faith I would get an answer to my prayers." Or, "please pray for me that I will have faith." This shows the lack of knowledge of God's Word. We already possess faith because God has given every believer a measure of faith (Rom. 12:3), but we need to demonstrate our faith by putting it into action and operation.

Faith is both a SUBSTANCE and EVIDENCE! Faith, like money is a tangible substance. But it is also evidence of what I want to purchase with it.
Faith is like having a title deed to property I inherited, but never saw with my physical eyes. However, because I have the title deed (substance), I can say with assurance (with evidence), I own a piece of real estate.

Faith is a Present Possession! Notice, Hebrews 11:1: *"NOW Faith IS."* Faith is not tomorrow, or sometime in the distant future, but NOW! Hope, which is the foundation of Faith, is tomorrow. Hope is future, faith is present. There is no conflict between faith and hope. Without faith we cannot receive. Without hope we have no foundation for faith. Hope is a good waiter, faith is the active receiver. (Emphasis mine)

Faith is a Belief and an Action joined together. We read in James 2:20-26, *"But do you want to know, O foolish man, that faith without works is dead? Was not Abraham our father justified by works when he offered Isaac his son on the altar?*

Do you see that faith was working together with his works, and by works faith was made perfect?

And the Scripture was fulfilled which says, 'Abraham believed God, and it was accounted to him for righteousness.' And he was called the friend of God.

You see then that a man is justified by works, and not by faith only. Likewise, was not Rahab the harlot also justified by works when she received the messengers and sent them out another way? "For as the body without the spirit is dead so faith without works is dead also."

I like Weymouth's translation of vs. 26, *"Belief without a corresponding action is worthless." We must have actions that go hand in hand with our faith.* For example, we read:

Noah believed God and **prepared** an ark for the saving of his household. (Heb.11: 7). He put action with his faith!

Abraham believed God and **took steps** to offer his son, his promised blessing, to God (Gen. 22).

Moses believed God and **forsook Egypt**, and **led the people** of God out of the land of bondage (Heb. 11:24-29).

The three Hebrews brothers **refused to bow** to the Kings image, believing God would deliver them, and He did (Dan. 3: 16-25)!

David believed God and **picked up the stones** and **charged** the giant and killed him (1Sam. 17: 40-58).

The disciples believed Jesus, **organized** the multitude to sit down in companies, then they **broke** the few loaves and fish to feed them. They acted on His Word and saw the miracle (Jn. 6: 1-14)!

To the man with the withered hand Jesus said first, "step forward". He did. He acted on the word of Jesus. *"Then Jesus said to him, 'Stretch out you hand', and he stretched it out, and his hand was restored as whole as the other"* (Mark 3:1-5).

Had this man not acted in obedience on what Jesus said, he would not have received his healing. He did not wait for a "feeling", or until he saw the miracle, before acting upon what the Lord said. Rather he acted, then, saw the miracle.

The corresponding action with your faith is absolutely necessary to obtain Salvation, The Baptism of the Holy Spirit, Divine Healing, or Answer to Prayer.

We can better understand what faith is when we determine what it is not:

Faith is NOT feelings- Feelings are in the realm of the natural senses. Faith is in the realm of the supernatural. Feelings say, "If I can see it, taste it, touch it, handle it, then I have it." I have asked many people after praying for their healing, "Are you healed? Invariably they would answer, "I don't know, I'm not sure, I hope so, or I don't feel like it."

They were basing their answer strictly on the physical senses. It seems logical to the mind if one continues to feel the pain or continues to see the symptoms, to conclude they are not healed and did not get the answer. That is because the mind has been programmed to think that way.

I well remember the night I was saved as a teen-age boy. I was kneeling at the altar fully broken, repentant, when the Pastor knelt down in front of me and asked, "How do you feel?" It confused me! I didn't even know what an altar was when I entered the church that night let alone understand salvation. With tears streaming down my face I cried, "I don't know, how am I supposed to feel?" Fortunately, the Pastor saw the problem and opened his Bible to Romans 10: 8-10, and asked me to read the following, *"But what saith it? The word is night thee, even in thy mouth, and in thy heart: that is, the word of faith, which we preach; That if thou shalt confess with thy mouth the Lord Jesus, and shalt believe in thin heart that God hath raised him from the dead, thou shalt be saved. For with the heart man believeth unto righteousness; and with the mouth confession is made unto salvation."* KJV

Then he asked me, "Do you confess the Lord Jesus Christ as your Savior?" Yes, I said, "Do you believe in your heart God raised Him from the dead?" Yes, I said. "Then, what does the verse say?" he asked. I said, "I AM SAVED!" Then everybody around me and the others at the altar together rejoiced and began weeping and hugging one another.

I suddenly had a calm assurance, an inner sense of peace, which later I came to understand as the "witness of God's Spirit with my spirit" (Rom. 8: 16) that I was saved, that Jesus Christ was truly MY Savior and I was ready to go to heaven.

However, it was not until I left the church that night, while walking down about seven steps, that I really felt something. I felt like I stepped out onto a cloud and walked in a realm I had never before known. The whole world seemed different. The stars, the town, the people, my parents and siblings all seemed different. I wondered how did they change, but it wasn't them that changed, it was me! That feeling of walking in a "glory cloud" continued for several weeks. But the firm assurance of my salvation has always been real in my heart over all these many years. Praise His Wonderful Name!

Now notice something: First it was **FACT**. God's Word said it! Second it was **FAITH**. I believed it! There was absolutely no doubt about it! Then third, I **FELT** it! Oh Glory!

This is the order, **FACT, FAITH, FEELINGS**. When we understand this and keep it in this order we will see results. This is just as true for healing, our finances, or whatever our need might be, as it is for salvation.

Satan, the thief tries to deceive the believer in thinking that because they didn't see or feel some tangible physical evidence, or see a change immediately in the symptoms, they didn't receive an answer (See 2Cor.10: 2-5).

We must recognize that feelings can deceive you. Feelings are like a barometer that can move up or down and confuse you. Feelings are like a sailboat, which goes whatever way the wind is blowing. Feelings, like the weather can change with the circumstances. Your feelings are one thing, Bible faith is another; and one has nothing to do with the other.

In a dear book entitled *Gems of Truth*, that I have had for nearly sixty years, is this little saying on feelings: "If a man's feelings do not feel as he feels they ought to feel, he is liable to get feeling his feelings until his feelings feel that he feels backslidden. Was it Noah's feelings that saved him or was it the ark?"**2**

But Hebrews 11: 1 describes faith as "the evidence of things not seen." Faith is the substance of things hope for, because it makes them real. It is the evidence of things not seen because it convinces us of their actual existence. Simply put, you have to believe you have it before you see or feel it!

Faith is NOT merely believing- Most people think *faith* and *belief* are the same thing. Most of us have been taught and brought up to think *believing is faith*, and *faith is believing*; but as long as Christians think and believe like this they seldom ever get answers to their prayers.

Thinking that belief is faith is also very deceiving. The Bible says "demons believe and tremble" (James 2: 19), and have a general kind of faith, and could say, *"Let us alone; what have we to do with Thee, thou Jesus of Nazareth? Art thou come to destroy us? I know knew Thee who thou art; the Holy One of God"* (Luke 4: 34). They believe, but they were still demons condemned to eternal punishment.

But does not the Bible say, "Believe on the Lord Jesus Christ, and thou shalt be saved, and thy house," you ask? (Acts 16: 31) Indeed it does! But you must understand the meaning of this passage from the original language. **The Amplified Bible** clarifies the meaning here of belief. *The Philippian jailer "brought them out (of the dungeon) and said, Men, what is it necessary for me to do that I may be saved? And they answered, Believe in the Lord Jesus Christ (give yourself up to Him, take yourself out of your own keeping and entrust yourself into His keeping as you will be saved, (and this applies both to) you and your household as well."*

The word *"believe"* here and in many other passages comes from the Greek word *pisteuo*, meaning: "to adhere to; cleave to; to trust; to have faith in; to rely on; to depend on." Now insert all this into the passage and clearly it is not talking about belief originating from the mind as one does with *mental assent*, but rather trust and acting upon what you believe with all your heart. That is saving faith!

Another passage where this is clearly seen is John 11: 25: *"Jesus said to her, I am (Myself) the Resurrection and the Life. Whoever believes (adheres to, trusts in, and relies on) Me, although he may die, yet he shall live."* (AMP)

It must be the combination of faith and belief to be saving faith. Faith and belief are two sides of the same coin. They both must be intact just like both sides of a coin of currency must be intact to spend. Otherwise, it won't work. If you don't understand this difference, you will never truly be able to exercise faith.

You must be as certain that you know when you are exercising faith as you are certain you are male or female. How long does it take you to answer a form question as to whether you are male or female? Not long, does it? You know that. If you don't know that you are in serious trouble!

Well, how do you know? Do you have to say, "Let me see—I'd better pray about it and see if I can get a confirmation—Maybe somebody will prophesy over me and tell me; " No! You ought to know. You ought to be able to say, "I'm a man, a male. I have all the standard equipment to prove it." Or, "I'm a woman, a female. I have the standard equipment to prove it." Likewise, we are confident with our prayer request because we are confident about God's Word!

Faith is NOT hope. While hope is a wonderful virtue, it is not faith. Hope is the foundation upon which faith rest. Notice Hebrews 11: 1 again, *"Now faith is the substance of things HOPED FOR."* If you do not have any hope, then faith will have no substance or substantial foundation to stand on. Without hope you are truly hopeless. (Emphasis mine)

Hope has a wonderful place as one of the ABIDING QUALITIES of the Christian life. When Paul, writing to the Corinthians, said *"And now abideth faith, hope, love, these three; but the greatest of these is love"* (1Cor. 13: 13), he was not inferring that hope and faith are not important. Each has its place, and one cannot be substituted for another. **We cannot substitute love for hope. Neither can we substitute hope for faith.**

Hope always has reference to the future. It is always in the future tense. Faith, however, is ALWAYS IN THE PRESENT TENSE

Hope says, "I believe I receive my healing or answer—sometime." That is not faith, that's hope because it is put into the future. Faith says, "I receive my healing or answer—now!"

Hope is a good waiter, waiting for the answer to come, but faith never comes home with an empty basket. Notice for instance, Ephesians 2: 8, 9 and Romans 10: 9, 10, 13:

> 8 "For by grace are ye saved through faith; and that not of yourselves: it is the gift of God:
> 9 Not of works, lest any man should boast."
>
> 9 "That if thou shalt confess with thy mouth the Lord Jesus, and shalt

believe in thine heart that God hath raised him from the dead, thou shalt be saved.

10 For with the heart man believeth unto righteousness; and with the mouth confession is made unto salvation.

13 For whosever shall call upon the name of the Lord shall be saved."

No where here does it say we are saved by hope. We are saved by grace through faith. That faith is God's gift to us! We have it, we use it, and we get results! This same principle is true for healing or answer to prayer.

Faith is NOT pity. We can feel deep sorrow and compassion for our needs or for another person's need and that is commendable, because God is a God of compassion, but that will not get us the answer to our prayers. God's desire is for all to be saved, but until one acts in faith one will not be saved. Just so with healing— God is unable to heal until our faith is put into action!

Faith is NOT some form of mysticism. Faith is not "a blind leap into the dark", or as something mysterious, indefinable and unintelligible; something super-spiritual and mystical. It is not superstitious religion such as you see in animism and other forms of human religions.

True faith is very practical and very simple. The life of Jesus as a man full of faith and the Holy Ghost is the glorious example of the simplicity of faith.

Faith is NOT mental assent. "John Wesley once said that the devil has given the church a substitute for faith, one that looks and sounds so much like faith that few people can tell the difference. This substitute he called "mental assent." Many people read God's Word and agree that it is true, but they are agreeing only with their minds. And that is not what gets the job done. It is heart faith that receives from God."

Mental assent says, "I know God's Word is true. I know God has promised healing, but for some reason I can't get it; I can't understand it." However, real faith in God's Word says, "If God's Word says it's so then it's so. It is mine. I have it now." Real faith says, "I have it even though I can't see or feel it."

Mental assent doesn't go far enough. It agrees with what the Word of God says, but it doesn't act upon the Word. Faith, however, is an action!

Mental assent is Head Faith not Heart Faith. The difference between head faith and heart faith can be demonstrated in the comparison between Thomas and Abraham. Thomas said, "I'll not believe until I can see Him," whereas Abraham staggered not at the promise of God…but was strong in faith."(See and compare John 20: 24-29 with Romans 4: 17- 21).

Notice the difference in Thomas' faith and Abraham's faith. Thomas had only a natural, human faith which said, "I'm not going to believe unless I can see and feel". Abraham, however, believed God's Word, considering not his own body—his own natural senses. If Abraham didn't consider physical knowledge or feelings, what did he consider then? The Word of God!

Too many times we focus our attention on the wrong thing. We consider our physical senses—the symptoms, and the circumstances rather than looking to God's Word.

What natural food is to the body the Word of God is to the spiritual man. That is why it is imperative we read, study, and mediate much in the Word of God which alone builds our confidence and assurance.

Faith is not CONGENIAL spiritual fellowship with others likeminded, or of like life-style. You can associate with all the great "faith teachers," faith ministries, and belong to a strong faith Church, and still not have faith. Simply going to a Faith Church will not give you faith any more than going to the Holy Land will make you holy! True faith is a complete spiritual trust and commitment; it is full and total reliance upon Christ, and Christ alone!

Faith is more easily described than defined.

In the book of Hebrews chapter eleven, we have an extensive and beautiful array of practical descriptions of the nature and evidence of faith.

1. v. 8 Faith is IRREVOCABLE OBEDIENCE

"By faith Abraham obeyed the call to go out to a land destined for himself and his heirs, and left home without knowing where he was to go." We read about Abraham in Romans 4:20, *"He staggered not at the promise..."*

2. v. 4 Faith is INTEGRITY

"By faith ABLE OFFERED a sacrifice greater (more excellent)than Cain's and through faith his goodness was attested, for his offerings had God's approval"

3. v. 7 Faith is INITATIVE

"By faith NOAH, divinely warned about an unseen future, took good heed and built an ark to save his household."

4. v. 11, 12, Faith is INSTRUMENTALITY

"By faith even SARAH herself received strength to conceive, though she was past age-and therefore from one man, and one as good as dead, there sprang descendants numerous as the stars..."

5. v. 17 Faith is ILLUSTRATION

"By faith ABRAHAM, when the test came, offered up Isaac...he was on the point of offering his only son..."

6. vv.24-26 Faith is IDENTITY

"By faith MOSES, when he grew up, refused to be called the son of Pharoah's daughter, preferring to suffer hardship with the people of God rather than enjoy the transient pleasures of sin. He considered the stigma that rest on God's Anointed greater wealththan the treasures of Egypt..."

7. vv. 28-31 Faith is INVOLVEMENT

"By faith he (Moses) celebrated the Passover and sprinkled the blood...By faith they crossed the Red Sea as though it were dry land..By faith the walls of

Jericho fell down after they had been encircled on seven successive days...By faith..RAHAB... had given the spies a kindly welcome."

8. v. 13 Faith is IMPULSION

"Faith made it possible for those who believed God's promises to persevere to keep on going on and on. Faith was always an impelling force in their lives. "All these persons died in faith. They were not yet in possession of the things promised, but had seen them afar ahead and hailed them" **WHAT IMPULSION!**

WHY? Because, *"They were looking for a country of their own"* (v. 16).

"They were "longing for a better country" (v.16).

"He was looking forward to the city with firm foundations whose architect and builder is God" (v. 10).

".......his eyes were fixed upon the coming day of recompense" (v. 26).

"He saw the invisible God" (v. 27). What drive, what impetus, what impulsion!

9. vv. 31-39 Faith is INVINCIBILITY

Because of faith those persons did not yield to their Circumstances—however dire and devastating!

They were Invincible in the face of terrible odds—hostile kingdoms, strong armies, ravening lions, the fury of fire, poverty, distress, misery, persecution, jeers, flogging, prison bars, martyrdom. THEY OVERCAME IT ALL!

10. v. 2 Faith is IMMORTALITY

"It is for their faith that men of old stand on record"

v. 4 *"Through faith ABEL continued to speak after his death"*

vs. 39, 40 *"These are commemorated for their faith"*

THEN, WE MOVE TO CHAPTER TWELVE OF HEBREWS which begins with a glorious declaration, "ALL OF THESE WITNESSES TO FAITH SURROUND US LIKE A CLOUD" (v. 1). Therefore in the light of this great reality, we are urged to *"lay aside every weight, and the sin which so easily ensnares us, and let us run with (patience) endurance the race that is set before us."* Let us be faithful!

Faith has measures or degrees.

In Romans 12:3 we read, *"For I say, through the grace given unto me......as God has dealt to each one a measure of faith."*

Such faith is a gift from God. It has its origin in God. We "live by the faith of the Son of God..." (Gal. 2:20). God is the author and source of faith. In Hebrews 12:2, we read, *"Looking unto the Jesus the author and finisher of our faith."* He is the **author** (source) and He is the **finisher** (perfector) of our faith.

The Measures of Faith are seen in a variety of experiences listed among God's people:

SOME HAD NO FAITH:

When the disciples were caught in a severe storm at sea, and Jesus was asleep on a pillow in the stern of the boat, they cried out, "Teacher, do You not care that we are perishing?" Then He arose and rebuked the wind, and said to the sea, *'Peace, be still!'* And the wind ceased and there was a great calm. But He said to them, *"Why are you so fearful, how is it you have no faith?"* (Mark 4:40, NKJV).

"And he said, I will hide my face from them, I will see what their end shall be: for they are a very forward generation, children in whom is no faith" (Duet. 32: 20).
"And that we may be delivered from unreasonable and wicked men: for all men have no faith" (2Thes. 3: 2).

SOME HAD LITTLE FAITH:

"Now in the fourth watch of the night Jesus went to them, walking on the sea. And when the disciples saw Him walking on the sea, they were troubled, saying, "It is a Ghost!" And they cried out for fear.

But immediately Jesus spoke to them, saying, "Be of good cheer! It is I; do not be afraid."

And Peter answered Him and said, "Lord, if it is You, command me to come to You on the water."

So He said, "Come." And when Peter had come down out of the boat, he walked on the water to go to Jesus.

But when he saw that the wind was boisterous, he was afraid; and beginning to sink he cried out, saying, "Lord save me!" (Matt.14:31).

"Wherefore, if God so clothe the grass of the field, which today is, and tomorrow is cast into the oven, shall he not much more clothe you, O ye of little faith" (Matt. 6: 30).

Little faith is better than No faith. Charles Spurgeon once said, "Little faith will take you to heaven, Great faith will bring heaven to you."

SOME HAD STRONG FAITH:

"He staggered not at the promise of God through unbelief; but was strong in faith, giving glory to God; and being fully persuaded that, what he had promises, he was able to perform" (Rom.4: 20, 21).

SOME HAD GREAT FAITH:

"Then Jesus went out from there and departed to the region of Tyre and Sidon.

And behold, a woman of Canaan came from that region and cried out to Him, saying, "Have mercy on me, O Lord, Son of David! My daughter is severely demon-possessed."

But He answered her not a word. And His disciples came and urged Him, saying, "Send her away, for she cries out after us."

But He answered and said, "I was not sent except to the Lost sheep of the house of Israel."

Then she came and worshiped Him, saying, "Lord, help me!"

But He answered and said, "It is no good to take the children's bread and throw it to the little dogs."
And she said, "True, Lord, yet even the little dogs eat the crumbs which fall from their master's table."
Then Jesus answered and said to her, 'O WOMAN, GREAT IS YOUR FAITH! LET IT BE TO YOIU AS YOU DESIRE." And her daughter was healed from that very hour" (Matt. 15:21-28). (Emphasis mine)

"When Jesus hear it, he marveled, and said to them that followed, Verily I say unto you, I have not found so great faith, no, not in Israel" (Matt. 8: 10).

SOME HAD MUCH FAITH:

"Now when Jesus had entered Capernaum, a centurion came to Him, pleading with Him,
saying, "Lord, my servant is lying at home paralyzed, dreadfully tormented."
And Jesus said to him, "I will come and heal him"
The centurion answered and said, "Lord, I am not worthy that You should come under my roof. But only speak a word, and my servant will be healed.
For I also am a man under authority, having soldiers under me. And I say to this one, 'Go,' and he goes; and to another, 'Come,' and he come; and to my servant, 'Do this,' and he does it"
When Jesus heard it, He marveled, and said to those who followed, "Assuredly, I say to you, I HAVE NOT FOUND SUCH GREAT FAITH, not even in Israel" (Matt. 8:5-13)! (Emphasis mine)

Notice that the Centurion had no visions, no dreams, no fleeces, nor any tangible evidence to depend on. All he had was the WORD of the Master! "Speak only a Word and my servant will be healed." His complete trust was in the SPOKEN WORD of Jesus.

The Mixture or Dynamic of Faith

"For indeed the gospel was preached to us as well as to them; but the word

which they heard did not profit them, not being mixed with faith in those who heard it" (Hebrews 4:2 NKJV)

Remember that James said, *"Faith without works is dead"*. If there are no actions to go along with what we ask and believe God for it will be worthless. The greatest "word of wisdom" to be found in Scripture is when Mary, the mother of Jesus said to the servants, *"Whatsoever He says to you, do it!"* (John 2:5).

BELIEF AND ACTION TOGETHER PRODUCE THE RESULTS OF FAITH

How Do We Mix Faith, you ask? Simply by our Confessions! Notice Romans 10:8, 9, 10,

> *"But what does it say? "The word is near you, even in your mouth and in your heart" (that is, the word of faith which we preach):*
> *that if you confess with your mouth the Lord Jesus and believe in your heart that God has raised Him from the dead, you will be saved.*
> *For with the heart one believes to righteousness, and with the mouth confession is made to salvation"*

There must be the corresponding action of our heart and mouth together to see the results of faith. This is how we mix the word with faith!

We have a beautiful example of this in Abraham. Look how he mixed works (actions) with his faith (see Rom. 4:17-20*)*. *"He did not waver (stagger) at the promise of God through unbelief, but was strengthened in faith, giving glory (or praise, a mouth exercise) to God"* (V.20, NKJV).

Abraham was fully convinced and persuaded that what God had promised, He was fully able to perform. Therefore, he was fearless in his confession of the word!

Will He Find Faith?

Jesus was always concerned about faith. He sought continually to awaken it in all who came to hear Him; He commended it with words of approval; He always rewarded it! Furthermore, He was disappointed when faith was absent because He knew what faith was capable of performing.

He was concerned about faith when His earthly ministry was coming to a close. He looked through the corridors of time and asked this piercing question: *"WHEN THE SON OFMAN COMES, WILL HE REALLY FIND FAITH ON THE EARTH?"* (Luke 18: 8) (Emphasis mine)

The validity of faith is in the OBJECT, never primarily in the SUBJECT. The all important issue is NOT THAT I BELIEVE, but IN WHOM DO I BELIEVE!

Jesus never asked a person to believe that he/she was
GOING TO BE HEALD, but rather believe THAT HE IS ABLE TO HEAL him or her!

AS FAR AS YOU ARE CONCERNED TODAY, "WILL THE SON OF MAN FIND FAITH ON THE EARTH WHEN HE RETURNS?" IF SO, THEN THE LAW OF FAITH WILL REWARD YOU!

Chapter Five

The Law of Frustration REPRODUCES Me

"And we know that all things work together for good to those who love God, to those who are the called according to His purpose. For whom He foreknew, He also predestined to be conformed to the image of His Son, that He might be the firstborn among many brethren" (Rom. 8:28, 29).

"For all things are for your sakes, that a grace, having spread through the many, may cause thanksgiving to abound to the glory of God. Therefore we do not lose heart. Even though our outward man is perishing, yet the inward man is being renewed day by day.
For our light affliction, which is but for a moment, is working for us a far more exceeding and eternal weight of glory, while we do not look at the things which are seen, but at the things which are not seen. For the things which are seen are temporary, but the things which are not seen are eternal" (2Cor. 4:15-18).

We read in Romans 8:20, in the Amplified version, *"For the creation (natural) was subjected to frailty----to futility, condemned to FRUSTRATION..."* (Emphasis mine)

HAVE YOU EVER BEEN FRUSTRATED? Have you ever had those times when NOTHING was working right, and everything seemed to be going wrong? Well, when you read what happened some years ago to a man in Barbados perhaps your problems will not seem so bad after all. His letter to his employers explained what happened when he went to repair a building damaged by a hurricane:

"At the top of the building I rigged up a beam with a pulley, and hoisted up a quantity of bricks by means of a barrel and rope. When I had fixed the building, there were quite a few bricks left over, which I wanted to take back down to the ground. I hoisted the empty barrel to the top, secured the rope at the ground level, and then went up and filled the barrel with the extra bricks. I did not realize that now the barrel had more bricks in it than it had ever had before.

"I went downstairs and carefully untied the rope to lower the bricks. Unfortunately, the barrel of bricks was heavier than I was, and before I knew what was happening the barrel started down, jerking me off the ground. I decided to hang on, and halfway up I met the barrel coming down and received a severe blow on my shoulder. Still clinging to the rope, I then continued to the top, when I banged my head on the beam and got my finger jammed in the pulley.

"When the barrel hit the ground, it burst its bottom, allowing all the bricks to spill out. I was now heavier than the barrel, so I started down again at high speed. Halfway down I met the barrel coming up, and received serious injuries to my shins.

"When I hit the ground I landed on the bricks, getting several painful cuts from the sharp edges. At this point I must have lost my presence of mind, because I let go of the rope. The barrel then came down, giving me another heavy blow on the head, and putting me in the hospital. I respectfully request a sick leave." **1**

It goes without saying FRUSTRATION is a common denominator in human experience. The Law of Frustration is perhaps the least understood, and taught, and yet it is one of the most important of Kingdom Laws.

If we understand it, co-operate and allow it to work for us, we will reap glorious benefits for time and eternity.

It will be very beneficial to understand that God established and ordained the Law of Frustration. He is in control, not the devil! For many "faith people" this law may seem strange and unacceptable, but it is, nevertheless, real and works in every believer's life!

According to Paul's statements in Romans 8:22, 23, and 26 there are three major groans in the world: The whole creation groans v. 22; we groan within ourselves, v. 23; and The Holy Spirit Himself groans in making intercession for us v. 26.

The whole creation groans and is under frustration. That we live in a FRUSTRATED WORLD, no sensible person will deny. Our world is filled with a multiplicity of complex crisis that result in utter frustration! The ever increasing crime rate, the escalation of violence, war, international fear, legalized murder, drugs, pills and tranquilizers are all related to frustration. It is a hopeless situation for those who do not know nor want God. However, for the people of God, we know that "ALL THINGS WORK TOGETHER for good"!

We know that our light affliction IS WORKING for us a far more exceeding and eternal weight of glory. Paul says we look through a glass darkly (1Cor. 13: 12).

When we look at THINGS that are seen, they may appear dark, dismal, discouraging and difficult to understand. You may feel like a vessel on an uncharted sea--- UNCHARTED TO US, BUT NOT TO HIM!

We must ever remind ourselves, *that "...ALL THINGS are for your sakes, that the abundant grace might through the thanks giving of many redound to the glory of God"* (2Cor 4:15).

Despite all the negative circumstances that come our way, Paul assures us by precept and example, we can be a Victor not a Victim, if we understand this Law of Frustration that is working in our lives for our benefit and God's glory.

"WHY?" can be a terrible wail in the heart of a Christian if Satan can get you in that tangle of questioning God: 'Why this?', 'Why Me?', 'Why now?', and etcetera.

Christians are not exempt from tribulations, test, and trials. The rain falls on the just and the unjust alike. In fact, JESUS SAID WE WOULD HAVE TRIBULATION: *"These things I have spoken to you, that in Me you may have peace. In the world you will have tribulation: but be of good cheer, I have overcome the world"* (John 16:33).

The Greek word for tribulation is *thlipsis*, from the root *thlibo*, which in turn is derived from *thalo*, meaning "to break." *Thlibo* means to crush, press, compress, squeeze. *Thlipsis* symbolically means grievous affliction or distress, pressure or burden upon the spirit" **2**

Thlipsis is also the Greek word for affliction (see Phil. 4:14). Affliction is not a disease, as some normally think. Not once is it used of a physical sickness or disease, but is translated as <u>tribulation</u> 20 times, <u>affliction</u> in the sense of <u>tribulation</u> 18 times; <u>burdened</u> (2 Cor.8:13); <u>anguish</u> (John 16:21); <u>persecution</u> (Acts 11:19); and <u>trouble</u> (1Cor. 7:28; 2Cor.1:4, 8). **3**

So count on it! As long as we are in the world we shall have tribulations, but "be of good cheer" Jesus said, "I have overcome the world." We too, can overcome the world through our identification with the victory of Jesus.

There is basically a Two-fold Purpose to the Law of Frustration:

> ➢ To Bring Sinners to Christ
>
> ➢ To Bring Christians into the IMAGE of Christ.

The Bible, history, and human experience tell us that MOST people never come to God by His GOODNESS. If that were so, then multitudes of people in the western world would already have been saved. But such is not the case. In fact, it is the very opposite! Multiplied thousands have good jobs, good health, good cars, homes, boats, insurance, retirement funds, and etcetera. They got the world by the tail and seem to be in control. Consequently, THEY NEVER THINK ABOUT GOD!

It is not until their world is jerked apart with a sudden tragedy— sickness, death in the family, serious trouble, loss of a job, etc, that God and prayer then becomes a consideration in their lives.

We see it time and again in America. We pass laws to put God out of our courts, congress, schools, and all public life. Then terrorism suddenly and un-expectantly strikes! The first thing people do is PRAY! It's when we have no control of the situation, we turn to God.

Frustration is the result of involvement in something over which you have no control. Much of people's frustration in the world is simply because they want to live their lives their way. It is the height of selfishness! Thus, God permits hardships and frustrations to come to turn them to Him.

Why, you ask, does God do this? It is because God has made us for something better than the things of this world. As Augustine said, "Thou Lord hast made us for thyself." C.S. Lewis said, "Automobiles (cars) were made to run on gas, man was made to run on God. If you don't run on God, you don't run."

We have a saying in America about the Missouri mule--because it is so hardheaded, you must take a 2x4 timber and whack it in the head TO GET ITS ATTENTION. Sometimes God must use drastic means to get our attention as well!

We must remember we cannot LEARN if we do not LISTEN! So, God must put a brick wall in front of people to stop them, to frustrate them! This is not only so for sinners, but Christian believers as well. If we run into the brick wall long enough, we might just stop and look for the door.

One reason why many Christians are not victorious, happy and maturing in Christ is because they haven't learned what the Law of Frustration is telling them. HOW CAN YOU BE HAPPY WHEN YOU ARE CONTINUALLY HITTING YOUR HEAD INTO THE BRICK WALL?

Dear Christian friend, when frustration comes, instead of "going to pieces", go to the bedroom-- fast, pray, seek God, and ultimately you will find yourself coming to a place of yielding to God.

> Frustration does bring people to God. This truth is woven all through the Word of God. You can find an entire chapter devoted to Love (1Cor.13); to Faith (Heb. 11); to Works (James 4); Gifts of the Spirit (1Cor. 12 & 14); the Second Coming of Christ (Matt. 24, 25). Just so, there is a chapter devoted to this Law of Frustration.

Psalm 107 ENLARGES UPON THIS LAW:

> In this chapter there are 44 examples of the Providence of God; 6 Classes of People; 14 Admonitions, and 15 Reasons to Praise the Lord. The 6 Classes of people are the Redeemed, Rebels, Fools, Sailors, Rich, and Poor. There are 6 Sections in the chapter dealing with these classes of people. 4

At the beginning of the five sections the writer repeats: *"OH, THAT MEN WOULD PRAISE THE LORD FOR HIS GOODNESS, AND FOR HIS WONDERFUL WORKS TO THE CHILDRE MEN!"*

Notice the first group in vs. 1-7: They were oppressed by the enemy, lost, no home, hungry, thirsty, their soul fainted in them, "THEN they cried out to the Lord in their trouble" (v.6).

This scenario is played out in the other five classes as well (vs.8; 15; 21; 31). Why are they redeemed and delivered? Frustration drove them to it! And I suspect that it was most probably frustration that brought you to Christ.

Look at some people who came to Jesus out of frustration:

> ➤ The Woman at Jacob's Well (John 4)
>
> ➤ The woman with the incurable issue of blood. (Mark 5:21-34)
>
> ➤ The Gentile woman whose daughter was vexed and grievously tormented with demons (Matt. 15:21-28)
>
> ➤ Blind Bartimaeus who refused to stop crying out to the Lord for mercy and healing (Mark 10:46-52)

When frustration comes, we too quickly want to blame the devil. It is true, some storms and problems are created by the Devil. For example, the storm at sea recorded in Mark 4:35-41. The fact that Jesus rebuked the storm was obviously an attempt of Satan to hinder Him and the disciples from reaching the other side. The devil didn't want the demonic on the other side to be delivered and have 2,000 demons leave him and enter the swine.

However, not all storms, problems and frustrations are from Satan. It requires close communion with the Lord and spiritual discerning of the situation to know its origin. But we can know!

In the account of the storm in which JONAH found himself struggling, we see a classic example of God's Law Of Frustration at work. God was responsible for the storm! Jonah refused to obey God, and the report is clear that GOD prepared the storm, the fish, the ship, the sailors, etc. It was frustration that drove Jonah to repentance and obedience; *"Now the Lord had prepared a great fish to swallow Jonah. And Jonah was in the belly of the fish three days and three nights. Then Jonah prayed to the Lord his God from the fish's belly.*
And he said: 'I cried out to the Lord because of my affliction, and He answered me. "Out of the belly of Sheol (hell) I cried, And you heard my voice" (Jonah 2: 1-2.).

The Book of Ecclesiastes provides a graphic description of the Law of Frustration at work. King Solomon, a man of wealth, wisdom, a botanist, a philosopher, a psychologist, a King and a diplomat is the central figure in the book. He had wine, women and song--He was a real Playboy—BUT, A VERY FRUSTRATED MAN! *"VANITY OF VANITIES, ALL IS VANITY,"* he cries! It was the Law of Frustration at work in his life to turn him back to God.

When God hedges up a sinful man's path with thorns, it is His way of drawing the person to Him. Scripture makes plain, "the way of the transgressors is hard" (Prov. 13:15b). "The Hebrew word for "hard" is *ethan*, meaning strong, rough. Sinners have more pain, suffering, and hardships in damming their souls than the righteous have, with all their cross-bearing, to save their souls. The way of the transgressor is hard, desolate, and fruitless." **5**

On numerous occasions, I have seen spouses who were rebellious and separated from their husband or wife, whose paths became so thorny and difficult, they returned to their spouse in repentance and the marriages were restored. This is the glorious work of the law of frustration.

The Believer and the Law of Frustration

This same law is employed to bring forth The Image of God's Son in Every Believer.
"And we know that all things work together for good to those who love God, to those who are the called according to His purpose,
"For whom He foreknew, He also predestined TO BE
CONFORMED TO THE IMAGE OF HIS SON, that
He might be the firstborn among many brethren" (Rom. 8:28, 29). (Emphasis mine)

I have seen it many times. For a while the man of God is a mediocre preacher--he preaches sermonettes, spends only a few minutes in daily prayer, and rushes about doing his "religious routine", feeling he is quite spiritual and doing well.

Then sudden and totally un-expected hardships, difficulties, stress and pressures come upon him, and like the sailors who reel to and fro, and stagger like a drunken man, and are at their "wits-end," in Psalm 107: 27, he also cries out to the Lord. He spends much time in the Word of God; he fasts, prays earnestly, and diligently seeks the Lord with all his heart, until he knows he has touched heaven.

Then eventually he is no longer a shallow preacher. He has touched the "sweet spot" in God! Every golfer understands hitting the "sweet spot". It's a glorious feeling. Likewise, when one hits the sweet spot in God, he has "prayed through", and is forever different.

There is a sweet spot in God, but it doesn't come from mediocre living. More often than not, it takes frustration to drive you to seek that special and unique place in God, but it will change your life!

Prayer doesn't change God, but it does change people and things! Paul describes this in Romans chapter seven. He is deeply troubled by the inner conflict he describes. He uses the personal pronoun 47 times in describing his plight. Then he cries out, *"O wretched man that I am! Who will deliver me from this body of death? I thank God---through Jesus Christ our Lord!"*

Then he moves directly into chapter eight and reveals the glorious answer and change that took place in his life. He is changed from personal ego to the Holy Spirit. Nineteen times he mentions the Holy Spirit in this chapter. This never would have happened if it were not for the Law of Frustration!

"But I want you to know, brethren that the things which happened to me have actually turned out for the furtherance of the gospel" (Phil. 1:12).

Dear friend, we have a choice, either to be changed or continue ramming our heads into the brick wall of frustration. We would be smart to start looking for the door.

Make no mistake, GOD WANTS TO CHANGE US! He wants to form, to fashion, to shape and mold us to the beautiful image of Christ.
This was Paul's prayer in Gal. 4:19: *"My little children, of whom I travail in birth again UNTIL CHRIST BE FORMED IN YOU."* (Emphasis mine)

In Romans 12:2, he says we are to be transformed. The word 'transformed', is taken from the Greek word *Meta-morphoo*, meaning to be transfigured by a supernatural change as in the transformation of Christ on the Mount (Matt. 17:2; Mk. 9:2).

Like the beautiful butterfly that came through various stages from the larva to the butterfly, we are changed and made into something beautiful by the grace and power of God. As the gospel song declares, "He made something beautiful of my life."

"But we all with open (unveiled) face beholding as in a glass (mirror) the glory of the Lord, are changed into the SAME IMAGE from glory to glory, even by the Spirit of the Lord" (2Cor. 3:18). (Emphasis mine)

The purpose for this transformation to His image is that we:

> ➤ GLORIFY GOD!
>
> ➤ THINK HIS THOUGHTS by having the mind of Christ;
>
> ➤ LIVE HIS WAYS by walking in the Spirit; and
>
> ➤ POSSESS HIS LIFE by keeping filled with the Sprit and the conscious dwelling and living in Him.

Pain urges us to find relief, Right? When we are thirsty, we seek water. When we are hungry, we seek food. When we are tired, we seek rest. AND WHEN WE ARE FRUSTRATED, WE SEEK GOD—HIS PLAN, HIS PURPOSE, HIS WILL, HIS FAVOR AND PEACE!

God is in the reproduction business and He uses *The Law of Frustration* to change us. So may our song ever be: *"Mold me, make me, fill me, use me."* So,

"Let the beauty of Jesus be seen in me, All His wonderful passion and purity. Oh, thou Spirit divine, all my nature refine, Till the beauty of Jesus be seen in me." **6**.

Then they will take note of us that we have been with Jesus!

Chapter Six

> ## *The Law of Love REFINES Me*

"Then one of the scribes came, and having heard them reasoning together, perceiving that He had answered them well, asked Him, "which is the first commandment of all?"
Jesus answered him, "The first of all commandments is: 'Hear, O Israel, the Lord our God is one.
And you shall love the Lord your God will all your heart, with all your soul, with all your mind, and with all your strength.' This is the first commandment.
And the second, like it, is this: 'You shall love your neighbor as yourself.' There is no other commandment greater than these" (Mark 12:28-32).

"A new commandment I give to you, that you love one another; as I have love you, that you also love one another.
"By this all will know that you are My disciples, if you have love for one another" (Jn.13:34, 35).

"If you love Me, keep My commandments" (Jn. 14:15).

"And we have known and believed the love that God has for us. God is love, and he who abides in love abides in God, and God in him.
Love has been perfected among us in this: that we may have boldness in the day of judgment; because as He is, so are we in this world.
There is no fear in love; but perfect love casts out fear, because fear involves torment. But he who fears has not been made perfect in love.
We love Him because He first loved us."
If someone says, "I love God.' and hates his brother, he is a liar; for he who does not love his brother whom he has seen, how can he love God whom he has not seen?
And this commandment we have from Him: that he who loves God must love his brother also" (1John 4:16-2).

"If you really fulfill the royal law according to the Scripture, "You shall love your neighbor as yourself," you do well; but if you show partiality, you commit sin, and are convicted by the law as transgressor" (James 2:8, 9).

"Keep yourselves in the love of God, looking for the mercy of our Lord Jesus Christ unto eternal life" (Jude v.21).

We have a channel on our TV called, "The Discovery Channel." Quite frequently there are some very interesting and enlightening programs. It is always a joy when you discover something new, something you had not previously known. Life is full of such wonderful discoveries if we are alert to capture them.

I well remember the joy I had as a child when first I discovered 2 plus 2 equals 4. Do you remember when you first discovered the multiplication table— and learned you could increase the sum endlessly? Exciting, was it not?

But a joy, far greater than discovering mathematical laws, is the discovery of the *Laws of The Kingdom of God*, and how they work for us now. It is through these laws God is reaching out to us for an abiding relationship of communion and fellowship with Him.

The uniqueness of Christianity is that it is a relationship of love, light, liberty, and likeness to God! Christianity is a person--the Lord Jesus Christ!
HE IS A MESSAGE OF LOVE!

One chapter could never embrace all that needs to be said about the Law of Love. Herein is the heart, the core and center of all that the Kingdom is and all it stands for.

When you observe the work of a great sculptor, he begins with a huge rough, untouched, unfinished stone. He selects the larger, more rugged tools to begin his work in forming and shaping the stone. As the work progresses, he selects smaller tools to carve out his dream. Not until he is ready for the final finishing stages does he select his most fine tools. These tools are smaller, and exact and precise. They are necessary for the sculptor to refine the image to its final completion.

> Love is God's finer tool! His Love refines our lives. There is nothing that will change you like the love of God. Thus, *The Law of Love Refines Us!*

God's Call To His People Is A Call To Love:

"...thou shalt love the Lord thy God with all thy HEART, and with all thy SOUL, and with all thy MIND, and with all thy STRENGTH" (Mark 12:30). (My emphasis)

But what is this love? It is not an EMOTION, such as is expressed with Eros (sensual love) or Philo (brotherly, friendly love). God's love is divine! In the Greek language it is called Agape. AGAPE LOVE IS AN ACT OF THE WILL. It is a firm resolution, a determination, born in a sense of value, and renewed day after day.

Agape, God's love requires the CONSTANT ACT OF THE WILL, choosing GOD and His way before anything else. It is totally UNSELFISH or UNSELF-NESS---IT SEEKS nothing for itself, not even God!   IT SEEKS GOD FOR HIMSELF!

This divine, agape love, ask no gifts, no rewards. It gives with no expectation of reward. Agape is loving God for His own sake—it wants nothing from God, save God Himself!

St. Teresa wrote: "Let everyone understand that the real love of God does not consist in tear-shedding, nor in that sweetness and tenderness for which we long, just because they console us, BUT IN SERVING GOD IN JUSTICE, FORTITUDE OF SOUL, AND HUMILITY."

Again, it is an act of will empowered by the grace of God which involves the whole or total person: WE ARE TO LOVE GOD WITH:

> "ALL THY MIND" --all the understanding until we have the "Mind of Christ" (Phil. 2:5; 4:8).

> "ALL THY SOUL" Our total emotions, will, and thoughts.
> Thus it requires the total denial of self—this is the first demand of discipleship Jesus requires—self-denial! *"And He said unto them all, If any man will come after me, let him deny himself, and take up his cross daily, and follow me"* (Luke 9:23).

Paul expresses self-denial in several different ways: *"For me to live is Christ, and to die is gain"* (Phi. 1:21) *"I am crucified with Christ: nevertheless I live; yet not I but Christ liveth in me: and the life which I now live in the flesh I live by the faith of the Son of God, who loved me, and gave himself for me."* (Gal. 2:20) *"But God forbid that I should glory, save in the cross of our Lord Jesus Christ, by whom the world is crucified unto me, and I unto the world?"*(Gal. 6: 14) *"For I determined not to know anything among you, save Jesus Christ, and him crucified"* (I Cor. 2:2).

John Wesley said, "I am no longer my own, but Thine."

Oswald Chambers wrote, "Give up right to ourselves."

Geo. Mueller declared, "...day I utterly died...my opinions my preferences, etc."

> "ALL THY HEART" To the depth of our innermost being.... our spirit wholeheartedly in love with God, to seek to be Holy. To be like God—with nothing contrary to God in our lives!

> "ALL THY STRENGTH" Wholeheartedly we serve Him. Faithfully we work for the Master with gladness and joy.

We do not work for ourselves, for others, the Church or the Denomination, BUT WE WORK FOR JESUS----

> WHERE?   EVERYWHERE!
> WHEN?   ALL THE TIME!
> WHY?   BECAUSE WE LOVE HIM!
> WHY?   BECAUSE HE FIRST LOVED US!

God's Love Is A Refining Love

If we are to possess the Kingdom of God and His Kingdom Possess us, we cannot escape the REFINING FIRES OF HIS LOVE.

If the Baptism of the Holy Spirit is anything, it is a baptism of divine love, because God is love. And such love has a refining fire. We read in Luke 3:16, 17, *"John answered, saying to them all, "I indeed baptize you with water; but One mightier than I is coming, whose sandal strap I am not worthy to loose. He will baptize you with the Holy Spirit and with FIRE."* (My emphasis)
His winnowing fan is in His hand, and He will thoroughly purge His threshing floor, and gather the wheat into His barn; but the chaff He will burn with unquenchable fire."

We are called to holiness to be vessels of honor to Him, because we are as Peter says, *"a chosen generation, a royal priesthood, a holy nation, His own special people, that you may proclaim the praise of Him who called you out of darkness into His marvelous light."* (1Peter 2:9) *"But as he which hath called you is holy, so be ye holy in all manner of conversation, Because it is written, Be ye holy; for I am holy."* (1Pet. 15, 16) *"…..holiness, without which no man shall see the Lord"* (Heb. 12:14).

The more God's love refines us the more we see ourselves *"seeking those things which are above, where Christ sitteth on the right hand of God."* (Col 3:1) and *"Mortifying our members which are upon the earth; fornication, uncleanness inordinate affection, evil concupiscence, and covetousness, which is idolatry: and putting off all these: anger, wrath, malice, blasphemy, filthy communication out of your mouth. Lie not one to another, seeing that ye have put off the old man with his deeds; And have put on the new man, which is renewed in knowledge after the image of him that created him"* (Col. 3: 5, 8, 9, 10).

Daily we must renew our minds with the Word of God. (Rom. 12: 2*)* *"And be renewed in the spirit of your mind"* (Eph. 4:23)*"by putting on the new man, which after God is created in righteousness and true holiness"* (Eph. 4: 24). There is no way of entering into the depth of God's Love without the renewing of the mind. There is no way to LIVE in the Kingdom of Love without our minds going through the process of change and transformation by the power of love's refinement.

Christians are in a constant spiritual warfare because Satan is a relentless foe *"seeking to steal, kill and destroy"* (Jn. 10: 10). The mind is the battle zone Satan seeks to capture and control, because he knows if he can control our thinking, he will control our believing and our confession. We overcome him in the arena of our minds by following Paul's instruction, *("For the weapons of our warfare are not carnal, but mighty through God to the pulling down of strongholds;) Casting down imaginations, and every high thing that exaltet itself against the knowledge of God, and bringing into captivity every thought to the obedience of Christ"* (2 Cor. 10: 4, 5). Victory always comes when daily we seek the mind of Christ. *"Let this mind be in you, which was also in Christ Jesus"* (Phil. 2: 5).

FOR THE WORLD TO SEE CHRIST THEY MUST SEE HIS LOVE IN US.

In the 13th chapter of First Corinthians, Paul unveils the finished product of the refining process of love. If you supply the name CHRIST in place of love, a beautiful revelation comes forth.

"Though I speak with the tongues of men and of angels, but have not CHRIST, I have become as sounding brass or a clanging cymbal.

And though I have the gift of prophecy, and understand all mysteries and all knowledge, and though I have all faith, so that I could remove mountains, but have not CHRIST, I am nothing.

And though I bestow all my goods to feed the poor, and though I give my body to be burned, but have not CHRIST, it profits me nothing.

CHRIST suffers long and is kind; CHRIST does not envy; CHRIST does not parade Himself, CHRIST is not puffed up;

CHRIST does not behave rudely. CHRIST does not seek His own. CHRIST is not provoked. CHRIST thinks no evil;

CHRIST does not rejoice in iniquity, but rejoices in the truth. CHRIST bears all things, CHRIST believes all things, CHRIST hopes all things, and CHRIST endures all things.

CHRIST never fails. But whether there are prophecies, they will fail; whether there are tongues, they will cease; whether there is knowledge, it will vanish away.

For we know in part and we prophesy in part,

But what that which is perfect has come, then that which is in part will be done away.

When I was a child, I spoke as a child, I understood as a child, I thought as a child; but when I became a man, I put away childish things.

For now we see in a mirror, dimly, but then face to face. Now I know in part, but then I shall know just as I also am known.

And now abide faith, hope, CHRIST, these three; but the greatest of these is CHRIST."

The Law of Love is about refining our lives into the image of Christ. Paul admonishes us in saying, *"If then you were raised with Christ, seek those things which are above, where Christ is sitting at the right hand of God.*

Set your mind on things above, not on things on the earth. For you died, and your life is hidden with Christ in God.

When Christ who is our life appears, then you also will appear with Him in glory" (Col.3:1-4).

For whom he did foreknow, he also did predestinate to be conformed to the image of his Son, that he might be called the firstborn among many brethren" (Rom. 8:29).

"But we all, with open face beholding as in a glass the glory of the Lord, are

changed in the same image from glory to glory, even as by the Spirit of the Lord" (2Cor. 3:18).

"My little children, of whom I travail in birth again until Christ be formed in you," (Gal. 4:19).

HAVE YOU EVER THOUGHT WHY YOU DIDN'T SUDDENLY DIE AND GO TO HEAVEN WHEN YOU WERE "BORN AGAIN"? In that precise moment when you were forgiven and cleansed from all your sins by the blood of Jesus, and your name was written in the Lamb's Book of Life, you were made righteous and holy enough to go, but you didn't. Why? Two Reasons:

One, because, God wants something from us—He wants our Fellowship and Communion here on the earth He created. The primary purpose for our creation and being here is to glorify God. In those days following the creation of Adam and Eve, Scripture says, God came down to walk with them in the cool of the day (Gen. 3:8). They were made in the image of God the Father, Son and Holy Spirit, and in their likeness to be the reflection of God's character and beauty glorifying Him (Gen. 1:26, 27)!

As the moon is a reflection of the Sun, God also wants us to be a perfect reflection of His holy character and love to glorify Him!

Two, we, the redeemed of the Lord, are the ONLY means whereby this GOSPEL OF THE KINGDOM can be spread to those whom God would have hear it and adhere to it, which of course, is every creature throughout the world (Matt. 28:18- 20; Mk. 16:15).

We are His lights in this world. His witnesses! We are the channels, the conduits for the expression of HIS LOVE TO OTHERS! That is why Jesus cautions us not to bury our light but let our lights shine so men can see our good works and glorify the Father in heaven (Matt.5: 16)!

DEAR FRIENDS, IT IS ALL ABOUT JESUS! CHRIST IS LOVE... If we do not have Christ, we are nothing and we can do nothing (John 15: 7*). But with "CHRIST IN YOU THE HOPE OF GLORY"* (Col.1:27) (My emphasis) *"We can do all things through Christ which strengthens us"* (Phil. 4:13). We can plant the seed of His Kingdom in the hearts of men everywhere! *"And this gospel of the Kingdom shall be* *preached in all the world for a witness unto all nations; and then the end shall come"* (Matt. 24:14).

AN ANALYSIS OF THIS AGAPE LOVE REVEALS THE FOLLOWING INGREDIENTS:

Please notice beginning with verse 4 in the 13th Chapter of First Corinthians.

1. LOVE IS LONG-SUFFERING, as opposed to impatient. It is passive...not in a hurry.

2. LOVE IS GRACIOUS AND KIND, as opposed to malice, ill will, and envy. Love in action never acts rashly.

3. LOVE IS OPPOSED TO ENVY AND JEALOUSLY. Love is always generous!

4. LOVE IS NOT EASILY PROVOKED, as opposed to rash, quick anger in conduct toward others. Love is courteous, polite, never rude, or discourteous.

5. LOVE IS HUMBLE, as opposed to pride, boastful, a big ego, a braggart, etc.

6. LOVE KEEPS NO RECORD OR ACCOUNT OF EVIL RENDERED, as opposed to revenge, ill-will, bitterness, un-forgiveness and retaliation.

7. LOVE IS RIGHTEOUS. It deplores sin! It never is glad when others do wrong; never rejoices in another's fall; and does not rejoice in iniquity. It is always slow to expose.

8. LOVE VAUNTETH NOT OR IS NOT PUFFED UP, as opposed to boastfulness; haughty, self righteous.

9. LOVE IS OPPOSED TO PRIDE in all its subtle forms and wrong doing.

10. LOVE IS, IN A WORD, UNSELFISH, as opposed to seeking its own way.

THINK ABOUT IT! Selfishness is the heart and core of all human problems. I have heard it said, "The five cardinal sins of the human race are: "Selfishness--- Selfishness--- Selfishness---Selfishness----Selfishness!"

"Now abides faith, hope, love, but the greatest of these is love" (1Cor.13: 13).

To see the power, performance and place of this love, please turn these two words "IS LOVE" around to "LOVE IS," which in turn forms a very POSTIVE STATEMENT. A statement of two absolutes! Notice,

"LOVE IS"

First, LOVE IS A FACT:

> *"For God so loved the world that He gave His only begotten Son, that whoever believes in Him should not perish but have everlasting life"* (John 3:16).

> *"But God demonstrates His own love toward us, in that while we were still sinners, Christ died for us"* (Rom. 5:8).

> *"And we have known and believed the love that God has for us. God is love, and he who abides in love abides in God and God in him"* (1Jn. 4:16).

> *"We love Him because He first loved us"* (1Jn. 4:19).

The greatest force in the universe is agape love! The very essence of God's nature and character is love. GOD IS TOTALLY, COMPLETELY, WHOLLY LOVE! Therefore, anything emanating or flowing forth from God is good, lovely, and wholesome.

Satan, however, is completely opposite. He is the total embodiment of hate! Truth has no place in him. He is a liar and the Father of lies, Jesus said (Jn. 8: 44). His kingdom of darkness is strong, but not omnipotent! It is powerful, but not ALL powerful, because it is built on the negative principle of hate.

Any institution or enterprise, whether it is the home, the school, the church, or the government that is built on hatred will not survive, it will ultimately crumble.

This mighty force of love has its source in God, for God is love. The world is ruled by two principle forces: Love or Hate: Light or Darkness: Life or Death: God or Satan. In John 10:10, Jesus verifies this very clearly, *"The thief does not come except to steal, and to kill, and to destroy. I have come that they may have life, and that they may have it more abundantly."*

Everything revolves around these two principal forces, love or hate, God or Satan. All world events in one way or another are related to either of these two factors.

This mighty FORCE of love is like a triangle. It begins with God, the top point of the triangle. That is the SOURCE of love, God. But this FORCE of love has a COURSE. It goes to the left and right bottom pointing to MAN. But it is not complete until it goes back and forth on the bottom points between people. *"Thou shalt love thy neighbor as thyself"* Then it returns back up to God! This is the triangle of love, loving God with all our hearts and loving our neighbors as ourselves!

There are some Christians, who have great difficulty in truly loving others. One of the reasons, I have observed, is they do not love themselves. Because they struggle to forgive themselves they in turn have difficulty loving themselves. But God, who is Almighty, can and does forgive us. Who then are we to not forgive ourselves? We will never understand the love and forgiveness of God! But it's real! We must cease from trying to rationalize it and place our trust in Him and receive His love and forgiveness and look in the mirror and say, "I forgive you." This takes an act of your will and when you do the floodgates of heaven's love and forgiveness will flood your soul, because Love is a Fact!

Second, LOVE IS A FORTUNE:

If you are filled with the love of God you are a wealthy person!

1. LOVE IS A FORTUNE BECAUSE LOVE IS A PROBLEM SOLVER: You will find it to be the:

> Best solver of problems in the Church.
> Best solver of problems in the Home.
> Best solver of problems between Jew and Gentile.
> Best solver of problems between labor and management.
> Best solver of problems between races, etc.

We will never solve any problems apart from LOVE.

2. LOVE IS A FORTUNE BECAUSE IT IS MORE VALUABLE:

> Than PROFOUND SPEECH - "Though I speak the tongues of men and of angels, but have not love, I have become as sounding brass or a clanging cymbal" (1Cor. 13:1).

> Than PROPHETIC ABILITY- "Though I have the gift of prophecy, and understand all mysteries, and all knowledge, **(that's a lot of knowledge)** and have not love, I am nothing (1Cor. 13:2).

> Than PERFROMING FAITH- "Though I have all faith so as to remove mountains, but have not love, I am nothing" (1Cor. 13:2).

> Than PUBLIC SACARIFICE - "Though I bestow all my goods to feed the poor, and though I give my body to be burned, but have no love, it profits me nothing" (1Cor. 13:3).

3. LOVE IS A FORTUNE BECAUSE:
(1Cor.13:4-7)

> It is Kind.
> It Forgives.
> It Covers Sin and Faults.
> It is Patient and Puts up with Wrong.
> It Returns good for evil.

Love is the essence of God manifested in the fruit of the Holy Spirit (Gal. 5:22).

> ➤ JOY is love exalted.
> ➤ PEACE is love in repose.
> ➤ LONGSUFFERING is love enduring.
> ➤ GENTLENESS is love in society.
> ➤ GOODNESS is love in action.
> ➤ FAITH is love on the battlefield.
> ➤ MEEKNESS is love in learning.
> ➤ TEMPERANCE is love in training.
> ➤ RIGHTEOIUSNESS is love enthroned.
> ➤ TRUTH is "love in freedom". 1

You may be the wealthiest person on the list of the world's top wealthy people, but without the love of God, you are worse than a pauper. You don't have to have an abundance of material things to be wealthy. Some of the wealthiest people I know have very little of this world's good. But they are rich toward God (See Luke 12: 16-21).

Third, LOVE IS A FASHION:

Walking in love is A Life Style!   *"Since you have purified your souls in obeying the truth through the Sprit in sincere love of the brethren, love one another fervently with a pure heart"* (1Pet. 1:22).

The word fervently means, "to boil over with heat," "blistering hot," "having or showing great warmth of feeling; intensely devoted." Our love of the brethren is not to be lukewarm, but hot!

THE WAY TO LOVE GOD AND OTHERS, IS FERVENTLY!

It is reported that Napoleon once told a fellow soldier in his army with the same name, but a poor soldier, "LOOK SOLDIER, EITHER BE A GOOD SOLDIER OR CHANGE YOUR NAME."

We can say the same for Christians. If we are in Christ's Army, and we are not living in the FASHION AND LIFE STYLE OF JESUS CHRIST, THEN, WE SHOULD CHANGE OUR NAME!

THERE IS NO SUBSTITUE FOR THIS LOVE. You are created to love. You are a product of love. **That means you are made for life, not death; for health, not disease; for success, not failure; for good, not bad.**

The life style of Jesus is the fashion of love. The love walk is the command of God for every Christian.

AND EVERYBODY CAN LOVE!   God doesn't expect everybody to sing, to play an instrument, to preach, etc., BUT HE KNOWS EVERYBODY CAN LOVE IF THEY SO CHOOSE.   Is that your choice?

LOVE IS A FACT, A FORTUNE, AND A FASHION: LOVE IS GOD, FOR GOD IS LOVE. NOW ABIDETH FAITH---HOPE---LOVE.

SO, when Faith becomes Sight and Hope is forever Realized, LOVE WILL BE HEAVEN'S ABIDING REALITY.

THIS IS THE MORE EXCELLENT WAY!

Chapter Seven

The Law of Giving REPLENISHES Me

"Give, and (gifts) will be given to you: good measure, pressed down, shaken together, and running over will they pour into (the pouch formed by) the bosom (of your robe and used as a bag). For with the measure you deal out (with the measure you use when you confer benefits on others), it will be measured back to you" (Luke 6:38, AMP).

From the first offering mentioned in Scripture (Gen.4: 3) to the last mention of offering in the Old Testament (Mal. 3: 8), we note that offerings played a vitally significant role in man's worship and relationship to God throughout the Old and New Testaments. When these offerings were presented correctly and with the right motive, God was pleased and His blessings abounded upon the people. It is evident that giving is a concept that dates back to man's beginning, and we dare not take the practice for granted or ignore it, lest we suffer serious consequences.

Giving always has a reciprocal effect upon the giver. We see a classic example of this principle spelled out for us in Psalm 41. Notice that for the generous act of considering or giving to the poor there are seven particular blessings mentioned: " v 1, deliverance in the time of trouble; v. 2 the LORD shall preserve him; the LORD shall revive or keep him alive; he shall be blessed upon the earth; deliverance from his enemies; v. 3 the LORD shall strengthen him (Hebrew *saad*, support; refreshing; healing) upon the bed of languishing (Hebrew *devai*, sickness, sorrow) and made to recovery in weakness" **1**

Notice this principle also in Isaiah 58: 10- 12. In verse 10, God say, If you will do two things, namely, feed the hungry and help those in trouble, He will do seven things: Your light will shine out like the beams of the sun on a clear morning; (v. 11) the LORD will guide you continually ; the LORD will satisfy your soul in the drought, meaning when there isn't anything God will created it for you; He will keep you healthy too; you will be like a well-watered garden, like an over-flowing spring, meaning you will be supplied in times of drought and national disaster; (v.12) the waste lands will be restored to a habitable state, and the blessings that should have been enjoyed for many generations will be yours.

The principle and practice of tithing, that was instituted hundreds of years before Moses and the Law, was a God ordained manner of acknowledging God's Sovereignty and Man's Stewardship. God is a Sovereign God. That is, He made everything and therefore He owns everything! God existed before there was a creation or a Garden of Eden. The garden was in place before Adam was created. Adam did not come on the scene before the garden, nor did he have ownership of the garden, once created and placed there; he was the caretaker, the steward or manager. Since the fall of Adam, however, Man has had this tendency to think he owns something when the Scripture clearly states, *"The earth is the Lord's and the fullness thereof; the world, and they that dwell therein. For he hath founded it upon the seas, and established it upon the floods"* (Ps. 24: 1, 2).

I am convinced when Christians receive this revelation of God's Sovereignty and Man's Stewardship it solves the problem about all the tithing issues that are prevalent among so many Churches and Christians today. Such silly statements as: "Tithing was under the old law," or "Tithing is only for the Old Testament or the Israelites" or "Tithing is not for New Testament Christians." And etc. Allow me to ask you a simple question. Is the Sovereign God of the Old Testament still Sovereign today? Is Jesus Christ LORD of all? Of course He is and there is only one way to truly acknowledge His Lordship and that is to acknowledge the fact HE IS OWNER! Ownership is the basis of Lordship! If He does not truly own us, then He is not Lord of our lives. We should carefully think about this the next time we sing in church the chorus, *"He is Lord, He is Lord, He is Risen from the dead and He is my Lord."* As the great missionary statesman, John R. Mott said, "He must be Lord of all or He is not Lord at all."

Tithing was never instituted because God needed the money, but rather so man would always know God owns everything, and this is his way to acknowledge God's sovereign ownership over everything, including his very life. We belong to God for we have been bought with a price (1Cor. 6:20; 7: 23). It is a sad commentary for so called New Testament Christians not to give the Lord at least the tithe amount that the people of God practiced in the Old Testament. We are told less than 2% of all Christians tithe. Less than 18% of Pentecostal/Charismatic Christians tithe. If the New Testament is BETTER than the Old, **and it is**, then common logic tells us we should do more than they did in the Old Testament with our giving!

It is not my intent in this chapter to go into lengthy discussion about the subject of tithing per se, but rather to point out the blessing that was attached to tithing and giving in particular in the New Testament. In Malachi chapter three God promised special blessings to those who faithfully brought all the tithes into the storehouse. The people lives were replenished as a result of faithful and obedient tithing and giving.

In the New Testament Christian living is a process of receiving and giving; receiving from God, and giving to others. We read in 2 Corinthians, 1:3, 4, *"Blessed be the God and Father of our Lord Jesus Christ, the Father of mercies and the God of all comfort, who comforts us in all our tribulation that we may be able to comfort those who are in any trouble, with the comfort with which we ourselves are comforted by God."*

It is the principle of reciprocity— we receive from God's bountiful hand that we may in turn give to others from our blessings. This wonderful principle is not something with which we were born. To the contrary, we were born with a selfish nature that only wants to take and not give. This, Jesus portrayed well in the story of the Prodigal son, who said to his father, *"Give Me"!* Not until he came to the end of himself in disgrace and humiliation, was he willing to humble himself and say to his Father, *"Make Me."*

God is a giving God (John 3: 16; Luke 12: 32), and when we are made "new creatures in Christ," we too have a giving nature, because we become partakers of His divine nature. (2Pet. 1: 4) It is totally a work of God in us! It is a work of His glorious grace in our hearts. We give from an inner desire and passion rather than an outward compulsion or performance of duty. Giving, whether it is the tenth or twentieth, ninety or one-hundredth is from a motivation of God's grace, love and faith that acknowledges His Lordship!

Paul makes the case for this manner of giving very clear in his Corinthian letter. It would do us all well to refresh ourselves from time to time mediating upon chapters 8 and 9 of 2nd Corinthians. In these chapters, Paul makes very clear that Christian giving is a grace. It is the unmerited favor and gift God has graciously bestowed upon us. These two chapters are very insightful about the grace of giving, and clearly show that the law (or principle) of giving truly replenishes us.

Webster defines the word replenish as, "To make full or complete again, as by furnishing a new supply." I LIKE THAT! That is precisely what happens as we faithfully exercise this marvelous law of giving. You simply cannot out-give God! I have learned that giving is the Master's key to masterful, abundant living, and I trust this lesson will enlighten, inspire and encourage you to abound in this glorious grace of giving.

When we "live to give," we shall never live to be in want for anything we need, because we are promised, *"My God shall supply all your need according to His riches in glory by Christ Jesus"*(Phil. 4:19).   When we clearly understand this beautiful law, giving is then never an obligation, but an opportunity. We give, not because *"we have to,"* but rather because we *"get to" and "want to."* Our giving is never out of a sense of fear, but joy; not out of guilt, but love; and not from a sense of duty, but privilege.

The Bible has many wonderful accounts about replenishing the supply after giving. The beautiful episode of Elijah the prophet and the widow woman is an excellent case in point. We read in 1Kings. 17: 7-16: *"And it happened after a while that the brook dried up, and because there had been no rain in the land. Then the word of the* Lord *came to him saying, "Arise, go to Zarephath, which belongs to Sidon, and dwell there. See, I have commanded a widow there to provide for you." So he arose and went to Zarephath. And when he came to the gate of the city, indeed a widow was there gathering sticks. **And he called to her and said, "Please bring me a morsel of bread in your hand.**" Then she said, "As the Lord your God lives, I do not have bread, only a handful of flour in a bin, and a little oil in a jar, and see, I am gathering a couple of sticks that I may go in and prepare it for myself and my son, that we may eat it, and die." **And Elijah said to her, "Do not fear; go and do as you have said, but make me a small cake from it first, and bring it to me; and afterward make some for yourself and your son.** For thus says the Lord God of Israel: **'The bin of flour shall not be used up, nor shall the jar of oil run dry, until the day the Lord sends rain on the earth.**'" So she went away and did according to the word of Elijah; and **she and he and her household ate for many days. The bin of flour was not used up, nor did the jar of oil run dry, according to the word of the Lord which He spoke by Elijah.**"* (My emphasis)

Oh, how many times across the past fifty seven years of ministry, have I seen this wonderful law demonstrated in our lives and the lives of many other believers.

I remember as though it was yesterday, many years ago as a young Methodist pastor, I was attending a tent revival. I had a one hundred dollar bill tucked away in my wallet that I had been saving up for a special need. I didn't have much to put in the offering that night, but the Lord spoke and said, "Give that one hundred dollar bill." I argued with the Lord. "But Lord, you know I am saving that for this special need." "Give the one hundred," He said. Finally, I surrendered and gave the money. Two weeks later, I was conducting a revival meeting many miles from home and the engine in my car blew up. I said, "Lord, what am I going to do?" I don't have any money, not even the one hundred dollars I was saving, but gave in that offering." He seemed to be silent, and the devil tried to condemn me for giving that one hundred dollars. But the devil never has the last word. God does! The pastor called a brother in his church that was a mechanic. He took my car to his garage and rebuilt the engine while I was conducting the meeting. When he finished, it was like a new car, but the bill was over eleven hundred dollars! I explained to the brother that I didn't have any money, but would be willing to either borrow some money when I got back home or pay him in installments. He said, "dear brother, you are a man of God, and you have given me so very much in these meetings, you do not owe me anything. It is a gift!" Oh, hallelujah! I gave God's servant one hundred, and God gave me in return, eleven hundred! My giving was replenished!

My friend, it pays to obey, and I learned early in life this law of giving works! You give and you will be replenished! When I began to see that giving was not an obligation and duty, but rather an opportunity and privilege that grace afforded me, I became literally liberated in my entire attitude about giving. It was then I began to "live to give"! This attitude and desire not only involved my finances, but my entire stewardship of life---my time, my talents, my gifts, my services---literally everything I am and have!

I have noticed over the years so many Christians struggle over the subject of tithes, offerings, and giving in general. Many, because they do not understand true Biblical Christian Stewardship, have been offended at such teaching and consequently changed churches or drop out of church all together. How sad and unfortunate!

Yet on the other hand, I have seen many believers understand God Sovereignty and Man's Stewardship, and receive this beautiful grace of giving, and watched their lives become mightily transformed and abundantly blessed spiritually, physically and materially.

It is not my purpose in this chapter to do a complete exegetical study of 2nd Corinthians chapters 8 and 9, but rather to point out some highlights of Paul's teaching and instruction concerning this marvelous grace of giving. He begins in verse one commending or bragging on the Macedonians about their giving to the poor and shows it is because of the grace of God. Thus, he is saying that Christian giving is a grace; it is a desire or disposition God has put into their hearts. As I previously mentioned, this does not come naturally, it is a God-given desire! Notice how he says it, *"We want to tell you further, brethren, about the grace (the favor and spiritual blessing) of God which has been evident in the churches of Macedonia (arousing in them the desire to give alms);*

The word for grace in the Greek language is *Charis*, meaning "benefit, favor, or gift." **2** It is the undeserved gracious benevolence of God. It is not natural, but supernatural. A grace is a divine disposition or benefit that God works in the heart of the believer. God's character is TO GIVE. When we have His nature, our character will also desire to give. As a result of this grace, giving will be as natural and breathing.

Anyone who has experienced this glorious grace will never need prodding, coaxing, or manipulation to give. You do not have to convince or pressure them into giving tithes and offerings. Giving will automatically and naturally flow out from this grace.

Next, noticed that Paul says even though one is having trouble and difficult financial times and deep poverty, it will not prevent one from having the grace of giving. *"For in the midst of an ordeal of severe tribulation, their abundance of joy and their depth of poverty (together) have over-flowed in wealth of lavish generosity on their part"(v. 2 Amp).*

Every Christian will face the furnace of affliction one time or another. It is God's way to prove (test) our obedience, faithfulness and loyalty. This was the purpose of Abrahams' test. *"Now it came to pass after these things that God tested Abraham, and said to him, "Abraham!" And he said, "Here I am." And He said, "Take now your son, your only son Isaac, whom you love, and go to the land of Moriah, and offer him there as a burnt offering on one of the mountains of which I shall tell you."* Keep in mind, this was the son Abraham had waited twenty five years for. He had been faithful to God during this entire period, and *"never wavered at the promise of God through unbelief, but was strengthened in faith, giving glory to God"* (Rom. 4:20). But now God was asking him to give up his blessing. Think how difficult this decision was from a human standpoint. Abraham, however, did as the Lord commanded. At that precise moment when he was about to slay his son *"the Angel of the Lord called to him from heaven and said, "Abraham, Abraham!" And he said, "Here I am."   And He said, "Do not lay your hand on the lad, or do anything to him; for now I know that you fear God, since you have not withheld your son, your only son, from Me"* (Gen. 22: 1, 2, 11, 12). (Emphasis mine)

God wanted to know if Abraham loved his blessing more than the one who blessed him. There is always the danger of loving the gift more than the giver of that gift.   Abraham proved that affliction would not stop him from giving to God. We must be careful with the gifts of God. Israel, you remember, was given a wonderful blessing of healing and life if they would obediently, *"look and live"* by looking at the serpent on the pole (Num. 21:8-9).   In time, however, they began to worship the serpent on the pole (God's blessing) rather than God (the One who blessed them), until it was destroyed under the reign of Hezekiah (2Kings 18: 4). In no matter what form idolatry presents itself God hates it with a passion!

Count on it, tests will come to reveal our hearts. The apostle Peter declares, *"In this you greatly rejoice, though now for a little while, if need be, you have been grieved (distressed) by various trials, that the genuineness of your faith, being much more precious than gold that perishes, though it is tested by fire, may be found to praise, honor, and glory at the revelation of Jesus Christ"* (1Pet. 1:6, 7). God's wonderful grace is available to keep us in such test and trials.

We are indebted to these Macedonian Christians for their example of generous giving, and the glorious plan of *Faith Promise Giving* that originates from them, and has been a blessing beyond description in mission work for many years. I have practiced Faith Promise Giving since my mission's professor introduced the plan to me more than fifty years ago. The late Dr. Oswald J. Smith built the world's largest missionary church on this plan of Faith Promise Giving. It truly is a grace of giving. What is Faith Promise Giving, you ask? We read in verse 3, *"For to their power, I bear record, yea, and beyond their power they were willing of themselves."* The NKJV explains it better, *"For I bear witness that **according to their ability**, yes, and **beyond their ability**, they were freely willing."* (Emphasis mine) Giving according to one's ability is giving from a known source of income—salary, wages, "selling what you have and give to the poor', etc. Giving beyond your ability is giving money you don't have or foresee how you can do it. There is only one way to give what you do not have, and that is by faith! You determine according to your faith how much you will trust God to provide for you to give to missions. When God sees your faithfulness to give from your ability to give, then He is faithful to provide what you trust Him to do through you by faith. I have seen this grace of giving work hundreds of times, not only in my personal life but the lives of hundreds of others. I always tell the people, God has no problem getting the money TO YOU if He knows He can get it THROUGH YOU!

Paul tells us that God wants us to abound in this grace of giving just as much as we abound in everything, in faith, and utterance, and knowledge and in all diligence (v. 7). Notice the replenishing affect described in chapter 9: 6 and 10; *"But this I say, He who sows sparingly will also reap sparingly; and he which sows bountifully will also reap bountifully." "Now may He who supplies seed to the sower, and bread for food, supply and* **multiply** *the seed you have sown and* **increase** *the fruits of your righteousness."* (NKJV) (Emphasis mine) The obvious is very clear here—God will replenish our giving!

Grace giving is giving from the heart. As J.B. Phillips, says, "God loves the man whose heart is in the gift." The poor widow woman is a classical example, as she put into the treasury her only two mites while the wealthy put in out of their abundance. Jesus said, *"Truly I say to you that this poor widow has put in more than all; for all these out of their abundance have put in the offerings for God, but she out of her poverty has put in all the livelihood that she had"* (Luke 21: 1-4).

> This is a demonstration how we should give: Freely (Matt. 10:8); Good measure (Lk. 6:38); As God has prospered (1Cor. 16:2); willingly (2Cor. 8:12); with purpose (2Cor. 9:7) and cheerfully (2Cor. 9:7) not grudgingly or of compulsion. The true grace of giving supplies the right attitude for our giving. Money given for wrong reasons or from wrong attitudes will not be *"an odor of a sweet smell, a sacrifice acceptable, well pleasing to God"* (Phil.4: 18).

A complete and unbiased study of our Lord's life reveals that the key to masterful living is GIVING! Jesus was a giver----He went about doing good and giving—that was His life style! He gave life to the dead; sight to the blind; food to the hungry; healing to the sick; hope to the hopeless; comfort to the bereaved, etc., etc. He is the perfect pattern for living to give!

May we, like the Macedonians, in seeking and desiring to have this grace and life of giving, give ourselves in complete and total surrender to the Lord (2 Cor. 8:5; Rom. 12: 1-2), acknowledging His Lordship over our lives, then our giving will be a grace and bountifully replenished.

PART III

KINGDOM REALITIES

Introduction

The Reality of Prayer (Part A)

The Reality of Prayer (Part B)

The Reality of Worship

The Reality of Praise

The Reality of Spiritual Warfare

The Reality of Fasting

The Reality of Christian Suffering

The Reality of Biblical Prosperity

Kingdom Realities

Introduction

There are many wonderful Kingdom realities to be discovered as we explore and live out the grand truths of the Word of God. These realities are the *mysteries of the Kingdom*, Jesus often referred to in His teachings about the Kingdom. For the purpose of this study, however, I want us to focus upon seven particular realities that are critically necessary for us to understand if we are to mature, and reach our full potential in God and function effectively in His Kingdom.

The doctrine of *Christian Perfection* is a little known doctrine among most Christians, and an almost unheard teaching in the modern-day pulpit. Perhaps it is because the word "*perfect*" frightens most Christians in this day of so much un-committed living. "None is perfect nor can be", they say. "We all sin every day-- so why teach people to be something they cannot be." This is tragic ignorance about what the Bible means concerning perfection, and Satan takes advantage of this ignorance to rob God's people from entering into the fullness of God, and enjoying the abundant life He has promised and provided.

The word *perfect* comes from the Greek word *teleios,* which means complete, or that which has reached maturity **1** (Matt. 5:48; 1Cor. 2:6; Phil. 3:15). The reason Christ gave the five *Ministry Gifts* (Apostles, Prophets, Evangelists, Pastors and Teachers) to His Church is to bring us into the fullness of Christ. Notice what Paul said in Ephesians 4:12-16, *"For the equipping (perfecting) of the saints for the work of ministry, for the edifying of the body of Christ, till we all come to the unity of the faith and the knowledge of the Son of God, to a perfect man, to the measure of he stature of the fullness of Christ; that we should no longer be children, tossed to and fro and carried about with every wind of doctrine, by the trickery of men, in the cunning craftiness by which they lie in wait to deceive, but speaking the truth in love, may grow up in all things into Him who is the head---Christ----from whom the whole body, joined and knit together by what every joint supplies, according to the effective working by which every part does its share, causes growth of the body for the edifying of itself in love."*

In these verses Paul describes seven blessings of perfection.

1. Maturity –no more like children (v 14).
2. Established in the faith - no more of doubtful mind or tossed to and fro like the waves (v 14; Jas. 1:5-6).
3. Rooted and grounded in truth – no more carried about by winds of doctrine (v 14; Jn. 8:32-36; Eph. 3:17; Col. 2:6-7; 2 Pet. 1:12).
4. Freedom from deception – able to discern truth from error (v 14; 2 Tim. 2:15; Heb. 5:11-14; Jn. 8: 32-36).
5. Ability to speak the truth in love (v 15; Rom. 15:14; Col. 3:16).
6. Constant growth in spiritual things (v 15; 1 Pet. 2:2; 2 Pet. 3:18).
7. Harmony with all others in Christ (v 16; 1Cor. 1:10; 2Cor.13:11). **2**

Finis Dake makes an excellent point about this, "Many seek to find out how many imperfections, failures, and carnal traits are allowable in religion, but few seek to bring Christians to the height of the gospel standard and to the un-limitations of the promises of God. The measure of the stature of the fullness is seldom mentioned much less demonstrated, while the stature of littleness, emptiness, and powerlessness of Christianity is often emphasized and demonstrated." **3**

When Paul wrote in Philippians 3:12, *"Not as though I had already attained, either were already perfect: but I follow after, if that I may apprehend that for which also I am apprehended of Christ Jesus,"* he was referring to a different state of perfection. The word perfect in this verse is from the Greek *"teleioo* meaning to make a full end or consummate. " **4** This kind of perfection refers to the complete and glorified state. "It does not imply that he was lacking in spiritual experience; that he was deficient in grace; that the body of sin was still cleaving to him; that he was yet struggling with an "old man" in him; that he was not yet sanctified." **5**

That is why Paul is not making a contradiction of himself in verse 15, when he says, *"Therefore let us, as many as are mature (perfect KJV), have this mind; and if in anything you think otherwise, God will reveal even this to you."*

Here Paul is using the word *teleios*—full growth, completeness, or maturity. He obviously had attained this level of perfection or maturity, for he states, *"Let us, as many as are perfect"* and again in 1Cor. 2:6 , *"howbeit we speak wisdom among them that are perfect: yet not the wisdom of this world, nor of the princes of this world, that come to nought."*

One of the great joys of parenting is to watch your children grow into strong mature people. Nothing is as sad as children who are handicapped and forever crippled with physical, mental, and emotional immaturity. Just so, God takes enormous delight in the growth and maturity of His children. This is what Jesus had in mind when He said, *"Therefore you shall be perfect, just as your Father in heaven is perfect"* (Matt. 5:48).

The word *teleios* is again used here and means complete in conformity to God's laws. A mature Christian must be:

1. Broken in spirit, burdened for others, meek, humble, hungry for righteousness, merciful, pure in heart, wise, patient, loving, joyful, and gracious (Matt. 5:3-12).
2. Salt to preserve and a light to shine (Matt. 5:13-16).
3. A teacher and keeper of truth (Matt. 5:17-19).
4. Free from hypocrisy, selfishness, and grudges (Matt. 5:20-24).
5. A peace-maker (Matt. 5:9, 25-26).
6. Free from lusts (Matt. 5:27-30).
7. A family man (Matt. 5:31-32).
8. Truthful (Matt. 5:31-37).
9. Non-resistant to mistreatment (Matt. 5:38-41).
10. Charitable, neighborly, and God like in society (Matt.5: 38-47). 6

Is such a state of mature growth possible for Christians today? Yes, absolutely! All this is possible through:

➢ The new birth (2Cor. 5:17; 1Jn.2:29; 3:5-10; 5:1-4, 18).
➢ By walking and living in the Spirit (Rom. 8:1-13; Gal. 5:16-26).
➢ By discipline and the proper use of Christian weapons (2Cor. 10:5-7; Eph.6:10-18; Col. 2:6-10; 3:3-10; 2Tim. 2:21).

Make no mistake about it dear Christian friend, God wants every believer to enjoy His fullness! The Bible is very clear about this. Jesus said, *"I have come that they may have life, and that they may have it more abundantly"* (John 10:10b).

Paul writes in Ephesians 3: 13-21, *"Therefore I ask that you do not lose heart at my tribulations for you, which is your glory. For this reason I bow my knees to the Father of our Lord Jesus Christ, from whom the whole family in heaven and earth is named, that He would grant you according to the riches of His glory to be strengthened with might through His Spirit in the inner man, that Christ may dwell in your hearts through faith; that you being rooted and grounded in love, may be able to comprehend with all the saints what is the width and length and depth and height— to know the love of Christ which passes knowledge; that you may be filled with all the fullness of God. Now to Him who is able to do exceedingly abundantly above all that we ask or think, according to the power that works in us, to Him be glory in the church by Christ Jesus throughout all ages, world without end. Amen."* (Emphasis mine)

To be filled with the fullness of God is just as possible today as then, and as possible as the other things prayed for here and in 1:17-23, *"That the God of our Lord Jesus Christ, the Father of glory, may give to you the spirit of wisdom and revelation in the knowledge of Him, the eyes of your understanding being enlightened; that you may know what is the hope of His calling, what are the riches of the glory of His inheritance in the saints, and what is the exceeding greatness of His power toward us who believe, according to the working of His might power which He worked in Christ when he raised Him from the dead and seated Him at His right hand in the heavenly places, far above all principality and power and might and dominion, and every name that is named, not only in this age but also in that which is to come. And He put all things under His feet, and gave Him to be head over all things to the church, which is His body, the fullness of Him who fills all in all."*

Paul gives a stern warning in Colossians 2:8, *"Beware lest anyone cheat you through philosophy and empty deceit, according to the traditions of men, according to the basic principles of the world, and not according to Christ."*

God's will is that we be complete and filled with the fullness of Christ. *"For in Him dwells all the fullness of the Godhead bodily; and you are complete in Him, who is the head of all principality (rule) and power (authority)"* (Col. 2:9, 10). (Emphasis mine) He doesn't want anybody or anything to defraud you of this glorious inheritance of His fullness.

I am convinced the understanding and practice of the previous *Laws of the Kingdom* and the following seven realities will bring you into the wonderful maturity, completeness and fullness of Christ God desires for you to enjoy <u>now</u> in the Kingdom of God.

Each of these realities is a book in itself and there are many good volumes written on them. It is my purpose, however, to share a general overview of each reality to enable the reader to realize what vast treasures of spiritual wealth and dynamics are available to him to live a victorious fruitful Christian life!

As you study these lessons, ask God to quicken your understanding and make these realities real in your life! As these truths become real to you, your life will take on a whole new meaning and purpose. You will discover the joy of Paul, "<u>for me to live is Christ!</u>"

Chapter Eight

The Reality of Prayer   Part A

"Then He spoke a parable to them, that men always ought to pray and not lose heart."

-Luke 18:1

The greatest lesson I have ever learned about prayer **is to pray!** The most important thing I could say about prayer is---**pray!** I am convinced, if there is any lack in our lives that lack somehow relates itself to the neglect of prayer. If there are any failures in our lives, those failures can somehow and in some way be traced to the lack of prayer. If we have any victories at all, those victories can be traced to the root of faithful prayer and praying in faith.

We must do more than read books on prayer, listen to tapes, watch videos, hear sermons and attend seminars on prayer—**WE MUST PRAY!** Over the years I have seen ministries come and go who sought to impact the church world with their "prayer movements" only to dissipate and die. Was it because their teaching was in error? No! Was it because they did a great deal of merchandising their tapes, books, videos, etc.? No! Was it because many churches refused to buy into their ministries? No! More usual than not, their failures were due to their personal neglect of really praying. They were saying all the right words about prayer, going to the right places to teach about prayer, but met with dismal failure. Why? Very simply, <u>they did not pray</u>!

To simply talk about prayer and not pray is a very serious danger and borders on insincerity and hypocrisy. It is worse than playing with fire or dynamite. Judas heard the Master teach and demonstrate the power of prayer, but that did not stop him from betraying Jesus. Had he been faithful to *"watch with Him one hour"* in prayer in the garden, as well as the many other occasions and opportunities he had, he very well could have been faithful and victorious and spared himself such eternal disgrace and damnation.

It is the <u>practice of prayer</u> that must become the passionate reality of our hearts and the discipline of our lives. We cannot afford to be glib and passive in our attitude about fervent praying. In his letter to the Colossians, Paul admonishes the believers to *"Continue earnestly in prayer, being vigilant in it with thanksgiving"* (Col.4: 2).You see his passion about prayer in the words—<u>continue</u>, <u>earnest</u>, <u>vigilant</u>, and <u>thanksgiving.</u>

We see similar passion about prayer with David. Psalm 63:1-8 is one of the numerous references that illustrate what I am talking about. *"O God, you are my God, earnestly I see you; my soul thirsts for you, my body longs for you, in a dry and weary land where there is not water. I have seen you in the sanctuary ands beheld your power and glory. Because your love is better than life, my lips will glorify you. I will praise you as long as I live, and in your name I will lift up my hands. My soul will be satisfied as with the richest of foods; with singing lips my mouth will praise you. On my bed I remember you; I think of you through the watches of the night. Because you are my help, I sing in the shadow of your wings. My soul clings to you; your right hand upholds me."*

Here is a man with a desperate desire for God. *"I earnestly seek you…"* *"My craving for you is stronger than my thirst for water!"* *"My deepest longing is for you!"*

I fear that all too often we prefer God, but we do not passionately desire Him. Yes, He's the God of our choice, but is He the God of our craving? We like Him a lot, but do we love Him with all our heart?

David sought the Lord in public worship. He "looked" for Him "in the sanctuary." He wanted to see God's "power and glory" on display.

David sought the Lord in his daily living. He said God's "loving-kindness," His "steadfast love" was "better than life" to him. "More to be desired than all the riches of gold and silver."

David sought the Lord in privacy. He said he would "remember" the Lord while lying on his bed, and he would "meditate" during the "night watches."

People who are passionate for God will desperately desire His presence. We are told by the writer to the Hebrews, *"God is a rewarder of those who diligently seek him"* (Heb.11: 6).Through the prophet Jeremiah God promised, *"You will seek me and find me when you seek me with all your heart."* (Jeremiah 29:13) Also he said, *"Call to Me, and I will answer you, and show you great and mighty things, which you do not know" (*Jeremiah 33:3*). "If you will look to God and plead with the Almighty, if you are pure and upright, even now he will rouse himself on your behalf and restore you to your rightful place. Your beginnings will seem humble, so prosperous will your future be"* (Job. 8:5-7).

Passionate, private, and priority time with God is absolutely essential if we are to know God and see the mighty display of His glory and presence. Cannon Liddon states, *"The great masters and teachers in Christian doctrine have always found in prayer their highest source of illumination. Not to go beyond the limits of the English Church, it is recorded of Bishop Andrews that he spent five hours daily on his knees. The greatest practical resolves that have enriched and beautified human life in Christian times have been arrived at in prayer."***1**

There is no greater example of a passionate praying man that the Lord Jesus Christ. The record shows He spent many whole nights in prayer. His custom was to pray much. He flowed in a continual communication with the Father. Among all the great qualities of his life, none is more predominate than his life of prayer. This same testimony can be said for the Apostle Paul, whose practice and teaching of prayer is amazingly wonderful. Daniel's passion for God found him taking time from very important government interest to seek God three times a day.

"The men who have most fully illustrated Christ in their character, and have most powerfully affected the world for Him, have been men who spent so much time with God as to make it a notable feature of their lives. Charles Simeon devoted the hours from four till eight in the morning to God. Mr. Wesley spent two hours daily in prayer. John Fletcher stained the wall of his room by the breath of his prayers. Sometimes he would pray all night; always, frequently, and with great earnestness. His whole life was a life of prayer. "I would not rise from my seat,' he said, 'without lifting my heart to God.' Luther said: "If I fail to spend two hours in prayer each morning, the devil gets the victory through the day. I have so much business I cannot get on without spending three hours daily in prayer." **2**

John Welch, the holy and wonderful Scotch preacher, thought the day ill spent if he did not spend eight or ten hours in prayer. He kept a plaid that he might wrap himself when he arose to pray at night. His wife would complain when she found him lying on the ground weeping. He would reply: "O woman, I have the souls of three thousand to answer for, and I know not how it is with many of them!" **3**

> The motto of Dr. Adam Clarke, contemporary of John Wesley, and author of the *Clarke's Commentary*, was "never be without a praying heart." **4**

In the book, *Prevailing Prayer,* Dr. Tony Anderson shares a brief report of his personal experience in one of the greatest revivals in American history, the revival at Asbury College in 1950. This mighty move of God was a direct result of his and several students who covenanted to make prayer their way of life. He said, "When I entered into this covenant of prayer it was not as an experiment; it is an imperative necessity in my life. It has been a delight to my heart to meet Him at the throne of grace while the day is young. It has become a fixed habit of life to pray; I consider it to be more important than my
daily bread." **5**

"My Lord has been pleased to increase the fruitfulness of my ministry. He has given the unspeakable pleasure of seeing many souls saved by His grace. I witness to the glory of my Christ, that He has blessed my humble ministry for more than forty years. But after I entered into a covenant of prayer with Him, and have faithfully kept watch with Him in the silent hours after midnight, He has given me more that seventeen thousand and five hundred souls, in less than two years." **6**

These are but a few of the multiplied thousands of testimonies that could be brought to our attention from saints of God who touched heaven, blessed earth, and shook hell with their passion for God in prayer.

IT IS THE WILL OF GOD THAT EVERY CHRISTIAN UNDERSTAND AND ENJOY THE REALITY OF PRAYER AND GET ANSWERS. STUDY AND PRACTICE THE FOLLOWING GUIDELINES AND YOUR PRAYER LIFE WILL BE ENRICHED IN THE AWESOME REALITIES OF THIS SPIRITUAL DISCIPLINE.

"And it came to pass, as He was praying in a certain place, when He ceased, that one of His disciple said to Him, "Lord teach us to pray, as John also taught his disciples" (Luke 11:1-13).

1. Prayer will become a reality when we understand the general principles of prayer and stay with this range and learn:

1. How to begin prayer (v2; Matt. 11:25).
2. Whom to address (v 2; Jn.14:13-15; 15:16; 16:23-26).
3. Whose NAME to revere (v 2).
4. Whose WILL to obey (v2).
5. Whose INTEREST to serve and have at heart (2; Matt. 22:37).
    1. HEART – all inward affections
    2. SOUL – all consciousness
    3. MIND—all thoughts
6. What to ask for (v 2-4).
7. How to KEEP CLEAR channels to God (v 4; 1Jn 3:21-22).
8. How to LIVE with our fellowman (v 4; Mk. 11:25-26; Eph.4).
9. How to LIVE free from sin (v 4; Rom.6:16-23; 8:12-13).

2. Prayer becomes a reality when we become bold as the friends of God—importune, urge with frequent solicitation, be tenacious in purpose, stubbornly adhering to a purpose; continue steadily, incessant, refuse to give an inch; be desperate, demanding, insistent, eager, and troublesome in pursuit of what God has promised (v 5-8; 18:1-8; Heb.4:14-16; 10:19-23,36).

3. When we believe in and have confidence in the absolute certainty of answered prayer with no wavering or doubt as to the final outcome (v 9-10; Mt. 7:7-11; 17:20; 21:21; Mk. 9:23; 11:22-24; Jn.14:12-15; 15:7; 16:23-26; Heb.11: 6; Jas. 1:5-8; 1Jn. 3:19-22; 5:14-15).

4. When we believe in and have confidence in the infinite Fatherhood of God, realizing that He is at least as interested in our welfare as an earthly parent, that He will give all things which are best to His children, and that He will give exactly what is asked according to His will and Word (v 11-13; Mt. 7:7-11; 1Jn. 3:19-22; 5:14-15; Ps. 84:11).

5. When we believe in and know beyond all possible doubt that it is the will of God for His children to get what they will and want (v 9-13; Ps.23:1; 34:9-10; 84:11; Mt. 17:20; 21:21; Mk. 11:22-24; Jn.15:7).
6. When we believe in and ask God for the Holy Spirit, the all-inclusive gift, who will enable us to pray and get answers (v 13; Rom.8:26-27; Eph.2:18; 6:18; Jude 20; Jn.7:37-39).

7. When we believe in and never question it—that God will answer each persons who prays right, not just a few special ones (v 9-13; Mt. 7:7-11; Mk. 9:23; 11:24; Jn.14:12-15; Rom.2:11). 7

Anyone who learns and practices well these lessons will get answers."

Prayer is a fascinating discovery

When we discover the reality of prayer we will realize prayer is an <u>adventure in Love,</u> because prayer is communion and communication with God and God is love! (1John 4:8).

We will realize prayer is an <u>adventure in Riches</u>, *"for the same Lord over all is rich unto all that call upon him"* (Rom.10: 12).

We will realize prayer is an <u>adventure in Power</u>, *"and when they had prayed, the place where they were assembled together was shaken; and they were all filled with the Holy Spirit, and they spoke the word of God with boldness"* (Acts. 4:31).

God promised, *"Call unto Me and I will answer thee, and show thee great and mighty things, which thou knowest not"* (Jeremiah 33:3).

May God richly bless you with deep and keen insight, and a deeper passion for the heart of God as you go forth in the venture and discovery of the *Reality of Prayer.*

Chapter Nine

The Reality of Prayer Secrets   Part B

*And whatever we ask we receive from Him, because we keep His commandments and do those things that are pleasing in His sight."--*1John 3:22

Some time ago I purchased a large suitcase specifically for my travels abroad. I noticed it had two sets of locks for security purposes. One type lock was a combination and the other required a key. Common sense, of course, tells one you must both know the combination and have a key made for the locks in order to open the luggage. That is simple logic and doesn't require a space scientists or technician to figure it out. The same principle holds true in getting answers to our prayers. If we do not understand the secrets or keys to getting answers, then as T.L. Osborne says, "our prayers will be nothing more than rituals."

Just before going to the cross, Jesus said concerning prayer, *"And in that day you will ask Me nothing. Most assuredly, I say to you, whatever you ask the Father in My name He will give you. Until now you have asked nothing in My name. Ask, and you will receive, that your joy may be full"* (John 16:23, 24).

Earlier in John 14:12-14, Jesus said, *"Most assuredly, I say to you, he who believes in Me, the works that I do he will do also; and greater works than these he will do, because I go to My Father. And whatever you ask in My name, that I will do, that the Father may be glorified in the Son. If you ask anything in My name, I will do it."*

You will note the word *ask* is used in both statements Jesus made. However, to avoid confusion and to show there is no contradiction between these two scriptures, we must understand that in the Greek text two entirely different words are used for the same English word *ask*.

The word "ask" in John 14:13, 14 relates to our power of attorney to use the Name of Jesus in doing the works of Jesus. I will deal with this aspect of prayer later.

First, notice Jesus said in John 16:23, 24 *"And in that day you will ask Me nothing."* <u>This is our first secret to prayer</u>. Jesus is referring to the time following His resurrection and ascension to the right hand of the Father. From that position Jesus is our mediator, intercessor, advocate and Lord. He stands between the Father and us to grant us access to the Father by virtue of His righteousness and eternal redemption.

So Jesus is telling us <u>we are not to pray to Him</u>, but we are to <u>Pray To The Father</u> in His Name! We praise Him! We glorify Him! We worship Him and tell Him how we love Him, but we do not pray TO Him. We pray to the Father through Him. Recently, I was visiting a very sick man and his brother was there also. The patient's brother led in prayer and never once addressed the Father. He continued praying, "dear Jesus, I ask you to touch my brother." He was very sincere, but how many know a football player can be very sincere and yet run with the ball to the wrong goal post. It takes more than sincerity! We must pray the way Jesus said! He said, *"Whatever you ask the Father in My name He will give you."* Then He adds, *"Ask, and you will receive, that your joy may be full."* Our joy is full when our needs are met and that is God's will for us. What a glorious secret!

Furthermore, we must realize there is a <u>difference in praying in the name of Jesus</u> and <u>for the sake of Jesus.</u> This is another vital key. I have heard people conclude their prayer, *"this I ask for Jesus' sake".* If you are asking God for healing or to supply your need, it is not Jesus who needs the healing or material need, it is YOU! It is not for His sake! It is for your sake. In the first place Jesus does not need the help and in the second place you don't have any credit to guarantee it if He did. It's the other way around. We need the help and He has the credit.

In addition, Jesus said we have the power of attorney to use His name. He said in John 14:12-14, *"Most assuredly, I say to you, he who believes in Me, the works that I do he will do also; and greater works than they he will do, because I go to My Father. And whatever you ask in My name, that I will do, that the Father may be glorified in the Son. If you ask anything in My name, I will do it."*

As I stated earlier, the word "ask" in this verse comes from the Greek word *aiteo* and means require or demand. It is obvious we cannot demand God, but with the power of attorney we can place a demand upon Satan and demons. This verse is talking about the works of Jesus and our legal right to do those same works. And we can do His works through His Name! See (John 14: 12)

This power of attorney is clearly defined for us in Mark 16:17-18, Jesus said *"And these signs will follow those who believe:* <u>*In My name*</u> *they will cast out demons; they will speak with new tongues; they will take up serpents; and if they drink anything deadly, it will by no means hurt them; they will lay hands on the sick, and they will recover."*

This is a very important key. **IF WE IN FAITH WILL EXERCISE OUR RIGHT TO USE THE NAME OF JESUS, WE WILL WITNESS WHAT HE SAID WOULD HAPPEN. NOTICE THE FIVE SIGNS OF THE BELIEVER:**

1. Cast out demons (Verse 17).
2. Speak with new tongues (Verse 17).
3. Take up serpents (Verse 18).This does not mean handling snakes, but if bitten by accident we have God's protection (See Acts 28:3-5).
4. Drink anything deadly, it will not hurt them (Verse 18). This of course also means by accident. We are not to tempt God.
5. Lay hands on the sick and they will recover (Verse 18).

We have all of this available to us by virtue of His name. This right and authority is given to all believers. We must learn to act upon His word and do it!

<u>We are to pray expecting results</u>. This is a vital key! So many people's prayers remind me of the proverbial "Mother Hubbard's dress"-- It covers everything, but touches nothing. So many pray useless words—covering everything but expecting nothing! Why should we pray if we cannot expect results?

I don't know of anything that could be more frustrating and discouraging than praying ceaselessly for days, weeks, and perhaps years without ever seeing any results. In fact, I remember well as a young teen age Christian praying the same prayer in the same form for several years without ever seeing results. But, oh how different once I learned how to really pray <u>according to the Word</u>. I began to see results!

Jesus said the Word of the Lord is truth and God didn't make promises to simply fill in spaces. In fact, God is so concerned about His promises to us that He challenges us to put Him in remembrance. The principle for this is seen in Isaiah

43:25, 26, where God says to Israel, *"I, even I, am He who blots out your transgressions for My own sake; And I will not remember your sins. Put Me in remembrance; Let us contend together; State your case, that you may be acquitted."*

In context here, God is urging Israel to remind Him of His promise of forgiveness. The same principle applies to all the promises of God. He desires that we <u>remind</u> Him of what has been promised to us. Kenneth Hagin quotes Smith Wigglesworth as saying, "God delights in His children having the audacity of faith to say, 'Lord, you promised it, so do it.'" **1**

This does not mean we are to be arrogant and careless with God. But it does mean we are reverently and boldly stand on the promise of God's Word and tell the Lord we are doing so, and expect Him to fulfill His promises.

It is precisely here where the "fight of faith" comes into the picture again. Prayer means fighting against demons and the host of darkness that are trying to hold back the answers and results. Paul says in Ephesians 6:12, *"For we do not wrestle against flesh and blood, but against principalities, against powers, against the rulers of the darkness of this age, against spiritual hosts of wickedness in the heavenly places."* When we understand the nature of this spiritual warfare and boldly take our stand against these demonic forces, we begin seeing results. We have the authority and right to demand Satan and demons to release their hold on lost souls, our money, and all other things God has promised us.

Another key is the <u>power of agreement</u> in prayer. In Matthew 18:19 Jesus said, *"Again I say to you that if two of you agree on earth concerning anything that they ask, it will be done for them by My Father in heaven."* Although we may get results praying ourselves, we greatly enhance our prayer power and results when two or more pray and agree together. The Bible says that one will put a thousand to flight but two will put 10,000 to flight. You can do ten times as much with someone agreeing with you as you can by yourself. It doesn't take a great number. Just two will do. My wife and I have learned that our agreeing together gets results!

The key word in this passage is the word *"agree"*. It comes from the Greek word *sumphoneo* from which we get our English word "symphony". It means "to sound together, each one joining in harmony with the other, each supporting the other." This grand symphony of oneness is portrayed in the glorious vision and revelation given to the Apostle John numerous times in the Revelation. He says in 19:1, 5, 6, *"After these things I heard a loud voice (singular) of a great multitude in heaven, (plural) saying, "Alleluia! Salvation and glory and honor and power to the Lord our God! Then a voice came from the throne, saying, "Praise our God all you His servants and those who fear Him, both small and great!" And I heard, as it were, the voice (singular) of a great multitude, (plural) as the sound (singular) of many waters (plural-nations and peoples), and as the sound (singular) of mighty thunderings, (plural) saying, "Alleluia! For the Lord God Omnipotent reigns!"*

Understanding Kinds or Types of Prayer

In Ephesians 6:18 Paul reveals there are different types or kinds of prayer. *"...praying always with all prayer and supplication in the Spirit, being watchful to this end with all perseverance and supplication for all the saints---"* Notice several other translations:

The Amplified Bible says, "Pray at all times (on every occasion, in every season) in the Spirit, with all (manner of) prayer and entreaty"

Goodspeed, "Use every kind of prayer and entreaty"

RSV- "praying with all prayer and supplication"

Philips- "Pray at all times with every kind of spiritual prayer"

Moffatt- "Praying at all times with all manner of prayer"

It is obvious there are different types of prayer. One type of prayer will work in one situation and another type in a different situation. It is similar to sports. Not all sports are alike. There are different types or kinds of sports, each with a different set of rules, likewise there are different kinds of prayer and we must pray each prayer according to the rule as set forth in the Word of God. It is, therefore, very important that we know and employ all types of prayers that we might be fully equipped. You will find Scripture reveals the following types of prayer:

1. *Prayer of Asking or Petition*: Matt. 21:22
        The simplest type of prayer–ask and receive

2. *Prayer of Guidance:* Acts 9:6; Jas. 4:2-3
        Need guidance concerning what to pray for

3. *Prayer of Consecration,* Dedication, and Surrender: Matt. 26:39; Luke 22:42 1Pet.5: 6-7
        Totally commit the situation and surrender it to God

4. *Prayer of Faith:* Jas. 5:15
        A supernatural knowing where God imparts faith

5. *Prayer of Worship:* Acts 13:1-4
        The act of ministering to the Lord and not to one another

6. *Prayer of Commitment*: Matt. 6:25-27; Phil. 4:6; 1Peter 5:7

7. *Prayer of Silence or listening*: Ps. 46:10
        Learning to listen to God speak

8. *Prayer of Importunity:* Lk.11: 5-10
        Persistent intercession for someone else

9. *Prayer of Agreement:* Matt. 18:19
        Two people harmonize in making a request

10. *Prayer of Humility.* 2Chron. 7:14; Mk. 9:29
        Humble ourselves by fasting

11. *Lord's Prayer*: Matt. 6:6-15
        a. Praise and Worship
        b. Intercession
        c. Petition
        d. Confession and forgiveness
        e. Protection and deliverance

12. *Prayer of the Holy Spirit:* Rom. 8:26-27
　　　　Groaning in the spirit and praying in tongues

13. *Prayer in the Name of Jesus:* Jn. 16:23-24
　　　　We have the power of attorney to use His Name

14. *Prayer of Remembrance:* Isa. 43:26
　　　　Prepare your case and remind God of His promises

15. *Prayer of Binding and Loosing*: Matt. 18:18
　　　　Bind the power of Satan operating in that situation

16. *Prayer of Unison:* Acts 1:14, 25, 2:42-47; 4:23-31; 5:41, 42;
　　12:5; 13:1:3; 14:23; 16:25, 26
　　　　Two or more are praying in company with each other.

Foundation to Answers - *(The following seven steps to answered prayer are adapted from Kenneth Hagin's Bible Prayer Study Course.)* 1

1. *Decide What You Need and Want From God and then find the Scriptures that definitely promise you those things.* James 1: 6-8; Matt. 18:19.
   a. A wavering man will not receive
   b. Be definite and specific; Mark 10:46-52; Matt. 9: 27-29; 8:1-3.
   c. Rom. 4:20-21: Feed on the Word and faith is built into your
   　　　Inner consciousness
   d. A promise from God's Word gives us confidence and victory

2. *Ask God For The Things You Want and Believe That You Have Them.* Matt. 7:7-8; Mk. 11:23-24
   a. Realize His plan for us is to make our needs known
   b. We do not have because we do not ask. James 4:2
   c. Believe that you receive before you see a tangible answer, that is, believe you have it before you get it. When do we believe? When we pray, when we ask.

3. *Let Every Thought and Desire Affirm That You Have What You Ask.* Joshua 1:8; 2Cor. 10:3-5; 1Pet. 5:6-9

4. *Discipline Your Mind.* Your thoughts are governed by observation, association and teachings. You refuse to doubt by directing your thoughts in line with the Word of God. Phil. 4:8

5. *Cultivate A Constant Meditation on the Promises Upon Which You Base Your Answer To Your Prayer.* Prov. 4:20-22; John 15:7; Joshua 1;8:
    a. Through mediation, or constant pondering and "chewing" on the Word of God.
    b. See yourself with the answer and God will make His Word good.

6. *Begin In Your Waking Moments Thinking on the Greatness and Goodness of God, and Count Your Blessings.* Phil 4:6

    a. Fill yourself with Psalm 37 when tempted to fret, worry or to be fearful.

7. *Give God the Praise.*

    a. Constantly Praise Him Before and After The Answer. Phil. 4:6-7

    b. Develop the discipline of thinking FAITH THOUGHTS and speaking FAITH WORDS. This habit will feed your faith and starve your doubts and lead your heart out of defeat into victory.

Bottlenecks In The Prayer Life — **Why some prayers are hindered.**

Tucked away in a passage of Scripture dealing with husband and wives relationships and responsibilities to one another is this interesting little phrase, *"that your prayers may not be hindered"* (1Pet. 3:7). I am certain every Christian has had an experience of praying and not receiving an answer. Upon examination you discover there was a hindrance. A bottleneck!

The word "bottleneck" is a term that became common during the production years of WWII. It meant, "a slowdown in war production caused by the scarcity of material, machinery, or skilled labor, essential to the given industry."

When applied to the Christian prayer life, bottleneck means "a slowdown of spiritual progress caused by a scarcity of proper praying so essential to the Christian in his life and work."

The Word of God promises that God answers prayer, but we often make it impossible for Him to answer our prayers because there is a bottleneck or hindrance standing in the way. Scripture clearly reveals a number of these hindrances.

1. *Praying Amiss or With The Wrong Motive.* James 4:3: *"You ask and do not receive, because you ask amiss, that you may spend it on your pleasures."*

    a. We ask amiss when our prayer is not in accord with the Word of God. 1John 5:14
    b. We ask amiss when we do not believe what we ask for. Mark 11:22-24
    c. We ask amiss when we fail to pray in the Holy Spirit. Rom. 8:26

2. *Praying With Sin In Our Lives will hinder prayer.* Sin will not only throttle, or 'clog' our prayer channel <u>it will completely stop it up!</u> Isaiah 59: 1, 2, says, *"But your iniquities have separated you from your God; And your sins have hidden His face from you, So that He will not hear."* That is very clear!

    David, who understood from personal experience reveals in Psalm 66:18, *"If I regard iniquity in my heart the Lord will not hear."*

    The apostle John clearly teaches that willful sinning and walking with God do not go together. 1John 1:6, *"If we say that we have fellowship with Him, and walk in darkness, we lie and do not practice the truth."*

3. *Praying When God Is Not First and Foremost In Our Lives hinders our prayers.* The prophet Ezekiel declares, *"Son of man, these men have set up their idols in their hearts, and put before them that which causes them to stumble into iniquity. <u>Should I let Myself be inquired of at all by them?</u>"*

Jesus makes very clear that the Kingdom of God must be the first priority of our lives. *"But seek first the kingdom of God and His righteousness, and all these things shall be added to you"* (Matt. 6:33).

God hates the sin of idolatry! An idol can be anything from the obvious millions of hand-made gods in India's temples, to the more subtle sophisticated system that produces a false sense of value that's engulfed the West. It is anything or anybody we put before God, or in the place of God. The subtle idolatry is the most lethal! It comes in the beautiful garments known as "secularism", "materialism", or "humanism", etc. But, Oh how deadly!

4. *Praying Without Compassion And Care For The Needy will hinder prayer.* Proverbs 21:13 says, *"Whoever shuts his ears to the cry of the poor will also cry himself and not be heard."*

God loves a cheerful giver! (2Cor. 9:7). God wants us to have a liberal spirit and practice Proverbs 3: 9, *"Honor the Lord with your possessions, And with the firstfruits of all your increase; So your barns will be filled with plenty, And your vats will overflow with new wine."*

5. *Praying With Unforgiveness In Our Hearts Will Hinder Prayer.* Jesus said in Mark 11:25, *"And whenever you stand praying, if you have anything against anyone, forgive him, that your Father in heaven may also forgive you your trespasses. But if you do not forgive, neither will your Father in heaven forgive your trespasses."*

There is a great danger when we entertain an offence and allow a spirit of bitterness, strife, resentfulness, malice, or any form of malevolence take root in our lives. The Hebrew writer admonishes, *"Pursue peace with all men, and holiness, without which no one will see the Lord: looking diligently lest anyone fall short of the grace of God; lest any root of bitterness springing up cause trouble, and by this many become defiled"* (Heb.12: 14, 15).

An unforgiving spirit will not only hinder your prayers but will destroy your health and life as well.

6. *Praying When There Is A Wrong Relationship Between Husband and Wife will hinder prayer.* Notice the instruction Peter gives, *"Likewise you husbands, dwell with them with understanding, giving honor to the wife, as to the weaker vessel, and as being heirs together of the grace of life, that your prayers may not be hindered"* (1Peter 3:7.)

Every husband is to love his wife and every wife is to honor her husband. A relationship of peace, love, joy and mutual respect for each other builds a healthy marriage and gets answers to prayer.

7. *Praying Without Faith Will Hinder Prayer.* The Apostle James tells us, *"If any of you lacks wisdom, let him ask of God, who gives to all liberally and without reproach, and it will be given to him. But let him ask in faith, with no doubting, for he who doubts is like a wave of the sea driven and tossed by the wind. For let not that man suppose that he will receive anything from the Lord; he is a double-minded man, unstable in all his ways"* (James 1:5-7.)

We must understand that unbelief is an insult to God. It was unbelief and hardness of heart that brought the rebuke from Jesus to His disciples. (Mark. 16:14)

8. *Praying When It Is Humanly Possible For Us To Answer Our Own Prayer will hinder prayer.*

A farm boy overheard his father praying for the needs of the poor in the community. He said to his father, "Daddy, I wish I had your corn." "What would you do with it?" the Father asked. "I'd answer your prayer," he said.

A good motto to follow is, "Pray as though all depended on God, and work as though all depended on you."

Some people pray for safety on the highway and then drive 80 to 90 miles per hour breaking the speed laws. Some pray for health and then indulge in overeating and eating all the wrong foods, drinking alcoholic beverages and abusing the body with narcotics and nicotine and so forth. We must mix common sense with our prayers.

Are you praying and not getting any answers? It would pay you to review these eight hindrances and examine your life in the light of each one to see what might be hindering your answer.

We must keep constant vigil on our lives. David cried out to the Lord, *"Search me, O God, and know my heart; Try me, and know my thoughts; And see if there is any wicked way in me, And lead me in the way everlasting"* (Psalm 139:23, 24).

MAY THIS ALWAYS BE OUR DESIRE AND PRAYER AS WELL!

Chapter Ten

The Reality of Worship

"O come, let us worship and bow down: let us kneel before the LORD our maker."
-Ps. 95:6

Deeply imbedded in the spiritual DNA and soul print of every human being is the crucial need and desire to worship. Every person will worship something or someone. The so called atheist who claims there is no God is a worshipper. He cannot avoid it! It is as much in human nature to worship as it is for you to breathe. Every idol erected, every altar built, every burning sacrifice that ever wafted its smoke to heaven is mute testimony to the truth that man was created with a deep inherent need to worship.

From the earliest records of human history we see man performing the act of worship. Early Biblical history is rich and full with records of man's role in worship. When man thinks independently of God, or he is too intelligent to worship, then he is all the more likely to succumb to some base form of idolatry. We read about it in Romans 1:21-32:

Because that, when they knew God, they glorified him not as God, neither were thankful; but became vain in their imaginations, and their foolish heart was darkened.
Professing themselves to be wise, they became fools,
And changed the glory of the uncorruptible God into an image made like to corruptible man, and to birds, and fourfooted beasts, and creeping things.
Wherefore God also gave them up to uncleanness through the lusts of their own hearts, to dishonour their own bodies between themselves: Who changed the truth of God into a lie, and worshipped and served the creature more than the Creator, who is blessed for ever. Amen.
For this cause God gave them up unto vile affections: for even their women did change the natural use into that which is against nature: And likewise also the men, leaving the natural use of the woman, burned in their lust one toward another; men

with men working that which is unseemly, and receiving in themselves that recompense of their error which was meet.

And even as they did not like to retain God in their knowledge, God gave them over to a reprobate mind, to do those things which are not convenient; Being filled with all unrighteousness, fornication, wickedness, covetousness, maliciousness; full of envy, murder, debate, deceit, malignity; whisperers,

Backbiters, haters of God, despiteful, proud, boasters, inventors of evil things, disobedient to parents,

Without understanding, covenant breakers, without natural affection, implacable, unmerciful: Who knowing the judgment of God, that they which commit such things are worthy of death, not only do the same, but have pleasure in them that do them.

The Scriptures are clear in describing the various forms or kinds of worship. Only one kind of worship is acceptable and pleasing to God. Notice,

Un-acceptable Worship

The Lord declared through His prophet Amos, *"I hate, I despise your feast days, and I will not smell in your solemn assemblies. Though ye offer me burnt offerings and your meat offerings, I will not accept them: neither will I regard the peace offerings of your fat beasts. Take thou away from me the noise of thy songs; for I will not hear the melody of thy viols"* (Amos 5:21-23).

It may come as a surprise to some that God actually hated the worship forms of His ancient people. But it is true and God is no more pleased today with worship that is not totally and completely focused upon Him and according to His Word.

Webster defines worship as *"to pay divine honors to, to have intense love or admiration for; adore or idolize; to venerate; to perform acts of homage to; to hold very dear."* Actually, the word "worship" comes from an Anglo-Saxon word meaning "worth". Worship is *worth-ship*. It is reverence paid to an object or person of worth. What or whom we worship reveals the object to which we put supreme worth and value upon. A.W. Tozer said, "Worship means to feel in the heart the awesome wonder and overpowering love in praise to God."

"Worship is the human spirit 'reaching out' to God, bowing down in humility and adoration before Him." Such an experience of worship will involve: (1) Revelation of God, (2) Recognition of God, and (3) Response to God.

Scripture is clear that God will accept the worship of some as He did with Abel and He will reject the worship of others as portrayed with Cain. So what is unacceptable worship?

False Worship

First and perhaps foremost is FALSE WORSHIP. False worship is idol worship and the Bible clearly shows God's burning hatred of idolatry. False worship is a direct violation of the Ten Commandments and an insult to God!

David gives a description of false worship in Psalm 115: 4-8, *"Their idols are silver and gold, the work of men's hands. They have mouths, but they speak not: eyes have they, but they see not: they have ears, but they hear not: noses have they, but they smell not: They have hands, but they handle not: feet have they, but they walk not: neither speak they through their throat. They that make them are like unto them; so is every one that trusteth in them."*

These are dead mute idols made by men's hands. This is blatant idolatry! This false idolatrous worship is a predominated practice in many areas of the world. In India, for example, Hinduism claims over 330 million gods. Hinduism is like a giant sponge—always room for another god.
Please note verse 8, *"they that make them are like them; so is every one that trusts in them."* This tells us we gravitate or surface to the level of *what* or *who* we worship. This is clearly evident as you observe the behavior of the many Hindus brought up in this form of idolatrous worship. Their facial expressions reveal the hallow emptiness of their souls. Their eyes express the deep darkness of satanic oppression and deadness. Such worship leaves the worshipper empty, morbid, depressed and unfulfilled.

Vain Worship

In Matthew 15:9, Jesus states that VAIN WORHIP is unacceptable worship.
"Then came to Jesus scribes and Pharisees, which were of Jerusalem, saying, Why do thy disciples transgress the tradition of the elders? For they wash not their hands when they eat bread. But he answered and said unto them, For God commanded, saying, Honour thy father and mother: and, He that curseth father or mother, let him die the death. But ye say, Whosoever shall say to his father or his mother, It is a gift, by whatsoever thou mightest be profited by me; And honour not his father or his mother, he shall be free. Thus have ye made the commandment of God of none effect by your tradition. Ye hypocrites, well did Esaias

*prophesy of you, saying, This people draweth nigh unto me with their mouth, and honoureth me with their lips; but their heart is far from me. **But in vain they do worship me**, teaching for doctrines the commandments of men." (Emphasis mine)*

The worship of the scribes and Pharisees had surfaced to a level of focusing all attention on the traditions, the symbols and images of worship rather than God Himself. Though very impressive their worship was empty of content. In their aggressive attempt to be very precise, meticulous, and accurate about HOW to worship and serve God, they neglected GOD! They forgot God who alone is worthy of worship!

We must never forget that the WHO of worship is more important than the HOW. We must never neglect the true Person of worship for some pattern, place or form of worship. To do so is to become guilty of "worshipping your worship" and that is vain, repugnant, and unacceptable to God who alone is worthy of true worship.

Ignorant Worship

In Acts 17: 22-34 we discover another form of unacceptable worship. It is IGNORANT worship. Notice what Paul encountered at Mars Hill in Athens, Greece. *"Then Paul stood in the midst of Mars' hill, and said, Ye men of Athens, I perceive that in all things ye are too superstitious. For as I passed by, and beheld your devotions, I found an altar with this inscription, TO THE UNKNOWN GOD. Whom therefore ye **ignorantly worship**, Him declare I unto you." (Emphasis mine)*

The Latin word from which we get our word 'religion' means "to bind back". The purpose and true goal of religion should be to bind man back to God from whom he has been cut off. True religion is to lead man into a saving knowledge, relationship, and meaningful worship of Almighty God. Any religion that does not do this is woefully lacking and seriously defective.

In Paul's encounter with the religious philosophers and wise men in Athens, he was taken to Mars Hill, the Areopagus, to explain this new doctrine he was preaching. Paul offers a very wise and beautiful response to their inquiry:

> *"Then Paul stood in the midst of Mars' hill, and said, Ye men of Athens, I perceive that in all things ye are too superstitious. For as I passed by, and beheld your devotions, I found an altar with this inscription, TO THE UNKNOWN GOD. Whom therefore ye ignorantly worship, him declare I*

unto *you.* *"God that made the world and all things therein, seeing that he is Lord of heaven and earth, dwelleth not in temples made with hands; Neither is worshiped with men's hands, as though he needed any thing, seeing he giveth to all life, and breath, and all things; And hath made of one blood all nations of men for to dwell on all the face of the earth, and hath determined the times before appointed, and the bounds of their habitation; That they should seek the Lord, if haply they might feel after him, and find him, though he be not far from every one of us: For in him we live, and move, and have our being; as certain also of your own poets have said, 'For we are also his offspring'. Forasmuch then as we are the offspring of God, we ought not to think that the Godhead is like unto gold, or silver, or stone, graven by art and man's device. And the times of this ignorance God winked at; but now commandeth all men every where to repent: Because he hath appointed a day, in the which he will judge the world in righteousness by that man whom he hath ordained; whereof he hath given assurance unto all men, in that he hath raised him from the dead.*
And when they heard of the resurrection of the dead, some mocked: and others said, we will hear thee again of this matter. So Paul departed from among them. Howbeit certain men clave unto him, and believed: among the which was Dionysius the Areopagite, and a woman named Damaris, and others with them" (Acts 17: 22-34).

Paul's first observation in Athens was the extreme devotion the people had to religious idols. They had erected statues to every conceivable god they could think of. However, in case they missed a god and so as not to offend that god, they erected an altar with the inscription: TO THE UNKNOWN GOD. This revealed their obvious ignorance.

The situation remains the same in this 21st century. Multitudes continue to worship in their shrines and at their altars without revelation, illumination, and inspiration. They could not be more sincere when they say, "I worship God in my own way." While we ascribe to every individual's right to worship, we must say, however, TRUE WORSHIP must be according to God's way, not man's way.

In describing the ignorance and folly of the pagan worshipers in his Roman letter, Paul said: *"who changed the truth of God into a lie, and worshiped and served the creature more than the Creator, who is blessed for ever. Amen."*

In his discussion about worship with the woman at the well in Samaria, Jesus told her about her ignorant worship: *"You worship you know not what"*(John 4: 22).

She was caught up in the debate about the <u>location of worship</u>, *"our fathers worshiped in this mountain, and ye say, that in Jerusalem is the place where men ought to worship"* (John 4: 20). How easy it is to become so engrossed in the PLACE of worship we miss the PERSON of worship.

Will Worship

A fourth type of unacceptable worship is WILL worship. In his letter to the Colossians Paul deals with the error and heresy of Gnosticism. He systematically sweeps away every false foundation men laid, warning the Colossian believers to *"beware lest any man spoil (or rob) you through philosophy, vain deceit, after the traditions of men, after the rudiments (or principles and ways) of the world, and not after Christ"* (Col. 2:8).

Will worship is any form of worship man chooses for himself apart from the true worship of God (Rom. 1:21-25). Some forms have a great show of refinement, humility, and asceticism, but they are powerless to deal with sin and the old man (v.23). They only feed self-righteousness and pride and do not change the heart. Paul refutes all this heresy by showing Christ's deity. The totality of God is embodied in Christ, he affirms (Col.1: 14-19). Paul clearly shows that our salvation is found only in Jesus Christ. Our salvation does not depend on our own discipline and rule keeping, but on the power of Christ death, resurrection, and the glorious grace of God alone!

Acceptable Worship

In His encounter and discussion with the woman at Jacob's well about the stirring issue of worship, Jesus said in response to her question about the place of worship, *"Ye worship ye know not what: we know what we worship: for salvation is of the Jews. But the hour cometh, and now is, when the true worshippers shall worship the Father in spirit and in truth: for the Father seeketh such to worship him.*
God is a Spirit: and they that worship him must worship him in spirit and in truth (John 4:22-24).

Here Jesus points out true worshippers and true worship. In verse 24, He said, *"God is a Spirit: and they that worship him must worship him in spirit and in truth."*

The focus of this woman's worship and those in her town for many years was Mount Gerizim (the Mount of Blessings). For the Jews, it was Mount Zion where their Temple was located. But the mountain never did anything to change this woman and meet her needs. Neither did the Temple in Mount Zion make any change in the multitudes that came to offer their annual sacrifices.

In this discussion with this woman, Jesus wanted her to see that it is NOT THE PLACE OF WORSHIP (the mountain or the temple) BUT THE PERSON! Only the Lord Jesus Christ could meet her needs, change her character, and satisfy her with living water. Today, many make a similar mistake in thinking that worship is identifying with a certain truth, a certain doctrine, with a certain place, a certain minister. Their whole identification with God is a location, by a street address, a building, or a preacher's name or church name or creed. And I can tell you, none of those things will ever change you! But change comes when we learn to worship God in spirit and in truth!

The Festival of Trumpets (Numbers 29: 1-6) and True Worship

God, in the Old Testament had given Israel three special holidays to observe. The Feast of Trumpets was one of these three great holidays celebrated in the seventh month (the Feast of tabernacles and Day of Atonement were the other two). These holidays provided a time to refresh the mind and body and to renew one's commitment to God. Here we see the importance of setting aside a time for both private and corporate worship.

In this Festival of the Trumpets there were four important principles demonstrated that can be used as guidelines for our corporate worship:

1. The people gathered together to celebrate and worship. There is something special about worshipping with other believers (see Acts 2:42-47; Hebrews 10: 19-25).

2. God ordered that no hard work be done during the special day. It takes time to worship, and setting aside a special day gives us the time to worship God as we should. It is the Lord's Day! "This honor has all His saints" (see Psalm 149).

3. The people gave God something of value by sacrificing one of their own animals as a burnt offering to him. True worship involves giving something of value to God to show our love and commitment to him.

What a joy to honor the Lord with our spiritual sacrifices---the sacrifice of ourselves (Rom. 12: 1-2); our praise (Hebrews 13: 15); and our possessions (Philippians 4:18).

4. Spending time away from the normal routine of life was symbolic of giving themselves to God and demonstrating their dedication. As we are careful to set aside a day or time of worship, we not only receive spiritual refreshing, but physical and emotional rest and renewal as well (see Matthew 11:28-30; Hebrews 4: 9, 10).

These were important principles to God's people then and the same principles should appear in our worship today.

True worship involves four important essentials:

1. True Worship Must Be Directed To God Alone!

The Lord God Jehovah of the Bible is a divine Person. He is not some nebulas, unknown, mute entity created by the hands and imaginations of men. All worship must be focused upon Him alone! Jesus makes this point abundantly clear when He rebuked Satan for tempting Him to fall down and worship him. *"Then saith Jesus unto him, Get thee hence, Satan: for it is written, Thou shalt worship the Lord thy God, and him only shalt thou serve"* (Matt. 4:10; Luke 4:8). (Referring to Deuteronomy 6:13; 10: 20, 21)

The Bible clearly teaches that God will not share His glory with any other. *"And God spake all these words, saying, I am the Lord thy God, which have brought thee out of the land of Egypt, out of the house of bondage. Thou shalt have no other gods before me"*(Exodus 20: 1-3). (See also Matt. 4:10, Rev. 19:10, 22:8, 9)

2. True Worship Must Be Directed To Christ Alone!

Jesus said, *"I am the way, the truth, and the life: no man cometh unto Father, but by me"* (John 14:6). Paul declares, *"For through him we both have access by one Spirit unto the Father"* (Eph. 2:18).

Worship that is not centered in and focused upon the Person and work of Christ is not acceptable worship.

3. *True Worship Must Be Generated By The Holy Spirit Alone!*

Jesus told the woman at Jacob's well, *"But the hour cometh, and now is, when the true worshipers shall worship the Father in spirit and in truth: for the Father seeketh such to worship him. God is a Spirit: and they that worship him must worship him in spirit and in truth"* (John 4: 23, 24).

Paul amplifies this in Philippians 3:3, *"For we are the circumcision, which worship God in spirit, and rejoice in Christ Jesus, and have no confidence in the flesh."*

To worship "in spirit" means with one's whole soul, mind, feelings, emotions, desires. There can be no half-hearted efforts in such worship. The worship manual of the Old Testament was the book of Psalms and the writer often said, *"I will praise the Lord with my whole heart, in the assembly of the upright, and in the congregation"* (Ps. 111:1. *"I will praise thee, O Lord, with my whole heart; I will shew forth all thy marvelous works"* (Ps. 9:1).

4. *True Worship Must Be Based On Truth Alone!*

"In spirit AND IN TRUTH", Jesus said. "In truth" means in harmony with full revealed and attested truth, not in fallacies, controversies, ceremonies, rituals and offerings.

In His high priestly prayer in John 17:17, Jesus said, *"Sanctify them through thy truth: THY WORD IS TRUTH."* He said in John 8:32, *"And ye shall know the truth, and the truth shall make you free."* (Emphasis mine)

If our worship is not ACCORDING TO TRUTH, it will be either vain, ignorant or will worship—all of which is unacceptable and rejected worship.

Characteristics of True Worship

The following points are taken from the editorial page of *The Herald,* written by the late Dr. Frank Bateman Stanger. 1

1.	Worship is *reverent*. "The Lord is in His holy temple: let all the earth keep silence before Him" (Hab. 2:20) "…Thy house…the place where thine honour dwelleth" (Ps. 26:8). "I saw the Lord sitting upon a throne….Above it stood the seraphim….And one cried unto another, and said, Holy, holy, holy, is the Lord of hosts…" (Isa. 6:1-3).

2.	Worship is *spiritual*. "…true worships shall worship the Father in spirit and in truth…God is a Spirit: and they that worship Him must worship Him in spirit and in truth" (Jn. 4:23, 24). "…My house shall be called the house of prayer…" (Mt. 21:13).

3.	Worship is *beautiful*. "…worship the Lord in he beauty of holiness" (1Chr. 16:29; Ps. 29:2; 96:9). "One thing have I desired of the Lord, that will I seek after; that I may dwell in the house of the Lord all the days of my life, to behold the beauty of the Lord, and to inquire in His temple" (Ps. 27: 4).

Beauty is unity. Beauty is harmony. Beauty is consonance with God's nature. Beauty is attraction.

4.	Worship is *joyful*. "Blessed are they that dwell in Thy house: they will be still praising Thee" (Ps.84:4). "And they worshiped Him, and returned to Jerusalem with great joy: and were continually in the temple, praising and blessing God" (Lk. 24:52, 53).

"And they continuing daily with one accord in the temple, and breaking bread from house to house, did eat their meat with gladness and singleness of heart, praising God…"(Acts 2:46, 47).

5.	Worship is *transforming*. It is spiritually transforming, first of all, because true worship is the occasion of the revelation of God's will. "…let us go up to the mountain of the Lord, to the house of the God of Jacob; and He will teach us His ways…" (Isa. 2:3; Mic. 4:2). "He went into the synagogue on the Sabbath day, and stood up to read…and when He had opened the book, He found the place where it was written...and He began to say...This day is this Scripture fulfilled in your ears" (Lk. 4:16, 17, 21).

Worship is also transforming because of the climate it provides for a person's affirmative response to the Divine will. "Then said I, woe is me! for I am undone: because I am a man of unclean lips...for mine eyes have seen the King, the Lord of hosts. Then...one of the seraphim...having a live coal in his hand...laid it upon my mouth and said...thine iniquity is taken away, and thy sin purged. Also, I heard the voice of the Lord, saying, Whom shall I send, and who will go for us? Then said I, Here am I; send me (Is. 6: 5-8).

Likewise, worship is a transforming experience because it leads to corporate decisions under the guidance of God's Spirit and to consequent strategic actions. "As they ministered to the Lord, and fasted, the Holy Spirit said, Separate me Barnabas and Saul for the work whereunto I have called them" (Acts 13: 2). "Then please it the apostles and elders, with the whole Church, to send chosen men of their own company to Antioch...and they wrote letters by them after this manner..."(Acts 15:22, 23). **1**

Seven Components of True Worship

I have been given the privilege to be in a traveling ministry for many years, both national and international, and thus have the opportunity to observe the styles of worship among many different peoples, cultures, denominations, churches, groups, and etc., etc.

I am convinced that scores of Christians live in ignorance about what is a true worship service and what worship should do in our lives. I don't profess to have all the answers, but I am confident if the following components are prevalent in the worship service, God will be glorified, the saints will be edified, and the world will be electrified by our witness to Christ.

1. Our worship must have *Glorification*. *"Offer unto God thanksgiving and pay thy vows unto the most High; And call upon me in the day of trouble: I will deliver thee, and thou shalt glorify me"* (Ps. 50:14, 15). *"What? Know ye not that your body is the temple of the Holy Ghost which is in you, which ye have of God, and ye are not your own? For ye are bought with a price: therefore glorify God in your body, and in your spirit, which are God's"* (1Cor. 6: 19, 20). *"If any man speak let him speak as*

the oracles of God; if any man minister, let him do it as of the ability which God giveth: that God in all things may be glorified through Jesus Christ, to whom be praise and dominion for ever and ever. Amen" (1Pet. 4:11).

2. Our worship must have *Manifestation*. *"I will not leave you comfortless: I will come to you....He that hath my commandments and keepeth them, he it is that loveth me: and he that loveth me shall be love of my Father, and I will love him, and will manifest myself to him"* (Jn. 14:18, 21). *"But the manifestation of the Spirit is given to every man to profit withal"* (1Cor. 12:7).

3. Our worship must have *Confrontation*. *"And when he is come, he will reprove (convict, convince) the world of sin, and of righteousness, and of judgment:"* (Jn. 16: 8) *"Jesus answered and said unto him, Verily, verily, I say unto thee, Except a man be born again, he cannot see the kingdom of God"* (Jn. 3:3).

4. Our worship must have *Edification*. *"But he that prophesieth speaketh unto men to edification, and exhortation, and comfort. He that speaketh in an unknown tongue edifieth himself; but he that prophesieth edifieth the church. I would that ye all spake with tongues, but rather that ye prophesied: for greater is he that prophesieth than he that speaketh with tongues, except he interpret, that the church may receive edifying." "How is it then, brethren? When ye come together, every one of you hath a psalm, hath a doctrine, hath a tongue, hath a revelation, hath an interpretation. Let all things be done unto edifying"* (1Cor. 14: 3-5, 26).

5. *Our worship must have Dedication. "I beseech you therefore brethren, by the mercies of God, that ye present your bodies a living sacrifice, holy, acceptable unto God, which is your reasonable service. And be not conformed to this world: but be ye transformed by the renewing of your mind,*
That ye may prove what is that good, and acceptable, and perfect will of God." (Rom. 12:1, 2) "Now concerning the collection for the saints, as I have given order to the churches of Galatia, even so do ye. Upon the first day of the week let every one of you lay by him in store, as God hath prospered him, that there be no gatherings when I come" (1Cor. 16:1, 2).

6. Our worship must have *Satisfaction*. *"As for me, I will behold thy face in righteousness: I shall be satisfied, when I awake, with thy likeness."(Ps.17:15) "Who satisfieth thy mouth with good things; so that thy youth is renewed like the eagle's"(Ps. 103:5). "For he satisfied the longing soul, and filleth the hungry soul*

with goodness." And Jesus said unto them, I am the bread of life: he that cometh to me shall never hunger; and he that believeth on me shall never thirst" (Jn. 6:35).

7. Our worship must have *Witnessing. "But ye shall receive power, after that the Holy Ghost is come upon you: and ye shall be witnesses unto me both in Jerusalem, and in all Judea, and in Samaria, and unto the uttermost part of the earth."(Acts 1:8) "....And at that time there was a great persecution against the church which was at Jerusalem; and they were scattered abroad throughout the regions of Judea and Samaria, except the apostles.....Therefore they that were scattered abroad went everywhere preaching the word." "Having therefore obtained help of God, I continue unto this day, witnessing both to small and great, saying none other things than those which the prophets and Moses did say should come: That Christ should suffer, and that he should be the first that should rise from the dead, and should show light unto the people, and to the Gentiles" (Acts 26:22, 23.)*

Cultivating a Proper Atmosphere for True Worship

➤ *By understanding that the worship service first and foremost is about glorifying God!*

The worship service is basically a spiritual experience. Therefore, it is imperative that a deep sense of reverence be witnessed throughout the worship service. This is accomplished when the worshipper brings with him to the service a sense of the personal reality of God and a keen desire to worship Him. *"Make a joyful noise unto the Lord, all ye lands. Serve the Lord with gladness: come before his presence with singing...Enter into his gates with thanksgiving, and into his courts with praise: be thankful unto him, and bless his name"* (Ps. 100:1, 4). *"I was glad when they said unto me, Let us go into the house of the Lord"* (Ps. 122:1). *"O come, let us sing unto the Lord: let us make a joyful noise to the rock of our salvation"* (Ps. 95:1).

➤ *By creating an attitude and atmosphere of reverence and worship through soft music, silence, and meditation in the sanctuary before the worship service begins.*

Confusion and distraction from worship abounds where the sanctuary is more like a "sports arena" rather than the house of worship prior to the service. You feel as though you are attending "an event" rather than a worship service. *"And Jesus went into the temple of God, and cast out all them that sold and bought in the temple, and overthrew the tables of the money changers, and the seats of them that sold doves, And said unto them, It is written, My house shall be called the house of prayer; but ye have made it a den of thieves"* (Mt. 21:12, 13).

➢ *By making proper preparations:* Such preparation must include quality time privately and corporately praying, planning, and preparing oneself spiritually, mentally, and physically for the worship service:

> - The Pastor(s) and his (their) preparation
> - The Worship Leaders (Choir Director's) preparation
> - The Choir or Worship Team's preparation
> - The soloist or those doing special music preparation
> - The congregation's preparation

➢ *By having a proper Call To Worship. It is advisable that the Pastor initiates the worship and then presents the worship team.* The call to worship brings the congregations attention to a focal point to worship together in harmony and unity.

➢ *True worship is a 'life-style', thus preparation is an ongoing process all week every week, not just something we do one or two hours on Sunday morning.*

➢ *By keeping all unnecessary chatter and "fellowship" for the fellowship hour either before or following the worship service.*

➢ *By "leading" the worship service—not driving, pushing, screaming at the people to participate.* Such practices that tend to want to "hype up" the people to participate only acerbates the situation and leaves the worshipper unfulfilled.

➢ *By understanding there is a difference between a "song" leader and a "worship" leader.* A true worship leader will not succumb to being some sort of cheerleader, but realizes the awesome responsibility of leading people into God's holy presence!

➢ *True worship is a united experience.* This requires a unity and beautiful harmony as each worshipper participates in every aspect of the service. When some stand, some sit, and others are doing other distracting things it shows the lack of discipline, devotion, direction and unity of heart and spirit. This can cause division and rebellion.

➢ *People should not be made to feel they have come to some sort of concert or performance by the choir or worship team, but have come to corporately worship the Lord.* Therefore, it is important to sing hymns and songs familiar to the congregation, so as to have their full participation. Choruses and songs that are written primarily for a soloist, duets, trios or quartets, should not be used for congregational singing.

➢ *A worship leader is to lead in worship not spend time talking and taking other liberties.*

➢ *The choir, worship team, musicians and others on the platform must realize they are part of the ENTIRE service.* It is inexcusable when they leave the platform to wander off into other rooms, go home, or whatever and not participate in the ministry of The Word and all other phases of the service.

➢ *It is important to have balance in the service.* Too much time can be given to singing and especially singing a line or two of a chorus repeatedly for an exorbitant period of time. There should be balance between standing and sitting. It is unfair to the elderly to expect them to stand for 45 to 50 minutes singing a chorus or two.

There should be balance between the contemporary and traditional styles of worship—a balance with the music, the selection of songs and hymns. **And let us not forget "spiritual songs"!** Paul gives instructions for worship songs in Ephesians Five—psalms for Scriptural singing, hymns with great messages, and spiritual songs. Please note it is spiritual songs, not spirited songs. Spiritual songs are sung by inspiration of the Holy Spirit. When we incorporate these three types of songs it brings balance, inspiration, and soul satisfaction to the worshipper.

➤ *By learning how to be sensitive to the Holy Spirit and flow "in the Spirit" as He wishes to manifest Himself.* Many times the Holy Spirit would speak to the congregation but our haste to move "in the flesh" quenches Him, and we miss the glorious blessing of His manifestation.

Oh how important to learn the moods of the Holy Spirit and how to flow with Him! *"How is it then, brethren? When ye come together, every one of you hath a psalm, hath a doctrine, hath a tongue, hath a revelation, hath an interpretation. Let all things be done unto edifying" (1Cor. 14:26). "But the manifestation of the Spirit is given to every man to profit withal" (1Cor. 12:7).*

The use of these principles will produce an atmosphere of worship that will be pleasing to God and satisfying and fulfilling to the worshiper.

> "O worship the King, all glorious above, O gratefully sing His Power and His love; Our Shield and Defender, the Ancient of Days, Pavilioned in splendor, and girded with praise."
>
> Frail children of dust, and feeble as frail, In Thee do we trust, nor Find Thee to fail; Thy mercies how tender, how firm to the end, Our Maker, Defender, Redeemer, and Friend." 2

Chapter Eleven

The Reality of Praise

"Praise is awaiting You, O God, in Zion."
--Ps. 65:1

One has said, "God is pleased with our praise and pained with the lack of it." The book of Psalms is a golden handbook on the subject of praise. In the 65th Psalm we see a prayer without a petition. It is full of praise and gratitude but no requests.

The story is told of an Army Chaplain who was called to see a dying Christian soldier. The Chaplain asked the young man if there was any message he wished conveyed to his loved ones. After receiving these, he was asked to pray. The Chaplain then asked if there were any special requests that he should make in his prayer. The dying man replied: "Chaplain, thank God for a praying mother, thank Him that He has saved me, thank Him for His promises and thank Him that He gave me dying grace at this moment." So the Chaplain knelt and prayed with never a request to offer, only thanks to God for His mercy and grace. Do we not oftentimes fail to praise Him as we should and is God not pained by the lack of it?

There is another story of two Angels sent out from heaven, each with a basket to bring back the prayers and praises of those on earth. The Angel of praise started with a large basket, while the collector of petitions had only a small one. But when they returned, the petitions overflowed the basket and filled a sack besides, while the Angel of praise only had three in his large basked. Too often this is true of us as we are always ready to pray for things we want, but having received them, we forget to thank and praise the Giver. Truly, it is fitting to praise you, Oh God!

Worship in the Old Testament was never complete without a sacrifice. There were various sacrifices for different needs depending upon the time of the year and the event being observed. Although the Old Testament sacrifices were fulfilled in Christ at Calvary, still, however in the New Testament there are three basic sacrifices Christians are to observe. In 1Peter 2:5, the apostle declares *"you also, as living stones, are being built up a spiritual house, a holy priesthood, to offer up* **spiritual sacrifices** *acceptable to God through Jesus Christ."* All New Testament Christians are priests building a spiritual house by making proper spiritual sacrifices. (Emphasis mine)

THE SACARIFICE OF THE PERSON

The first spiritual sacrifice for the New Testament believer is the sacrifice of his total person. As the great Scottish missionary John R. Mott frequently said: "Jesus must be Lord OF ALL or He will not be Lord AT ALL". Paul is emphatic about this in Romans 12:1: *"I beseech you therefore brethren, by the mercies of God,* **that you present your bodies a living sacrifice**, *holy, acceptable to God, which is your reasonable service."* Scripture is very clear that God will be pleased with nothing less than the absolute total surrender of our whole person---spirit, soul, and body to Him! We read in First Thessalonians 5:2: *"Now may the God of peace Himself sanctify (set you apart) you completely; and may your whole spirit, soul, and body be preserved blameless at the coming of our Lord Jesus Christ."* (Emphasis mine)

When a certain lawyer representing the Pharisees tested Jesus with his inquiry: "What is the greatest commandment in the law?" Jesus said to him, *"You shall love the Lord your God with all your heart, with all your soul, and with all your mind. This is the first and great commandment"* (Matt. 22:34-38). This is the spiritual sacrifice with which God is well pleased, our total being.

THE SACRIFICE OF THE PURSE

The second New Testament spiritual sacrifice for the believer is the sacrifice of our possessions. We read in Philippians 4:18, *"Indeed I have all and abound. I am full, having received from Epaphroditus* **the things which were sent from you, a sweet smelling aroma, an acceptable sacrifice,** *well pleasing to God."* *(Emphasis mine)*

The context of this passage of Scripture is quite explicit that Paul is speaking about a financial offering. He states in verses 15 and 16, *"Now you Philippians know also that in the beginning of the gospel, when I departed from Macedonia, no church shared with me concerning giving and receiving but you only. For even in Thessalonica you sent aid once and again for my necessities."*

The offering of "first-fruits" spoken of in the Old Testament as "the tithe" and expounded by Paul in the Corinthian Letter as "the grace of giving" is the believer's acknowledgement of the sovereign ownership of God, and thus a spiritual sacrifice.

THE SACRIFICE OF PRAISE

"By him therefore let us offer the sacrifice of praise to God continually, that is, the fruit of our lips, giving thanks to his name" (Hebrews 13:15).

God desires to have a people who will not only pray but also praise Him. We were created for this. Man's primary and supreme   purpose for existence is to glorify God!   Offering praise, the fruit of our lips to the Father is one of the many ways we glorify Him. *"I will offer to You the sacrifice of thanksgiving, And will call upon the name of the Lord,"* is the heartbeat of the Psalmist (Ps.116: 17). Notice he said, "I will" offer praise. We must "will" to do it regardless of our circumstances or feelings! In Psalm 119:108 the Psalmist makes this quite clear: *"Accept, I pray, the freewill offerings of my mouth, O Lord."* In Psalm 34:1, David strongly affirms his determination to praise the Lord: *"I WILL bless the Lord at all times: His praise shall continually be in my mouth."*

The Bible is full of stories of victorious men because they were faithful to praise the Lord. Once such story is recorded in 2Chronicles 20:15 when Jeshohaphat was King over Judah. When the mighty armies of the Moabites, the Ammonites, and the inhabitants of Mount Seir came against Jehoshaphat and the kingdom of Judah, God said: *"Be not afraid nor dismayed by reason of this great multitude; for the battle is not yours but God's"* (2Chronicles 20:15). *"And Jehoshaphat bowed his head with his face to the ground and all Judah and the inhabitants of Jerusalem bowed before the Lord, worshiping the Lord. Then the Levites of the children of the Kohathites and of the children of the Korahites stood up to praise the Lord God of Israel with voices loud and high"* (vv.18-19). Think of it, without raising the arm of resistance, Jehoshaphat prayed, sought God's help, and lifted up the voice of praise in advance for the victory, and victory was certainly theirs. And that is what God is commanding each of us in a personal way, as we face our "enemy"---to "fear not", to "stand still", to "praise the Lord" to "see the salvation of the Lord", for the battle is not ours, but God's!

The power of praise brought down the walls of Jericho when Joshua and his army marched around the city seven times on the seventh day and shouted praise to God (Joshua 6). Paul and Silas were delivered from prison and won the jailer and his family to Christ because at the midnight hour (the darkest hour of the night) they sang songs and offered praise to God (Acts 16). It is interesting to me that in this terrible dilemma Paul and Silas didn't react to this cruel treatment with resentment nor resignation, but with REJOICING! They knew the power of praise!

We often hear the familiar statement, "Prayer Changes Things." I am convinced that prayer is vitally necessary, but I have also learned it's the continual praise we offer before and after prayer that brings the victory! PRAISE CHANGES THNGS! When it seems like you are not contacting God in prayer, try praising Him and He will flood your soul with His divine and delightsome presence because He promised to live in or take up habitation in our praises (Psalm 22:3).

Perhaps you do not like the noise that praise brings, or you feel it unnecessary and seemingly very foolish. I would ask-- do you feel the same way at ball games? David, King of Israel certainly did not allow such thinking to hinder him as he exhorted his people in Psalm 98:4, *"Make a joyful noise unto the LORD, all the earth: make a loud noise, and rejoice, and sing praise."* In fact, we are commanded to praise the Lord, *"Let everything that has breath praise the LORD. Praise the LORD"* (Psalm 150:6)!

I often ask, "Are you breathing?" If it looks foolish to raise your hands, and lift your voice in praise, just remember, *"God has chosen the foolish things of the world to put to shame the wise, and God has chosen the weak things of the world to put to shame the things which are mighty"* (1Corinthians 1:27). When it seems uncomfortable or you just don't feel like praising the Lord, then remember Paul's stirring words of admonition: *"Let us offer the sacrifice of praise to God"* (Hebrews 13:15).

One of the reasons so many do not receive from God is because they have not learned the secret of giving praise to God. True thanksgiving and praise is the indication of faith, and faith is the muscle that moves the hand of God. Have you ever noticed that when someone promises you a gift, or a dinner, a job or increase in salary, you immediately say, "Thank you!" though you have not yet received anything except a promise. Do we trust men more than we trust God and His promises?

We all want to be overcoming Christians! However, being overcoming Christians requires more than praying, we must also be praising Christians. The poise of praise is the pathway to victory. The apostle Paul shares this secret after having been surrounded by many negative circumstances: adversities of enemies, hunger, nakedness, storms, jails, beatings, stoning and in the face of execution, he cried out: *"Thanks be to God who gives us the victory through our Lord Jesus Christ"* (1Corinthians 15:57).

In all actuality, praise is more powerful than prayer. Praise without prayer might be presumption. But prayer without praise is unbelief. Praise anticipates the victory. Praise acknowledges that the answer is on its way. Praise testifies that God is more powerful than the devil or any situation the devil can bring upon us. Praise witnesses to the goodness and might and mercy and wisdom of God.

Praise is the "hymn of committal." Praise proclaims that the burden is no longer on our shoulders, but on the Lord. Praise testifies that no matter what the outcome we will be "glad and rejoice." Praise shouts, "My worries are over, my struggling is ended. God has taken over.   The battle is now His concern, not mine. I am free to stand still, to cease to fight, to see the salvation of the Lord!"

Praise is the power that puts you over and not under. Praise confesses, *"I have been crucified with Christ; it is no longer I who live but Christ lives in me; and the life which I now live in the flesh I live by faith in the Son of God, who loved me and gave Himself for me"* (Galatians 2:20).

Praise shouts, *"You are of God, little children, and have overcome them, because He who is in you is greater than he who is in the world"* (1John 4:4). Prayer frightens the devil, but praise puts him to rout. Prayer makes the devil tremble, but praise causes him to flee. Prayer begs God, but praise thanks Him in advance. Before Jesus commanded Lazarus to come forth from the grave, He said, *"Father, I thank You that You have heard Me"* (John 11:41).

Prayer brings our petitions to God, but praise takes home the answer. Prayer changes things, but praise shouts down the walls so we can take the city (Joshua 6:20). Yes, dear friend, pray much, pray without ceasing, but don't fail to keep your mouth continually filled with His praises, because praise is always proper spiritual etiquette (Psalm 33:1).

The Bible furnishes volumes of material about praise. It is not my intent to be exhaustive on this subject in the chapter, but rather to point out its reality. The following outline is shared to give the reader a grasp of the broad scope and reality of praise with the prayer that you will give some serious time and thought about the reality of praise.

A. WHY SHOULD WE OFFER PRAISE?

1. Because God's Word exhorts to offer praise (Ps. 147:1).

"Praise ye the LORD: for it is good to sing praises unto our God; for it is pleasant; and praise is comely" (Ps. 147:1).

"Make a joyful shout to God, all the earth! Sing out the honor of His name; Make His praise glorious (Ps 66:1-2).

"Oh come, let us sing to the LORD! Let us shout joyfully to the Rock of our salvation" (Ps 95:1).

"Oh, sing to the LORD a new song! Sing to the LORD, all the earth. Sing to the LORD, bless His name; proclaim the good news of His salvation from day to day. Declare His glory among the nations, His wonders among all peoples" (Ps.96:1-3).

Please see: Ps. 33:1; 34:3; 92:1,2; 98:1; 100:1,2; 105:1; 106:1; 107:1; 111:1; 112:1; 113:1; 118:1; 134:1,2; 135:1,2,3; 136:1,2,2,3,; 146:1; 147:1; 148:1; 149:1; 150:1: Rom. 15:11; Eph. 1:6,12,14; Phil. 1:11; Heb.2:12; 13:15; Rev. 19:5.

2. Because praise gives exaltation and glory to God (Ps. 50:23).

"Whoever offers praise glorifies Me; And to him who orders his conduct aright I will show the salvation of God."

3. Because we receive strength through praise (Ps. 84:4-5).

"Blessed are those who dwell in Your house; They will still be praising You. Selah

Blessed is the man whose strength is in You, Whose heart is set on pilgrimage."

4. Because the power of praise brings purity into our lives (Ps.27:21).

   "As the fining pot for silver, and the furnace for gold; so is a man to his praise."

   "But who may abide the day of his coming? and who shall stand when he appeareth? For he is like a refiner's fire, and like fullers' soap:

   And he shall sit as a refiner and purifier of silver: and he shall purify the sons of Levi, and purge them as gold and silver, that they may offer unto the LORD an offering in righteousness (Malachi 3:2-3).

5. Because praise is good for our mental, emotional and spiritual health (Ps. 92:1).

   "It is a good thing to give thanks unto the LORD, and to sing praises unto thy name, O most High:"

   Praise brings joy and the joy of the Lord is our strength (Nehemiah 8:10).

   "Why art thou cast down, O my soul? And why art thou disquieted within me? Hope thou in God: for I shall yet praise him, for the help of his countenance." Then verse 11, "for I shall yet praise him, who is the health of my countenance, and my God" (Ps. 42: 5, 11; 43:5).

   Not only do I praise Him for the 'help' of HIS countenance" (v.5) but in so doing He becomes the "Health of MY countenance." (v. 11).

6. Because praise is "comely" or proper behavior for the believer (Ps. 33:1).

   "Rejoice in the LORD, O ye righteous: for praise is comely for the upright."

7. Because God declares He will dwell or live in the praises of His people (Ps. 22:3).

   "But thou art holy, O thou that inhabitest the praises of Israel"

   The word "inhabit" means to "tent", to "tabernacle," to "dwell" or "take up residence." See Eph. 3:17 and Col. 3:16.

8. Because praise keeps our perspective and vision in balance. Hebrews 12: 2, *"Looking unto Jesus the author and finisher of our faith;"*

   We are *to "enter into his gates with thanksgiving and into his courts with praise"* (Psalm 100:4). Thus, praise brings us into His presence and forces us to behold His face. As we gaze upon Jesus we then see the whole picture of our purpose in proper perspective.

9. Because praise ministers to God (Ps. 149:3-4).

   "Let them praise his name in the dance: let them sing praises unto him with the timbrel and harp. For the LORD taketh pleasure in his people:"

   See Acts 13:2

10. Because praise is a mighty weapon in our defense against the enemy (Ps. 149: 6-9).

11. Because praise can change your surrounding environment (Acts 16: 25-40).

12. Because praise is the language of heaven (Rev. 7:9-12; 11:16-18; 15:1-4; 16: 4-6; 19: 1-7).

    "Thy will be done, as in heaven, so in earth."

B. WHEN SHOULD WE PRAISE THE LORD?

1. We should offer praise continually (Heb. 13:15; Ps. 34:1; 35:27; 70:4; 71:6; Luke 24:53).

2. We should offer praise at night (Ps. 134:1-3).

3. We should offer praise during the day (Ps. 119:164).

4. We should offer praise daily (Ps. 72; 15; Acts 2: 46-47).

C. WHERE SHOULD WE OFFER PRAISE?

1. We should offer praise in our homes (Ps. 149:5).

2. We should offer praise in the congregation (Ps. 22:22; 35:18; 149:1; Acts 2: 46-47).

3. We should offer praise in all the lands (Ps. 100: 1).

4. We should offer praise in the harvest fields (Ps. 108: 3).

5. We should offer praise before unbelievers (Ps. 40: 3, Acts. 16: 25-40).

6. We should offer praise in God's holy mountain, Mount Zion, Jerusalem (Ps. 99:9; 147:12).

7. We will offer praise in heaven (Rev. 7: 9-12). **1**

D. HOW SHOULD WE OFFER PRAISE?

1. We should offer praise verbally with our mouths (Ps.8: 2; Matt. 21:16; Ps. 40:3; 51:15; 71: 8; 71:15).

2. We should offer praise that can be heard. (Ps. 66:8; 98:4).

3. We should offer praise with shouting (Ps. 47:1; 35:27; 132:9)

4. We should offer praise through singing (Ps. 47:6; 100:2; 126:2; Isaiah 51:11; 1Cor. 14:15; Eph. 5:19; Col. 3:16).

5. We should offer praise through thanksgiving (Ps 69:30; 1Cor. 14: 16,17)

6. We should offer praise with a joyful noise (Ps. 66:1, 2; 95:1), because "Thou wilt show me the path of life: in thy presence is fullness of joy; at thy right hand there are pleasures forevermore" (Ps. 16:11).

7. We should offer praise with a strong cry (Isaiah 12:6).

8. We should offer praise through laughter (Ps. 126:1, 2, 3).

9. We should offer praise through speaking with other tongues (Acts 2: 11; 10: 46).

Please note all the previous ways have to do with our mouths. Oh let us magnify the LORD with our mouths.

10. We should offer praise by lifting up our hands (Ps. 28: 2; 63: 4; 134:2; Nehemiah 8: 6; 1Tim. 2:8; Heb. 12:12).

11. We should offer praise by clapping our hands (Ps. 47:1).

12. We should offer praise by kneeling before Him (Ps. 95: 6; See Eph. 3:14; Phil. 2:10).

13. We should offer praise by falling prostrate before Him (Nehemiah 8:6).

14. We should offer praise with musical instruments (Ps. 150).

15. We should offer praise to God with the dance (Ps. 150: 4). **2**

E. HINDERANCES TO PRAISE

1.   Satan is your number one hindrance and obstacle to praise (John 10:10; 1Thess. 2: 18).
       But Satan is defeated!   (Luke 9:1; Mark 16:17; Rom. 16:20; Heb 2:14)

2.   Sin will hinder your praise (Isaiah 59:2; 1John 1: 6-10).

3.   Guilt will hinder your praise. (John 8:11; Rom. 8:1; Eph. 4:22-32).

4.   Pride will hinder your praise. (Proverbs 13: 10; 1Tim. 3:6; 1John 2:16).

5.   Fear will hinder your praise (Job 4:14; 1:9; Proverbs 29:25; 1John 4:18. But note 2Tim. 1:7).

6.   Circumstances will hinder your praise (Isaiah 61:3)

7.   A wrong concept and picture of God will hinder your praise (Luke 11:13).

No one becomes a dynamic athlete without first beginning and continuing a systematic program of exercise and appropriate work-outs. Likewise, the believer must begin with a determined act of his will to offer praise to God. You must discipline yourself into the "poise of praise" continually if you are to ever see the glorious fruit of praise become a reality.

Along with your time of prayer, set ample time to offer praise to God. Then cultivate keeping praise on you mind and lips as much as possible during each day. Look around you, there are so many reminders of God for which we can give Him praise.

We are creatures of habits and as you continue to speak praise (both verbally and non-verbally) you will consciously and unconsciously develop a "holy habit," the habit of praise!

It is a journey you will never regret!

Chapter Twelve

The Reality of Spiritual Warfare

"For we wrestle not against flesh and blood, but against principalities, against powers, against the rulers of the darkness of this world, against spiritual wickedness in high places" - (Eph. 6: 14)

The prophet Hosea states very clearly *"My people are destroyed for lack of knowledge"* (Hosea 4:6). There is most probably no area where God's people are more lacking in Biblical understanding than Spiritual Warfare! Unfortunately, most Christians give very little consideration to Satan and don't believe in demons and demonic activity. Satan, the number One enemy of God and His children, could not be more pleased than when we deny his existence or ignore his operations.

We need an awakening to Satan and his devils, because he IS VERY REAL! He is as real as God the Father, the Son, the Holy Spirit and Angels! In his book, *Dealing With the Devil,* C.S. Lovett raises a very provocative and plausible question, "Why put on the whole armor of God (Eph. 6:11) if there is no enemy?" [1]

It would not be possible, nor is it the author's purpose, to share all the Bible has to say about this subject in this lesson. My intent, however, is to awaken as many as possible to the reality of spiritual warfare. We must understand if we are going to serve and please God, we are in a battle! Spiritual warfare is real, and we must know how to engage the enemy and "fight this fight of faith."

If we are going to be victorious, overcoming Christians, we must know how to engage this arch enemy of God and man with a strategy of victorious warfare. Notice the strategy.

UNMAKSING THE ENEMY

Unseen does not mean unreal. The whole range of the "spirit-world" is as real, if not more so, as the physical world we see with natural sight. One of the most important lessons you can ever learn is that Satan is not an abstract influence, disease germ, evil principle or idea, he is a real person.

The Devil or Satan is an evil personality, head of the kingdom of darkness and evil spirits. Jesus rebuked the Pharisees, *"Ye are of your father the devil, and the lusts of your father ye will do. He was a murderer from the beginning, and abode not in the truth, because there is no truth in him. When he speaketh a lie, he speaketh of his own: for he is a liar, and the father of it"* (John 8:44). Matthew reports, *"He (Jesus) said unto them, an enemy hath done this." "The enemy that sowed them is the devil..."* (Matt. 13: 28, 39). Peter exhorts us, *"Be sober, be vigilant, because your adversary the devil, as a roaring lion, walketh about, seeking whom he may devour"* (1Peter 5:8).

W.E. Vine, in his *Expository of New Testament Words*, states concerning the personality of the Devil, "Satan is not simply the personification of evil influences in the heart, for he tempted Christ, in whose heart no evil thought could ever have arisen (John 14:30; II Cor. 5: 21; Heb 4: 15); moreover, his personality is asserted in both the O.T. and the N.T., and especially in the latter, whereas if the O.T. language was intended to be figurative, the N.T. would have made this evident." **2** H. Orton Wiley states, "The origin of evil must be traced ultimately to personality." **3**

The Scriptures gives us many warning about this personality of evil. Paul warns and instructs us to *"Put on the whole armor of God, that ye maybe able to stand against the wiles of the devil"* (Eph. 6:11). In his Corinthian letter he says, *"For such are false apostles, deceitful workers, transforming (i.e., 'fashioning') themselves into the apostles of Christ. And no marvel; for Satan himself is transformed ('fashioneth himself') into an angel of light. Therefore it is no great thing if his ministers also be transformed ('fashioned themselves') as ministers of righteousness; whose end shall be according to their works"* (2 Cor. 11: 13-15). Simon Peter had a perfect insight into the reality of Satan and admonishes us, *"Be sober, be vigilant; because your adversary the devil, as a roaring lion, walketh about, seeking whom he may devour"* (1 Peter 5:8). Again Paul says, *"Lest Satan should get an advantage of us: for we are no ignorant of his devices"* (2Cor. 2: 11).

There are three main descriptions or names of this evil personality in Scripture:

---

a. "Satan" – used in the O.T. and N.T. a total of 55 times;
b. "Devil" and "Devils" –used a total of 111 times and,
c. "Serpent" –used 5 times in the O.T. and 5 times in the N.T., a total of 10 times.

Other names given him are: Accuser (Rev. 12:10); Adversary (1 Pet. 5: 8, 9); Angel of Bottomless Pit (Rev. 9:11); Beast (Rev. 19:19); Beelzebub (Matt. 10: 25; 12: 24); Deceiver (Rev. 12:9); Devourer (1Pet. 5:8); Dragon (Rev. 12:7); Evil One (1John 2:14); The Enemy (Matt. 13:39) God of this world (2Cor. 4:4); Liar and Murderer (John 8:44); Prince of this world (John 12:31); Prince of the power of the air (Eph. 2:2); Tempter (1Thess. 3:5); Wicked One (Matt. 13:19, 38);That Wicked One (1John 5:18).

Satan is not Omnipotent (all powerful), but he is a powerful enemy. He is not Omniscient (all knowing), but he is crafty. He is not Omnipresent (everywhere at once), but he is busy. When he was cast out of heaven, (Luke 10:18) one-third of the Angels fell with him. There are those that are bound (Rev. 9:11, 14; 11:7; 17; 8; 2Pet. 2: 4; Jude 6-7), and those that are still loose with Satan and will be cast down in the future tribulation (Rev. 12:7-12; Eph. 6: 10-17). These angels are subject to Christ (1Pet.3:22); evil (Ps. 78: 49); organized into principalities and powers (Eph. 1: 21; 3:10; 6:10-17; Col. 3:10; Rev. 12: 7-12), and Hell is prepared for them (2Pet. 2:4).

In addition, there is a vast host of demons or demonic spirits. "These are disembodied spirits and do not seem to be able to operate in the natural except through possession of man and beasts who have bodies for them to operate through. They can teach (1Tim 4:1); steal (Matt. 13:19; Luke 8:12); fight (Eph 6:10-18); get mad(Matt.8: 28; Rev.12:12); tell fortunes (Lev.20:27; Acts 16:16) be friendly (called *familiar spirits* sixteen times (Lev.20:6, 27); can go out and come back into men as they will, unless cast out and rejected (Matt.12: 43-45); travel (1Kings 22:21-24); speak (Mark 1:34; 5:12; Acts 8:7); imitate departed dead (2Sam. 28: 3-9;1Chron.10: 13; Isa. 8:19; Deut.18:11).

"They are able to cause dumbness and deafness (Matt.9:32, 33; Mark 9:25); blindness (Matt. 12:22); grievous vexation (Matt.15:22) lunacy and mania (Matt 4: 23-24; 17: 14-21; Mark 5: 1-18); uncleanness (called *unclean spirits*) twenty-one times,(Luke

---

4:36); supernatural strength (Mark 5: 1-18); suicide (Matt 17: 15; John 10:10) fits (Mark 9:20); lusts (John 8:44; Eph. 2: 1-3; 1John 2: 15-17); counterfeit worship (Lev. 17:7; 32: 17; 2Chron. 11:15; Ps.106: 37; 1Cor. 10:30; Rev. 9: 20); error (1John 4:1-6; 1Tim. 4:1); sickness and diseases (Matt. 4:23-24; Acts 10: 38); torments (Matt. 4: 23-24; 15:22); deceptions (1Tim. 4:1-2; 1John 4: 1-6); lying (1Kings 22: 21-24) enchantments and witchcraft (2Chron. 33:6); heresies (1Tim. 4:1); false doctrines (1Tim.4:1); wickedness (Luke 11:26); fear (2Tim.1:7);worldliness (1John 2:15-17; 1Cor. 2:12); bondage (Rom. 8:15); discord (Matt. 13: 39; 1Kings 22:21-24); violence (Matt. 17:15); betrayals (John 13:2; 1Kings 22:22-23);oppression (Acts 10: 38); sin (John 8:44); persecution (Rev. 2:10; 1Pet. 5:8); jealousy (1Sam. 16:14; 18:8-8-10); false prophecy (1Sam. 18:8-10; 1Kings 22: 21-24) and cause every evil they possibly can to come to man and God." **4**

UNMASKING THE"WILES"AND METHODS OF THE ENEMY

Ephesians 6:11".....the wiles of the devil." 2Cor.2:11 "....his devices."

We dare not be ignorant concerning the many methods of operation Satan and demons will use against us in this spiritual warfare. Since he cannot attack God directly, his strategy is to attack God's master-creation, MAN.

The following are some of the methods Satan uses in this warfare: lying (John 8:44; 2Cor. 11:3); tempting (Matt. 4:1); robbing (Matt. 13:19); harassing (2Cor. 12:7; Job 1 and 2); hindering (Zech. 3:1; 1Thess. 2:18; Eph. 6:12); sifting (Luke 22:31); imitating (2Cor. 11:14, 15; Matt. 13:25); accusing (Rev. 12: 9, 10); smiting with disease (Luke 13: 16; 1Cor. 5: 5); possessing (John 13: 27); and killing and devouring (John 8: 44; 10:10; 1Pet. 5: 8).

The devil's cleverest "wile" (i.e., trickery or deception) is to convince men that he does not exist. He is a master at deception and counterfeiting! In the 'last days' Jesus said deception would be one of his greatest weapons of destruction. See Matt. 24 where Jesus warns us about the danger of deception four times.

Every believer must understand he is in a battle against principalities, powers, against spiritual hosts in heavenly places. Paul describes it in Eph. 6:12 *"For we are not wrestling with flesh and blood (contending only with physical opponents), but against the despotism, against the powers, against (the master spirits who are) the world rulers of this present darkness, against the spirit forces of wickedness in the heavenly (supernatural) sphere."*(Amplified)   Please note: this magnifies the importance of prayer, privately and corporately. We read in 2Cor. 10: 4, 5 *"For the weapons of our warfare are not carnal ('of the flesh'), but are mighty through God to the pulling down of strongholds; casting down imaginations, and every high thing that exalteth itself against the knowledge of God, and bringing into captivity every thought to the obedience of Christ."*

Thank God all who so desire can be delivered from Satan's clutches and power. This is the powerful promise of Acts 26:18, *"To open their eyes, and to turn them from darkness to light, and from the power of Satan unto God, that they may receive forgiveness of sins, and inheritance among them which are sanctified by faith that is in me."* Furthermore Paul declares, *"Who hath delivered us from the power of darkness, and hath translated us into the kingdom of his dear Son"* Col. 1:13).

ENGAGING THE ENEMY BY UNDERSTANDING HIS TRICKS, WILES AND DEVICES

There are five critical areas in which Satan does his diabolical work of deception and destruction that must be understood if we are to be victorious over him:

1. **DIVERSON**—2Cor. 4:4 *"In whom the god of this world hath blinded the minds of them which believe not, lest the light of the glorious gospel of Christ, who is the image of God, should shine unto them."* It is the devil's business to blind men to the things of God by focusing their attention on other things, such as:

    a. Possession. Luke 12:15, *21 "And he said unto them, take heed, and beware of covetousness: for a man's life consisteth not in the abundance of the things which he possesseth...So is he that layeth up treasure for himself, and is not rich toward God."* 2Tim. 6:10 *"For the love of money is the root of all evil: which while some coveted after, they have erred from the faith, and pierced themselves through with many sorrows."*

b. <u>Pleasure.</u> 2Timothy 3: 4, 5 *"Traitors, heady, high-minded, lover of pleasures more than lovers of God; having a form of godliness, but denying the power thereof: from such turn away"* Such are the signs of the last of the "last days." Luke 8:14 *"....and the pleasures of this life...."*

c. <u>Position.</u> Matt. 20: 21 *"And he said unto her, What wilt thou? She saith unto him, Grant that these my two sons may sit, the one on they right hand, and the other on the left, in they kingdom."* Mark 9: 34 *"But they held their peace: for b y the way they had disputed among themselves who should be the greatest."*

d. <u>Performance.</u> Luke 10:*17 "And the seventy returned again with joy, saying, Lord, even the devils are subject unto us through thy name."*

e. <u>Popularity.</u> John 12: 43 *"For they loved the praise of men more than the praise of God."* Proverbs 29: 25 *"The fear of man bringeth a snare...."*

2. **DELUSION**—2Cor. 4:4 *"In whom the god of this world hath blinded the minds...."* Delusion is a misleading of the mind; false belief; a fixed misconception.

a. The unconverted
(1) Rely on their own righteousness—"I'm as good as your church members." Or "I'm as good as anyone in your church." But Matt. 5:20 records Jesus, *"For I say unto you, that except your righteousness shall exceed the righteousness of the scribes and Pharisees, ye shall in no case enter into the kingdom of heaven."*
(2) Some of them say, "I am all right." But Proverbs 14: 12 and 16: 25 declares, *"There is a way which seemeth right unto a man, but the end thereof are the ways of death."*
(3) Or, they say, "I do good works." But Ephesians 2: 8, 9 is very clear, *"For by grace are ye saved through faith; and that not of yourselves: it is the gift of God: Not of works, lest any man should boast."*

b. The religious "professor"
(1) Rely on the church membership. But: Jesus said, "I am the way…" (John 14:6)
(2) Rely on baptism. But: Gal. 6:15 *"For in Christ Jesus neither circumcision availeth anything, nor uncircumcision, but a new creature."*

(3) Rely on good works. But: Titus 3: 5 *"Not by works of righteousness which we have done, but according to his mercy he saved us, by washing of regeneration, and renewing of the Holy Ghost."* Romans 3: 20 *"Therefore by the deeds of the law there shall no flesh be justified in his sight: for by the law is the knowledge of sin."* Gal. 2:16 *"Knowing that a man is not justified by the works of the law, but by the faith of Jesus Christ, even we have believed in Jesus Christ, that we might be justified by the faith of Christ, and not by works of the law: for by the works of the law shall no flesh be justified."*

General William Booth of the Salvation Army feared the day would come when men would "have Christianity without Christ, religion without the new birth, and profession without possession." In other words he feared men would take church membership for conversion, baptism for regeneration, and mere appearance for reality.

c. The Believer
   (1) Over-emphasize feelings. But: Rom. 1:17 *"....The just shall live by faith."* See (Gal. 3:11; Heb. 10: 38). See the account of Philip meeting the eunuch from Ethiopia on the road toward Gaza in Acts 8: 26-39. Notice verse *35 "...preached unto him Jesus"* (FACT). Verse 37 *"...I believe"* (FAITH) .Verse 39 *"...he went on his way rejoicing"* (FEELING).
   (2) Over-emphasize non-essentials. This is the essence of Phariseeism. If Jesus came back to look for the Pharisees, where would he be most apt to look today?
   (3) To do the right thing in the wrong way—in an ugly spirit. We can be right in principle, but wrong in spirit. Which is worse—to be wrong in principle? Or wrong in spirit?

d. The Sects or Cults
   (1) Jehovah Witnesses
   (2) Christian Science
   (3) Unity and New Thought
   (4) New Age
   (5) Mormonism
   (6) Etc. It is feared that these, and others who distort God's Word, wrest the Scriptures "unto their own destruction." See 2 Peter 3:16

Note: (Two excellent books that go into detail concerning the cults is *The Kingdom of Cults,* by Dr. Walter Martin and *Encyclopedia of Cults and New Religion,* by John Ankerberg and John Weldon).

3. **DIVISION**—1Cor. 1: 10 *"....that there be no divisions among you..."* 1Cor 3:3 *"For ye are yet carnal: for whereas there is among you envying ('jealousy'), and strife, and divisions, are ye not carnal, and walk as ('after the manner of') men?'* 1Cor. 11:18 *"....I hear that there are divisions among you."* Rom. 16: 17 *"Now I beseech you, brethren, mark them which cause divisions and offences..."* Acts 20: 30 *"Also of your own selves shall men arise, speaking perverse things, to draw away disciples after them."*
   a. One of Satan's most effective weapons is the "wedge" and he is sufficiently skilled in its use to know that it is most effectively driven by using the small, thin edge to make entrance.
   b. The devastating work of Satan creating scandals, strife and divisions has been and is the saddest chapter in the history of Christendom.

4. **DOUBT** –Geneses 3: 1-4 *"Now the serpent was more subtle than any beast of the field which the Lord God had made. And he said unto the woman, Yea, hath God said, Ye shall not eat of every tree of the garden?....And the serpent said unto the woman, Ye shall not surely die:"* Both the question and the statement were calculated to put a doubt in Eve's mind.

   ➢ Doubts about God's existence. But: Heb. 11:6 *"But without faith it is impossible to please him: for he that cometh to God must believe that <u>he is</u>, and that he is a rewarder of them that diligently seek him."*
   ➢ Doubts about Jesus Christ—His Deity, His saving power, His miracles, His resurrection, etc.
   ➢ Doubts about the Bible, its authenticity, its reliability, etc.
   ➢ Doubts about Future Punishment
   ➢ Doubts about Judgment
   ➢ Doubts about the New Birth, The Baptism of the Holy Spirit, Holy Sanctified living, etc.

5. **DELAY**—Put off seeking the Lord
   (1) By tempting us to presume. Presuming to choose our own time to be saved.
   (2) By tempting us to pretend. Being unreal with God and with one's own conscience.

(3) By tempting us to postpone. But: Proverbs 27: 1 *"Boast not thyself of tomorrow; for thou knowest not what a day may bring forth."* Proverbs 29: 1 *"He that being often reproved hardeneth his neck, shall suddenly be destroyed, and that without remedy."* Isaiah 55: 6 *"Seek ye the Lord while he may be found, call ye upon him while he is near:"* Be wise like the Psalmist: Psalm 119: 59, 60 *"I thought on my ways, and turned my feet unto thy testimonies. I made haste, and delayed not to keep thy commandments."* 2Cor. 6: 2b *"....Behold, now is the accepted time; behold, now is the day of salvation."*

In his booklet, *Power Encounter (Spiritual Warfare)*, my dear friend and co-laborer, Dr. Hugh Skelton shares a brief list of some of the tactics (wiles) of Satan:

"Intimidates — 1Pet. 5:8; Interferes —1Thess. 2: 18; 2Cor. 4:4; Counterfiets— 2Cor. 11:14; Intensifies situations that should be normal –2Cor. 2:11; Deceitful—Rev 12:9; 20: 1-10; Tempts men— Mk. 1:13; 1Cor. 7:5; Causes offense—Matt. 16:23; Hinders the gospel —Acts 13:110; 1 Thess. 2:18; Steals the Word—Matt. 13: 19; Luke. 8:12; Causes delay and compromise—Acts 24: 25; 26:28; Makes war on the saints –Eph. 6: 10-18; Accuses the brethren –Rev. 12:10" **5**

Obviously I have not given here an exhaustive list of all the tactics and wiles in Satan's arsenal, but enough to show how dangerous, how deadly, and deceitful he is in his passion to "steal, kill and destroy" (John 10:10). We must be equipped and "battle-ready"!

UNDERSTAND HOW TO OVERCOME THE DEVIL

By Guarding Our Minds

The power of suggestion is an awesome weapon and Satan is very skillful in the execution of it. Martin Luther said, "An idle mind is the devil's workshop." We must close the door to our minds and thought-life to Satan and keep a vigilant guard, lest he take advantage of us. Paul admonishes us in 2Cor. 10: 3-5 *"For though we walk in the flesh, we do not war after the flesh: (For the weapons of our warfare are not carnal, but mighty through God to the pulling down of strongholds;) Casting down imaginations, and every high thing that exaleth, itself against the knowledge of God, and bringing in captivity every thought to the obedience of Christ."*

The greatest single need for every believer is to have the Mind of Christ. Paul declares, *"Let this mind be in you, which was also in Christ Jesus:"* (Phi. 2: 5). We do this by following his instructions in Phil. 4:6-9, *"Be careful for nothing; but in everything by prayer and supplication with thanksgiving let your requests be made known unto God. And the peace of God, which passeth all understanding, shall keep your hearts and minds through Christ Jesus. Finally, brethren, whatsoever things are true, whatsoever things are honest, whatsoever things are just, whatsoever things are pure, whatsoever things are of good report; if there be any virtue, and if there be any praise,* **THINK** *on these things. Those things, which ye have both learned, and received, and heard, and seen in me,* **DO***: and the God of peace shall be with you"* (Emphasis mine).

By Being Strong in The Lord And In The Power Of His Might

If anyone understood spiritual warfare apart from the Lord Jesus Christ, it was the Apostle Paul! From the day of his conversion to Christ on the road to Damascus, until his execution in a Roman prison, Satan used every conceivable method he could to destroy Paul's life and ministry. He cunningly used people, perils (dangers) of every kind, persecutions, prisons, privation of food, water, rest, etc, but in it all he was triumphant and victorious because he was strong in the Lord. "None of these things move me" he declared! Then he opens up to us the secret of this strength and might in Ephesians 6: 11-18:

a. "loins girt about with truth" verse 14
b. "the breastplate of righteousness" verse 14
c. "feet shod with the preparation of the gospel of peace" verse 15
d. "above all, taking the shield of faith" verse 16
e. "the helmet of salvation" verse 17
f. "the sword of the Spirit, which is the word of God" verse 17
g. "praying always...and watching thereunto" verse 18

By Resisting the Devil In Faith

The apostle Peter tells us in 1Peter 5: 8, 9 *"....whom resist in the faith..."* James gives the same instruction in James 4:7 *"Submitting yourselves therefore to God. Resist the devil, and he will flee from you."*

Faith is an awesome weapon! This is displayed graphically as you walk through Faith's "Hall of Fame" in Hebrews chapter eleven. The phrase "Through faith" and "By faith" is repeated no less than nineteen times. We resist in faith! In the chorus of a great gospel song we sing, "Faith in the Father, Faith in the Son, Faith in the Holy Ghost, victories are won!" The apostle John affirms it in 1John 5: 4, *"For whatsoever is born of God overcometh the world: and this is the victory that overcometh the world, even our faith."*

By Using the Word Of God

What a lesson we learn from our Lord Jesus Christ as he overcame the Devil in the wilderness of temptation. Jesus never argued, debated or reasoned with the enemy, He said, "Satan, it is written!" (Matt. 4: 4, 7, 10) Likewise, we must use the Word against every assault of the wicked one! We read in 1John 2: *14b "....young men, because ye are strong, and the word of God abideth in you, and ye have overcome the wicked one."*

The confession of the Word of God without wavering brings the victory! When the Devil says, "you are sick", declare "by His stripes I am healed" (Isa. 53:5).

➤ When he says, "you are weak", declare, *"The Lord is the strength of my lif."* (Ps. 27: 1).

➤ When he says, "you are defeated", declare, *"We are more than conquerors through Christ"* (Rom. 8: 37).

➤ When he says, "you can't pay your bills", declare*, "My God shall supply all my need according to His riches in glory by Christ Jesus"* (Phil 4: 19).

➤ When he talks fear, then boldly say, *"For God has not given me a spirit of fear; but of power, and of love, and a sound mind"* (2Tim. 1: 7).

> ➤ When he tries to discourage you, declare, Phil. 1: 6, *"Being confident of this very thing, that He who has begun a good work in me will complete it until the day of Jesus Christ."*
>
> ➤ When he seeks to condemn you, speak Romans 8: 1, *"There is therefore now no condemnation to those who are in Christ Jesus, who do not walk according to the flesh, but according to the Spirit."*

By Using the Name of Jesus and Pleading The Merit Of His Blood

We have the authority of His Name. Jesus said in John 14: 13, 14, *"And whatsoever ye shall ask in my name, that will I do, that the Father may be glorified in the Son. If ye shall ask any thing in my name, I will do it."* Now notice John 16: 23. 24 *"And in that day ye shall ask me nothing. Verily, verily, I say unto you, Whatsoever ye shall ask the Father in my name, he will give you. Hitherto have ye asked nothing in my name: ask, and ye shall receive, that your joy maybe full."*

Please note the word "ask" in both passages. John 14: 13, 14 says ask Jesus, whereas John 16: 23, 24 say ask the Father. Is there a contradiction here? Of course not! This is made clear in the original text which shows two different words used for our English word "ask." In John 14 the word *"aiteo"* (meaning require or a demand of something due) is used, whereas in John 16 the word *"erotao"* (meaning beseech, entreat, pray) is used. Christ has given us authority over the enemy (Matt. 10: 1).6

> Furthermore, Satan hates the blood of Christ because the shed blood of Christ totally defeated him at Calvary. As believers we have the power of His Blood to defeat him in every engagement. Rev. 12: 11 says *"they overcame him by the blood of the Lamb, and the word of their testimony."*

THE DEVILS DOOM

I would not want to close this lesson without striking the glorious note of victory now and one day the ultimate victory when Satan meets his final doom! There are many Scriptures revealing the complete defeat of Satan and all rebels and of their eternal confinement in eternal Hell. We read in Matt. 25: 41 *"Then shall he say also unto them on the left hand, Depart from me, ye cursed, into everlasting fire, prepared for the devil and his angels."* Rev. 20: 10 *"And the devil that deceived them was cast into the lake of fire and brimstone, where the beast and the false prophet are, and shall be tormented day and night forever and ever."* The Hebrew writer says *in Heb. 2: 14b "....that through death he might destroy him that had the power of death, that is, the devil."*

Yes, we are in warfare! But we have the victory! Be encouraged with the words of Charles Wesley hymn, *"Soldiers of Christ Arise"*:

> *Soldiers of Christ, arise, And put your armor on, Strong in the Strength which God supplies Through His eternal Son; Strong In the Lord of hosts, And in His mighty power, Who in the Strength of Jesus trusts Is more than conqueror.*
>
> *Stand, then, in His great might, With all His strength endued; But take, to arm you for the fight, The panoply of God; That, Having all things done, And all your conflicts passed, Ye May o'er-come thro' Christ alone, And stand entire at last.*
>
> *From strength to strength go on; Wrestle, and fight, and pray; Tread all the powers of darkness down, And win the well-fought Day: Still let the Spirit cry, In all His soldiers, "Come!" Till Christ the Lord who reign on high, Shall take the conquerors home.* 7

Chapter Thirteen

The Reality of Fasting

"Is this not the fast that I have chosen:" – Isa. 58:6

The practice of fasting has its roots deep in Hebrew history. Although there is no reference of anyone fasting before the days of Moses, the fact that mourning and prayer was such a typical feature among the patriarchs and people of the Old Covenant, it can be presumed they did fast before the days of Moses.

In the Pentateuch, the first five books of the Old Testament written by Moses, it should be noted that Moses gives very little attention to fasting, except upon the solemn Day of Atonement. On this occasion he enjoined the people to fast. In Leviticus 23:27, Moses talks about *"afflicting your souls."* In Hebrew this means, "You shall humble yourself deeply before God inwardly by sorrow, and by judging and loathing yourselves; and outwardly by fasting and abstinence from all carnal comforts and delights." **1**

Fasting is a sound Biblical doctrine! To fast means to abstain from food- that which was used to bring about the fall of man. Your faith needs prayer for its development and full growth, and your prayer needs fasting for the same reason. Fasting has done wonders when used in combination with prayer and faith.

The Purpose of Fasting

1. To humble the soul before God (Ps. 35:13).
2. To chasten the soul (Ps. 69:10).
3. To crucify the appetites and deny them so as to give entire time to prayer (2Sam. 12:16-23; Matt. 4:1-11).
4. It manifests earnestness before God to the exclusion of all else (1Cor.7: 5)
5. It shows obedience (Matt. 6:6-18; 9:15; Luke 5:33).
6. It gives the digestive system a rest.
7. It demonstrates the mastery of man over appetites.

8. It strengthens and aids in temptation.
9. It helps to attain power over demons.
10. It develops faith.
11. It crucifies unbelief.
12. It aids in prayer (Matt. 4:1=11; 17:14-21). **2**

In his booklet, *Biblical Fasting and Prayer*, R.D. Flory shares ten reasons why we should make the practice of fasting a vital part of our lives:

1. To minister unto the Lord (Acts 13:2, 3).
2. To increase your faith (Matt. 17:1921).
3. To give yourselves to prayer (1Cor. 7:5).
4. To walk in the Spirit (Romans 8).
5. Fasting brings *heart*-faith to believe in the Words and promises of Jesus.
6. To have faith to pray for the sick, to lay hands on them and see them healed, delivered of demon oppression.
7. To obtain faith to be used by the Lord for the salvation of souls. Fervent intercessory prayer with fasting will break the chains of indifference, laziness and desperation and transform your life into a firebrand in the Hand of the Lord.
8. Fasting will bring you faith to be filled with the Holy Spirit and to stay filled with the Holy Spirit, so that He, the Holy Spirit may live His life in and through you.
9. Prayer with fasting is the most powerful armor that God has given to each member of His Body.
10. Fasting and prayer will give you faith to realize in your own life (Isaiah 58:8-14). In these verses God promises you as a result of Biblically fasting:
    a. Revival in your spirit.
    b. A new power of concentration in your mind.
    c. And to restore health to your body. **3**

Fasting In the Old Testament

From time to time it was customary for the Jews to fast for periods of 24 hours: from the sundown of one day to the sundown of the next.

In Joshua 7:6 we see Joshua and his leaders fasted before God on their faces because of their defeat in the battle of Ai. The tragedy of defeat was the result of their sin of disobedience in the "sacred or devoted thing", 7:1, 11, 12, 15. From morning until evening, about 12 hours they lay before the Lord with torn clothes and dust on their heads.

In 1 Samuel 31 we have the record of the tragic end of King Saul and his sons on the battlefield against the Philistines. *"And when the inhabitants of Jabesh Gilead heard what the Philistines had done to Saul, all the valiant men arose and traveled all night, and took the body of Saul and the bodies of his sons from the wall of Bath Shan; and they came to Jabesh and burned them there. Then they took their bones and buried them under the tamarisk tree at Jabesh, and fasted seven days"* (1Sam. 31:11-13).

After Uriah's wife gave birth to David's son, the Lord struck the child and he became very ill. David lay on the ground and fasted seven days. When the servants told him the child was dead, *"David arose from the ground, washed and anointed himself, and changed his clothes; and he went into the house of the Lord and worship. Then he went to his own house; and when he requested, they set food before him, and he ate. Then his servants said to him, "What is this that you have done? You fasted and wept for the child while he was alive, but when the child died, you arose and ate food." So he said, "While the child was still alive, I fasted and wept; for I said, 'Who can tell whether the Lord will be gracious to me, that the child may live? "But now he is dead; why should I fast? Can I bring him back again? I shall go to him, but he shall not return to me"* (2:Sam. 12: 15-23).

When God's thundering message of judgment came to Ahab through the prophet Elijah the Tishbite, Ahab *"tore his clothes and put sackcloth on his body, and fasted and lay in sackcloth, and went about mourning. And the word of the Lord came to Elijah the Tishbite, saying, "See how Ahab has humbled himself before Me? Because he has humbled himself before Me, I will not bring the calamity in his days; but in the days of his son I will bring the calamity on his house"* (1Kings 21:27-29).

We read in Ezra 8:21-23 that Ezra and the 1754 males in his company proclaimed a fast at the river of Ahava, and sought for God's protection on their journey from Babylon to Jerusalem. *"So we fasted and entreated our God for this, and He answered our prayer."*

Nehemiah spent many days mourning and fasting over the plight of the Israelites in captivity. Like Daniel, he prays and makes confession to God on behalf of the captives. *"So it was, when I heard these words, that I sat down and wept, and mourned for many days; I was fasting and praying before the God of heaven"* (Neh.1: 4).

When it was revealed to Queen Esther that wicked Haman had conspired with success to secure a decree from the king for the concerted destruction of all the Jews in the kingdom, she put her life in jeopardy to request an audience with the king. She sent a message to Mordecai, *"Go, gather all the Jews who are present in Shusham, and fast for me; neither eat nor drink for three days, night or day. My maids and I will fast likewise. And so I will go to the king, which is against the law; and if I perish, I perish!"* (Esther 4:15-16).

The result of this combined fast was the deliverance of all the Jews, and the fatal destruction of wicked Haman for his evil plot to destroy the Jews.

Daniel was a man given much to prayer and fasting. We read his prayer of confession on behalf of all Israel beginning in 9:3, *"Then I set my face toward the Lord God to make request by prayer and supplications, with fasting, sackcloth, and ashes."* In chapter 10:1-3 Daniel reports of mourning and fasting for 21 days when God gave him visions and revelations concerning things to happen in the future.

Another example of fasting in the Old Testament is found in the Book of Joel. The prophet Joel calls Israel to a consecrated fast and repentance for their backsliding. Only if they did this would they be relieved of suffering and find restoration.

In the book of Jonah we read how the nation of Nineveh was spared judgment and destruction because the King and all the people and their animals neither ate nor drank anything. They fasted, prayed, repented and turned from their evil ways and God had mercy on them.

One of the clearest and most detailed references to fasting in the Old Testament is found in the 58th chapter of Isaiah. In verses 3-5 Isaiah describes ten things that do not constitute a proper or acceptable fast:

1. Practices about which we complain (v.3).
2. Afflicting the soul to attract God (vs.3-5).
3. Doing pleasures (v.3).
4. Exacting all labor (v.3).
5. Contentions and debates (v.4).
6. Smiting with the fist of wickedness (v.4).
7. Making voice to be heard in public (4).
8. Bowing the head like a bulrush to make an impression on others (v.5).
9. Spreading sackcloth as ashes under us (v.5).
10. Having a sad countenance, disfiguring the face, and making a show to be seen of men (in fasting or any other practice (Matt. 6:16-18). **4**

In verses 6-14 he enumerates what comprises a true and acceptable fast:

1. To lose the bands of wickedness (v.6).
2. Unto the heavy burdens (v.6).
3. Let the oppressed go free (v.6).
4. Break every yoke (vs.6, 9).
5. Deal bread to the hungry (v.7).
6. Shelter the cast out (v.7).
7. Cover the naked (v.7).
8. Not covering up your own faults (v.7).
9. To call upon and cry to God (v.9).
10. Cease accusing others (v.9).
11. Stop speaking vanity (v.9).
12. Having compassion on the hungry (v.10).
13. To satisfy the afflicted soul (v.10).
14. Keep from desecrating Sabbaths (v.13).
15. Abstain from doing own pleasure on Sabbaths (v.13).
16. Love and delight in Sabbath (v.13).
17. Call the Sabbath holy to the Lord (v.13).
18. Call the Sabbath honorable (v.13).
19. Honor God in all things (13).
20. Live an unselfish life (13).
21. Live for God and not own pleasure (v.13).
22. Speak God's word, not your own (v.13).
23. Abstain from food. **5**

Then he pronounces twenty blessings from observing a true fast:

1. Then (after doing the 8 things of vs.6-7) you shall have light as day (v. 8).
2. Your health will spring forth speedily (v.8).
3. Your righteousness will go before you (v. 8).
4. God's glory will be your rear guard (v.8).
5. <u>Then</u> you will <u>call</u> and receive answers to prayer (v.9).
6. You will cry and God will answer you (v.9).
7. <u>Then</u> (after doing the 6 things of vs. 9-10) your light will rise in obscurity (v.10).
8. Your darkness will be as the noonday (v.11).
9. The Lord will guide you continually (v.11).
10. He will satisfy you in drought (v.11).
11. He will make your bones fat (v.11).
12. You will be like a watered garden (v.11).
13. You will be like an unfailing spring of water (v.11).
14. Your waste places will be built (v12).
15. You will raise up the foundations of many generations (v.12).
16. You will be called, The repairer of the breach (v.12).
17. You will be called, The restorer of paths to dwell in (v.12).
18. <u>Then</u> (after doing the 9 things of v.13) you will delight yourself in the Lord (v.14).
19. I will cause you to ride upon the high places of the earth (v.14).
20. I will feed you with the heritage of Jacob your father, for I have spoken it from My mouth. **6**

It must be kept in mind that the Jews are being addressed here, not the Gentiles, or the New Testament Church. However, the principles remain the same for the general practice of fasting.

Fasting In the New Testament

The first reference to fasting in the New Testament begins with Anna the prophetess, *"the daughter of Phanuel, of the tribe of Asher,. She was of great age, and had lived with a husband seven years from her virginity; and this woman was a widow of about eighty-four years, who did not depart from the temple, but served God with fastings and prayers night and day"* (Luke 2:36,37).

Following that is the introduction of the ministry of Jesus in the wilderness of temptation in Matthew 4:2, *"And when He had fasted forty days and forty nights, afterward He was hungry."*

In His Sermon on the Mount Jesus addresses the issue of *fasting* and points out that there is a wrong way to fast and a right way to fast, just as He does with the principles of *giving* and *praying*. In Matthew chapter 6, Jesus links together these three indispensable principles that are necessary for our spiritual growth and development. He clearly shows that these three can be done in the right way or they can be done wrong. The believers *giving, praying,* and *fasting* should never be directed by man nor to man, but unto the Lord, as a ministry to God out of a heart full of love and thanksgiving for all that He has done for us on the Cross.

Of these three: *giving, praying, fasting*, the least understood and practiced by most Christians is the spiritual principle of fasting. But to maintain spiritual balance and to have the life of Jesus more fully manifested in your life, and thereby overcoming the flesh, the world, and the devil, fasting must become a vital discipline and practice in your life.

It is to be noted here that Jesus did not say, *"If"* you give, *"If"* you pray", *"If"* you fast, but He said, *"When"* you give, *"When"* you pray, *"When"* you fast. It's a foregone conclusion. Giving and praying are not options to be selected or rejected as we wish, and neither is the principle of fasting.

Furthermore, it must be remembered that the power is in Jesus and what He accomplished for us on the Cross. There is no power in giving--the power is in Jesus. Giving is the demonstration of your willing obedience to be the channel through whom Jesus may flow as He desires. There is no power in prayer--the power is in Jesus. Prayer is the contact and preparation to position you to receive. There is no power in fasting—the power is in Jesus. Fasting is the obedient yielding to God that He may do thorough you what He could not do otherwise.

Notice what Jesus said about fasting. *"Moreover, <u>when you fast</u>, do not be like the hypocrites, with a sad countenance. For they disfigure their faces that they may appear to men to be fasting. Assuredly, I say to you, they have their reward.*

But you, <u>when you fast</u>, anoint your head and wash your face, so that you do not appear to men to be fasting, but to your Father who is in the secret place; and your Father who sees in secret will reward you openly" (Matt. 6:16-18).

Our fasting is a personal matter before the Lord. We are not to announce or boast of fasting. It is vain to fast then tell others how many days you have been fasting. It is only as you keep it privately to the Lord you will see the open reward.

When the question arose why His disciples ate and drank while the disciples of John and the Pharisees fasted often, Jesus retorted, saying, *"Can the sons of the bride-chamber mourn as long as the bridegroom is with them? But the days will come when the bridegroom will be taken away from them, then they will fast"* (Matt. 9:15).

The time came when Jesus did leave His disciples, but He did come back, and He's with us today.

Fasting In the Book of Acts—the Early Church

Although prayer is mentioned many times in the Book of Acts, only a few references are made to fasting. In the ten-day period between the Ascension of Jesus and the day of Pentecost, the 120 had gathered in the upper room in obedience to the Lord's instruction to wait for the promise of the Father. We read in Acts 1:14, *"These all continued with one accord in prayer and supplication, with the women and Mary the mother of Jesus, and with His brothers."* Nothing is said here about fasting as they were praying and waiting for the promise of the Father. It can only be assumed, however, they did fast based upon of what Jesus said in Matt. 9:15, *"But the day will come when the bridegroom will be taken away from them, and then they will fast."*

Acts chapter 10 gives a report of an unsaved Gentile by the name of Cornelius who was *"a devout man and one who feared God with all his household, who gave alms generously to the people, and prayed to God always."* He was fasting when the angel of God came to him in a vision and instructed him to send for Simon Peter, who when he would come, would tell him what he must do.

Upon Peter's arrival, Cornelius said, *"Four days ago I was fasting until this hour; and at the ninth hour I prayed in my house, and behold, a man stood before me in bright clothing....* (Acts 10:30).

In chapter 13, various prophets and teachers had assembled together in the church that was at Antioch. *"As they ministered to the Lord and fasted, the Holy Spirit said, "Now separate to Me Barnabas and Saul for the work to which I have called them." Then, having fasted and prayed, and laid hands on them, they sent them away"* (13:2-3).

We see another occasion for fasting in chapter 14: 23, *"So when they had appointed elders in every church, and prayed with fasting, they commended them to the Lord in whom they had believed."*

We see in chapters 13 and 14 the purpose of fasting was connected to commissioning to ministry and appointment of elders for ministry in every local church. In chapter 27: 9, fasting is related to danger and trouble.

It is important to notice that Jesus never made any <u>kind of fast</u> a commandment or rule to follow. In fact, nowhere in the New Testament are we given instructions about fasting. There are instructions about observing the Lord's Supper, water baptism, gifts of the Holy Spirit, praying and giving, but none on fasting. This is not to say we don't need to fast. Fasting for the right reasons in the right way pays mighty dividends. All believers are supposed to fast but no regulations or set rules are given as to how long or how often. This is determined by individual desire and need (Matt. 9:14-15; 1Cor. 7:5; Acts 13:1-5).

WHEN SHOULD WE FAST?

1. When so led by the Holy Spirit (Matt. 4:1).
2. When one is under chastening (2Sam. 12:16-23).
3. When one is under judgment (1Kings 21:27).
4. When one is in need (Ezra 8:21).
5. When one is in danger (Esther 4).
6. When one is worried (Dan.6:18).
7. When one is in trouble (Acts 27:9, 33).
8. When one is in spiritual conflict (Matt. 4:1-11).

> 9. When one is desperate in prayer (Acts 9).
> 10. When one is to make a major decision, for example when Jesus fasted before selecting His disciples (Matt. 4).
> 11. When sorely tempted with the flesh, the world, or the devil (Matt. 4).
> 12. When under persecution and suffering (2 Cor.11:22-33).
> 13. When needing greater power for a ministry need (Mark 9:29).
> 14. When one longs for more of Christ (Phil. 3:10).
> 15. When commissioning to ministry (Acts 13:1-3).

HOW LONG SHOULD WE FAST?

The Scriptures do not set forth any hard and fast rule about the length of the fast. Of the thirty-five fasts mentioned in the Bible, we see a range from one day to forty days:

ONE DAY FAST:

> David.....2Sam.3:35; 2Sam. 1:12
> Judah....Neh. 9:1-4; Jer. 36:6
> Daniel...Dan. 9:3, 20-27
> Pharisee...Luke 18:9-14
> Israel....Judges 20:26-35; 1Sam. 7:6-14
> Darius...1 night Dan. 6:18-24

THREE DAY FAST:

> Esther, Mordecai....Est. 4:13-16; 5:1; 9:3
> Many people..........Mt. 15:32-39
> Paul...........Acts 9:9, 17

SEVEN DAY FAST:

> David.........2Sam.12:16-23
> Israel........1Sam. 31:13

FOURTEEN DAY FAST:

> Paul and 276 men.....Acts 27:33-34

TWENTYONE DAY FAST:

Daniel........Dan. 10:3-1

FORTY DAY FAST:

Moses........Dt. 9:9, 18, 25-29; 10:10
Joshua.....Ez. 24:13-18; 32:15-17
Elijah........1Ki. 19:7-18
Jesus........Mt. 4:1-11 7

These forty-day fasts without food and water should be noted in the context in which they are recorded. Moses could go 40 days without food and water because he was in the supernatural presence of God. Elijah went 40 days in the strength of Angel's food. Jesus fasted 40 days without food and water because "He was led by the Spirit" and angels ministered to Him.

It is impossible to live long periods of time without water, unless you are supernaturally preserved, as was Jesus in the wilderness.

HEALTH GUIDE TO FASTING

Whether you are on a brief or long fast, careful preparations should be made to make certain you get the maximum benefits of the fast without damaging your health. If you have any health problems, then the fast should be done under careful supervision.

A one to three day fast doesn't normally take a great deal of preparation. Many Christians fast one to three days and continue to engage in daily work and routine. This is not the best practice, however. The less you are involved with other duties, and etc, the better is it for maximum results in the fast. Furthermore, one should make certain that adequate amounts of pure water are taken on a regular schedule regardless of the length the fast. Water is a cleanser and the more water you drink the easier it is for your body to rid itself of toxins and poisons that have built-up in your muscles over time.

Beginning the fast

Any time frame longer than three days for the fast requires careful preparation. You should break into the fast gradually by slowly cutting back from solid foods and caffeine drinks to soft foods and water until you are able to stop all foods and drinks except pure water. This will enable your body to adjust to the change and make it more suitable to carry on the fast.

During the fast

It is important to arrange the best atmosphere possible for an extended fast. You should select a place where it is quite and comfortable. Sleep on a comfortable bed, get up daily, have a light bath (sponge baths) and dress. Maintain proper lighting for reading and depending on the season of the year, have proper ventilation of either heat or air condition.

You should be aware that your body will undoubtedly experience various changes throughout the fast. During the early part of the fast you might experience some headaches, nausea, and weakness as your body cleanses itself of various toxins and wastes. Once you are through this stage you most probably will experience hunger for a brief period. Once the hunger dissipates you will begin to sense new strength, a vital quickening in your body and senses as a result of the cleansing of toxins and poisons.

Normally at this period in the fast, as you give yourself to earnestly seeking the face of the Lord, searching your heart and meditating upon the Word of God, you will notice yourself becoming more sensitive to the Holy Spirit and what He is speaking to you. It is quite normal to have an awesome sense of God's presence and mighty breakthrough as you intercede for various people and situations. Make certain you have a pen and notepad always available to record those things the Holy Spirit makes real to you. If it works better for you have a tape recorder, keep it also where it is convenient to reach and use

It is in this high spiritual moment you realize the power and reality of fasting and prayer, and that it is more than worth all the time and self-denial you have dedicated to it.

Ending the fast

Once you realize you want to stop the fast, it is vitally important to bear in mind that breaking the fast, like beginning the fast, must be done very carefully. It is extremely important to remember the fast should be broken slowly to allow your body time to readjust to foods.

The first day or two you should drink only juice then slowly add some soft foods for a couple of days. After several days then begin eating lightly more solid foods, until you are able to eat a complete meal of solid food.

Following the fast you should give yourself sufficient time to evaluate and meditate upon the total experience of your fast. As always, keep in mind your fast was unto the Lord. It's neither necessary nor important that others know anything about the fast. Allow the Lord to reward you openly in His own time and way.

IS THE PRACTICE OF FASTING FOR CHRISTIANS TODAY?

In my travels to many different people groups throughout the world I have noticed one very common underlining denominator---FOOD! People love to eat! In America the national pastime is no longer baseball, but eating! The landscape of our culture is punctuated with shrines to the "golden arches", "pizza temples", "china gardens", and an unbelievable array of fast food chain restaurants. We have been convinced through constant propaganda that unless we have three large meals per day, with numerous snacks in between, we are on the verge of starvation (we eat, not because we NEED to eat, but because it's TIME to eat).

Christians who have bought into this worldly "mind-set" find fasting rather difficult, out of place and out of step with the times. But there are very good reasons supporting the fact that modern Christians should engage in the discipline of fasting.

One, Jesus expects it of us. He had more to say about fasting than about baptism and the Lord's Supper. In fact, there is more teaching in the New Testament on fasting than repentance and confession! Moreover it was His practice and He said, not "if" but "when" you fast, implying He expected all His disciples to do the same.

Fasting played a prominent role in the early New Testament Church. It is seen among the brethren at Antioch (Acts 13:1-3) and the churches of Galatia (Acts 14:21-23).

Paul, you remember commanded us to imitate him as he imitated Christ. (1Cor.11: 1). They both fasted. Fasting was very important to Paul. He listed fasting among those things that proved him as a minister of Jesus Christ (2Cor. 11:23-28).

Every great spiritual awakening recorded in church history was preceded by men of God who were noted fasters---Savonarola in Florence, Italy, Martin Luther in Germany, John Calvin in Geneva, John Knox in Scotland, John Wesley in England, George Whitefield, Jonathan Edwards, Francis Asbury, Peter Cartwright, and Charles G. Finney, D.L. Moody and a host of others in America.

> The gravity of the hour, the enormity of the task of world evangelization, and the challenge of the opportunities for spiritual awakening and the greatest harvest of souls we have ever witnessed should impel us to practice the spiritual discipline of fasting.

We are called to live the overcoming life over the flesh, the world, and the devil. Fasting is an excellent spiritual exercise that helps put to death the desires and passions of the flesh and energizes one's faith, love, and commitment to Jesus Christ.

If you have never engaged in this spiritual discipline and have no health reasons not to fast, let me encourage you to make the habit of fasting, a definite part of your life and service to God. IT DOES MAKE A DIFFERENCE!

Chapter Fourteen

The Reality of Christian Suffering

"Yet if any man suffer as a Christian, let him not be ashamed; but let him glorify God on this behalf" (1Pet. 4:16).

One of the stark realities of our universe is the fact of human suffering. We see it every day throughout the world! Humanity world-wide suffers from the tragedies of wars and human conflicts; physical calamities in nature such as earthquakes, hurricanes, tornadoes, floods, and fires; physical sicknesses, diseases, plagues, pestilences and infirmities; poverty and economic distress. There is an undeniable connection between human existence and human suffering.

From one of the oldest sources of literature we see men grappling with the mystery of suffering in general and why the righteous suffer in particular. *"For affliction comes not forth from the dust, neither does trouble spring forth from the ground. But man is born to trouble as the sparks and the flames fly upward"* (Job 5: 7).

Human suffering was never meant to be! God's man in his original state was one totally free from any form of suffering. So this begs the question: WHY? Why all the suffering from ancient history until our modern times? Wise men, sages, and philosophers have sought to give us the answer, but to no avail. Only the Bible gives the correct answer! In a very simplistic and straightforward way the man whom God placed in the garden in the beginning disobeyed God, and from that moment pain was introduced. Human suffering in all its many forms is the result of Adam and Eve's sinful and willful disobedience to God.

Sickness and disease is a most definite reality, none can deny. It is not the purpose of this chapter, however, to explore why Christians get sick or to discuss the broader aspects of human suffering but to focus on the reality of *Christian suffering* and how Christian believers are to respond to it.

Let's be very clear! Christians **have suffered**, **do suffer**, and **will continue to suffer** until Jesus comes and sets up His kingdom of millennial reign. Jesus said, *"These things I have spoken unto you, that in me ye might have peace. In the world ye shall have tribulation: but be of good cheer; I have overcome the world"* (Jn.6:33). Tribulation is most definitely a form of suffering and Christians will have tribulations. We will look at that in more detail later in this chapter. It is important, however, to understand what the Bible says about Christian suffering, and what Christians are to do in their response to it.

We in the western world, however, have very little understanding about the incredible sufferings and tribulations our fellow believers in China, India, numerous African countries and many other areas of the world are experiencing each day for Christ's name sake. One of the most well kept secrets in the Western church world is the reality of the Persecuted Church. More Christians suffer martyrdom today than all previous centuries combined.

The apostle Peter shares a significant insight into Christian suffering in 1Peter 4:12: *"Beloved, think it not strange concerning the fiery trial which is to try you, as though some strange thing happened unto you: But rejoice, inasmuch as ye are partakers of Christ's suffering; that, when his glory shall be revealed, ye may be glad also with exceeding joy"* (KJV).

Finnis Dake has done an excellent piece of work in rightly dividing the Scripture on this subject of Christian suffering. I am indebted to his Annotated Study Bible for some of the following material.

FACTS ABOUT CHRISTIAN SUFFERING

1. All that live godly in Christ Jesus shall suffer persecution (1Pet. 4:12; 2Tim.3:12).
2. One should rejoice when a partaker of the sufferings of Christ (1Pet. 4:13; Mt. 5:10-12).
3. The greater the suffering the greater the joy and glory (1Pet. 4:13; Rom. 8:17-18).
4. Besides the greater glory to come the Christian has the Holy Spirit upon him now to enable him to endure (1Pet. 4:14; Rom. 8:26-27).
5. Christian sufferings glorify God (1Pet. 4:14; Rom. 8:17-18).

6. It is an honor, not a shame, to suffer as a Christian (1Pet. 4:16; Heb. 11:24-26).
7. Though sufferings begin with Christians they end in an eternal weight of damnation to the ungodly (1Pet. 4:17-18).
8. Sufferings should be borne by Christians, in patience as in the will of God, realizing that God is always faithful to His own in their sufferings (1Pet. 4:19; 1Cor. 10:13). **1**

WHAT CHRISTIAN SUFFERING DOES NOT CONSIST OF

In this fourth chapter of 1Peter we find what Christian suffering does not consist of. Notice verse 15, *"But let none of you suffer—*

1. As a murderer
2. As a thief
3. As an evildoer
4. As a busybody

Furthermore, let none of you suffer from all the crimes listed in Rom. 1:18-32; 1Cor. 6: 9-11; and Gal. 5: 19-21. **2**

Christians who are passionately following the Lord Jesus Christ will live in holiness and righteousness, and not indulge in all the *"works of the flesh."* The Pauline message is clear about God calling His people to holiness. *"Be ye not unequally yoked together with unbelievers: for what fellowship hath righteousness with unrighteousness? and what communion hath light with darkness?*

And what concord hath Christ with Belial? or what part hath he that believeth with an infidel? And what agreement hath the temple of God with idols? For ye are the temple of the living God; as God hath said, I will dwell in them, and walk in them; and I will be their God, and they shall be my people. Wherefore come out from among them, and be ye separate, saith the Lord, and touch not the unclean thing; and I will receive you, And will be a Father unto you, and ye shall be my sons and daughters, saith the Lord Almighty. Having therefore these promises, dearly beloved, let us cleanse ourselves from all filthiness of the flesh and spirit, perfecting holiness in the fear of God" (2Cor. 6:14-7:1 KJV).

"For God hath not called us unto uncleanness, but unto holiness. He therefore that despiseth, despiseth not man, but God, who hath also given unto us his Holy Spirit" (1Thess. 4:7, 8).

Another example, among many, revealing our call to holiness is seen in 1Peter 1:15, 16: *"But as he which hath called you is holy, so be ye holy in all manner of conversation; Because it is written, Be ye holy; for I am holy."*

Living holy lives protects us from sufferings from all these things Paul shares in the above scriptures.

TWENTY-ONE FORMS OF CHRISTIAN SUFFERING

Christians have and will continue to suffer from any or all of the following forms of suffering as made quite clear from the following scriptures.

1. Persecutions for righteousness (Mt. 5:10; 13:21; Mk 10:30; Jn. 15:20).
2. Revilings and slander (Mt. 5:11-12; 10:25; Acts 13:45; 1Pet. 4:4).
3. False accusations (Mt. 10:17-20).
4. Scourgings for Christ (Mt. 10:17).
5. Rejection by men (Mt. 10:14).
6. Hatred by the world (Mt. 10:22; Jn.15:18-21).
7. Hatred by relatives (Mt. 10:21-36).
8. Martyrdoms (Mt. 10:28; Acts 7:58).
9. Temptations (Lk.8:13; Jas.1:2-16).
10. Shame for His name (Acts 5:41).
11. Imprisonments (Acts 4:3; 5:18; 12:4).
12. Tribulations (Acts 14:22; 2Th.1:4).
13. Stonings (Acts 14:19; 2Cor. 11:25).
14. Beatings (Acts 16:23; 2Cor. 11: 24-25).
15. Being a spectacle to men (1Cor. 4:9).
16. Misunderstanding, necessities, defamation, and despisings (1Cor. 4: 10-13).
17. Trouble, affliction, distresses, tumults, labors, watchings, fastings, and evil reports (2Cor. 6:8-10; 11:26-28).
18. Reproaches (Heb. 13:13; 1Pet. 4:14).

19. Trials (1Pet. 1:7; 4:12).
20. Satanic opposition (Eph. 4:27; 6:12).
21. Groaning and travailing because of the curse (Rom. 8:17-26). **3**

It is important here for the reader to notice that in all these twenty one categories of suffering described in the New Testament, none has any reference to sickness.

SIX THINGS CHRISTIANS SHOULD _NOT_ SUFFER

1. <u>With sin</u> which Christ suffered to cleanse us from completely (Mt. 1:21; 26-28; 2Cor. 5:17-21; Rom. 1:21-32; 1Cor. 6:9-11; Gal. 5:5; 19-21; 1Pet. 4:15; 1Jn. 1:7-9; 2:29; 3:8-10; 5:1-4,18).

2. With <u>Sickness</u> for which Christ died to take away from men (Isa.53; Mt.8:16-17; Jn.10:10; Acts 10:38; Jas. 5:14-16; 1Pet. 2: 24). Even provision has been made to keep the Christian immune from sickness (Ps.34: 9_10; 91: 1-12) as well as to give him power to heal others (Mt. 17:20; 21:22; Mk. 9:23; 11:22-24; 16:15-20; Lk.24:49; Jn.14:12-15; 15:7, 16; 16:23-26; Acts 1:4-8; 2:38-39; 5:32; 1Cor.12; Jas.5:14-16).

3. With <u>Failure in business</u> or <u>poverty</u> (Ps 1:3-4; 23:1-6; 34:9-10;37:1-8; 84:11 and scriptures under point 2, above).

4. With <u>Bad habits</u> (Rom.6:14-23; 8:1-13; 1Cor. 6:9-11; 2Cor. 5:17-21; Gal. 5:16-26; Col. 3:5-10; Tit. 2:11-13; Heb. 4:14-16; 7:25; 1Jn. 1:7-9; 2:29; 3:8-10; 5:1-5,18).

5. With <u>Lack of spiritual power</u> (Mt. 17:20; Mk. 9:23; 16:15-20; Lk. 24:49; Jn.4:12-15; Acts 1:4-8; 2:38-39; 1Cor.12).

6. With <u>Failure in prayer</u> (Mt.17:20; 21:22; Mk. 9:23; 11:22-24; Jn. 14:12-15; 15:7, 16; 16:23-26; Heb. 1:6; Jas. 1:5-8; 1Jn. 3:21-24; 5:14-16).**4**

The apostle Paul clearly states that Christ has redeemed us from the curse of the law (Gal.3:13). Christ came to heal all that were oppressed by the devil, not oppressed by God (Mt. 8:17; Lk.13:16; Jn.10:10; Acts 10:38; 1Pet.2:24). I embrace and fully support the following statement by Finnis Dake: "To follow truth we should cease blaming God for sickness, pain, poverty, and calamity, and count them as curses or enemies of both God and man, then cooperate with God and look to Him for deliverance and immunity from such." **5**

SIX THINGS CHRISTIANS ARE TO DO IN SUFFERING

1. Be happy in suffering (1Pet.3:14; Mt.5:10).

2. Be not afraid of man (1Pet.3:14; Mt. 10:28).

3. Be not troubled by trouble (1Pet.3:14).

4. Take suffering as unto God and hold Him sacred in your heart (1:Pet.1:15).

5. Be ready to give an account of your life, conduct, and hope (1Pet.1:15).

6. Maintain a good conscience by good behavior (1Pet.1:16). **6**

TRIUMPHANT TRUTH FOR TROUBLING TIMES

As we probe deeper into this subject of *Christian Suffering*, I would encourage you to give much time meditating on the following scriptures:

Rom 5:3-5 *"And not only so, but we glory in **tribulations** also: knowing that tribulation worketh patience 4 And patience, experience; and experience, hope: And hope maketh not ashamed; because the love of God is shed abroad in our hearts by the Holy Ghost which is given unto us"* (KJV)

Phil 4:14
*"Notwithstanding ye have well done, that ye did communicate with my **affliction**"* (KJV)

Ps 34:19
"Many are the **afflictions** of the righteous: but the LORD delivereth him out of them all" (KJV)

1 Thess 3:1-7
" Wherefore when we could no longer forbear, we thought it good to be left at Athens alone;
And sent Timotheus, our brother, and minister of God, and our fellowlabourer in the gospel of Christ, to establish you, and to comfort you concerning your faith:
That no man should be moved by these **afflictions**: for yourselves know that we are appointed thereunto.
For verily, when we were with you, we told you before that we should suffer **tribulation**; even as it came to pass, and ye know.
For this cause, when I could no longer forbear, I sent to know your faith, lest by some means the tempter have tempted you, and our labour be in vain.
But now when Timotheus came from you unto us, and brought us good tidings of your faith and charity, and that ye have good remembrance of us always, desiring greatly to see us, as we also to see you:
Therefore, brethren, we were comforted over you in all our **affliction** and distress by your faith:" (KJV)

1 Peter 5: 8-11
"Be sober, be vigilant; because your adversary the devil, as a roaring lion, walketh about, seeking whom he may devour:
Whom resist stedfast in the faith, knowing that the same **afflictions** are accomplished in your brethren that are in the world.
But the God of all grace, who hath called us unto his eternal glory by Christ Jesus, after that ye have suffered a while, make you perfect, stablish, strengthen, settle you.
To him be glory and dominion for ever and ever. Amen" (KJV).

James 5:13-15
"Is any among you **afflicted**? let him pray. Is any merry? let him sing psalms.
Is any sick among you? let him call for the elders of the church; and let them pray over him, anointing him with oil in the name of the Lord:
And the prayer of faith shall save the sick, and the Lord shall raise him up; and if he have committed sins, they shall be forgiven him" (KJV).

2 Tim 3:10-13
"But thou hast fully known my doctrine, manner of life, purpose, faith, longsuffering, charity, patience,

Persecutions, afflictions, which came unto me at Antioch, at Iconium, at Lystra; what **persecutions** I endured: but out of them all the Lord delivered me.

Yea, and all that will live godly in Christ Jesus shall suffer **persecution**.

But evil men and seducers shall wax worse and worse, deceiving, and being deceived" (KJV).

Heb 11:32-39
And what shall I more say? for the time would fail me to tell of Gedeon, and of Barak, and of Samson, and of Jephthae; of David also, and Samuel, and of the prophets:

Who through faith subdued kingdoms, wrought righteousness, obtained promises, stopped the mouths of lions,

Quenched the violence of fire, escaped the edge of the sword, out of weakness were made strong, waxed valiant in fight, turned to flight the armies of the aliens.

Women received their dead raised to life again: and others were tortured, not accepting deliverance; that they might obtain a better resurrection:

And others had trial of cruel mockings and scourgings, yea, moreover of bonds and imprisonment:

They were stoned, they were sawn asunder, were tempted, were slain with the sword: they wandered about in sheepskins and goatskins; being destitute, **afflicted**, tormented;

(Of whom the world was not worthy:) they wandered in deserts, and in mountains, and in dens and caves of the earth.

And these all, having obtained a good report through faith, received not the promise" (KJV).

2 Cor 1:3-11
"Blessed be God, even the Father of our Lord Jesus Christ, the Father of mercies, and the God of all comfort;

Who comforteth us in all our **tribulation**, that we may be able to comfort them which are in any trouble, by the comfort wherewith we ourselves are comforted of God.

For as the sufferings of Christ abound in us, so our consolation also aboundeth by Christ.

And whether we be **afflicted**, it is for your consolation and salvation, which is effectual in the enduring of the same **sufferings** which we also **suffer**: or whether we be comforted, it is for your consolation and salvation.

And our hope of you is stedfast, knowing, that as ye are partakers of the sufferings, so shall ye be also of the consolation.

For we would not, brethren, have you ignorant of our trouble which came to us in Asia, that we were pressed out of measure, above strength, insomuch that we despaired even of life:

But we had the sentence of death in ourselves, that we should not trust in ourselves, but in God which raiseth the dead:

Who delivered us from so great a death, and doth deliver: in whom we trust that he will yet deliver us;1 Ye also helping together by prayer for us, that for the gift bestowed upon us by the means of many persons thanks may be given by many on our behalf" (KJV)

2 Cor 4:7-12

"But we have this treasure in earthen vessels, that the excellency of the power may be of God, and not of us.

We are troubled on every side, yet not distressed; we are perplexed, but not in despair;

Persecuted, but not forsaken; cast down, but not destroyed;

Always bearing about in the body the dying of the Lord Jesus, that the life also of Jesus might be made manifest in our body.

For we which live are always delivered unto death for Jesus' sake, that the life also of Jesus might be made manifest in our mortal flesh.

So then death worketh in us, but life in you" (KJV).

2 Cor 6:3-10

"Giving no offence in any thing, that the ministry be not blamed:

But in all things approving ourselves as the ministers of God, in much patience, in **afflictions**, in necessities, in distresses,

In stripes, in imprisonments, in tumults, in labours, in watchings, in fastings;

By pureness, by knowledge, by longsuffering, by kindness, by the Holy Ghost, by love unfeigned,

By the word of truth, by the power of God, by the armour of righteousness on the right hand and on the left,

By honour and dishonour, by evil report and good report: as deceivers, and yet true;

As unknown, and yet well known; as dying, and, behold, we live; as chastened, and not killed;

As sorrowful, yet alway rejoicing; as poor, yet making many rich; as having nothing, and yet possessing all things" (KJV).

2 Cor 11:22-28

"Are they Hebrews? so am I. Are they Israelites? so am I. Are they the seed of Abraham? so am I.

Are they ministers of Christ? (I speak as a fool) I am more; in labours more abundant, in stripes above measure, in prisons more frequent, in deaths oft.

Of the Jews five times received I forty stripes save one.

Thrice was I beaten with rods, once was I stoned, thrice I suffered shipwreck, a night and a day I have been in the deep;

In journeyings often, in perils of waters, in perils of robbers, in perils by mine own countrymen, in perils by the heathen, in perils in the city, in perils in the wilderness, in perils in the sea, in perils among false brethren;

In weariness and painfulness, in watchings often, in hunger and thirst, in fastings often, in cold and nakedness.

Beside those things that are without, that which cometh upon me daily, the care of all the churches" (KJV).

Acts 14:19-22

"And there came thither certain Jews from Antioch and Iconium, who persuaded the people, and, having stoned Paul, drew him out of the city, supposing he had been dead.

Howbeit, as the disciples stood round about him, he rose up, and came into the city: and the next day he departed with Barnabas to Derbe.

And when they had preached the gospel to that city, and had taught many, they returned again to Lystra, and to Iconium, and Antioch,

*Confirming the souls of the disciples, and exhorting them to continue in the faith, and that we must through much **tribulation** enter into the kingdom of God"* (KJV).

John 16:33

*"These things I have spoken unto you, that in me ye might have peace. In the world ye shall have **tribulation**: but be of good cheer; I have overcome the world"* (KJV).

In John 10:10b Jesus said… *I am come that they might have life, and that they might have it more abundantly"* (KJV). However, here in John 16:33 He is warning His followers they too shall suffer tribulations. He wants us to understand that the Christian life is characterized with both negative and positive factors. Just as the battery in an automobile produces power to operate because it is balanced with two poles: one negative, the other positive, the Christian life is a mix of both the good and the bad. In the maturing process of our spiritual life and development which is in a constant process of being shaped more and more into the image of Christ, the need for both negative and positive forces are imperative to make it happen.

This means we must understand God's principle of balance. From the smallest cell in your body to the vast cellular bodies in the universe, everything in God's creation is in balance. Likewise, our spiritual life must be in balance. There is a spiritual equation that portrays this truth about balance:

> If we have the Word without the Spirit---we "dry up."
> If we have the Spirit without the Word---we "blow up."
> If we have the Word with the Spirit---we "grow up."

I want to say emphatically, any teaching or preaching that emphasizes ONLY prosperity, blessings, and personal success results in a shallow existence. It produces "cotton candy" Christians with no substance and depth! Conversely, any teaching or preaching that emphasizes ONLY suffering, hardships, sickness and afflictions, tends to give people a sense of guilt, subjecting them to a 'spirit of fear', and other forms of legalistic bondage, depression, and sin-consciousness.

Our victory and ability to grow and mature in the grace and knowledge of our Lord Jesus Christ requires that we understand this indisputable law of balance in God's book. I would neither be honest with you nor correct in my exegesis of the Holy Scriptures to suggest to you that the Christian life is ALL a joy ride or ALL a trail of tragedy and hardship. It is a combination of both! In the following study it is my purpose to show how both the positive and negative factors work together for us a more exceeding and eternal weight of glory.

> If you have read all the suggested scriptures above, you will note that I have high-lighted two dominate words which appear repeatedly: 1) *"Tribulation"* 2) *"Affliction"*. Both of these words come from the same original word, *thlipsis* which derives from the root *thlipo*. Where ever *thlipsis* is found, it is never in connection or conjunction with disease and sickness! **This is a very important observation for the reader to understand.**

> *Thlipsis* is translated "tribulation" 20 times, meaning "pressure, squeeze, and press". It is translated "affliction" in the sense of tribulation 18 times. *Thlipsis* is translated in other scriptures as:

1. **"Burdened"** – 2Cor 8:13: *"For I mean not that other men be eased, and ye burdened"* (KJV)
2. **"Anguish"** –John 16:21: *"A woman when she is in travail hath sorrow, because her hour is come: but as soon as she is delivered of the child, she remembereth no more the anguish, for joy that a man is born into the world"* (KJV).
3. **"Persecution"**—Acts 11:19: *"Now those who had been scattered by the persecution in connection with Stephen traveled as far as Phoenicia, Cyprus and Antioch, telling the message only to Jews* (NIV).
4. **"Trouble"**—1 Cor.7:28: *"But if you marry, you have not sinned; and if a virgin marries, she has not sinned. Yet such will have trouble in this life, and I am trying to spare you* (NASU).

From the Greek *"thlipsis,"* we have the Latin rendering *"tribulon,"* meaning the "beating rod" used for thrashing wheat. With this background in mind, look with me to John 16:33: *"These things I have spoken unto you, that in me ye might have peace. In the world ye shall have tribulation: but be of good cheer; I have overcome the world."*

First, notice *"In the world you shall have tribulation."* Although we are not OF the world, that is, we are not molded, squeezed into shape; motivated and mastered by the world's godless system; nor master-minded by "the god of this world", nevertheless, we are IN the world. And as long as we are IN IT, there will be tribulation, pressure and trouble. Count on it! We are constantly faced with test, trials, temptations, disease, poverty, persecution, trouble, anguish, Satanic attacks, heart-breaking reversals in all we attempt to do and accomplish.

We must never forget everyone faces tribulation—Jesus the Son of God was confronted with it! The Scriptures plainly teach that Jesus learned obedience by the things He suffered (Hebrews 5:8). But He triumphed over all suffering and He promises us the similar victory. You might remember a popular gospel song several years ago, *"Through It All."* It has a relevant message in the verse that states: "If I never had a problem, I would never know if God could solve them." If you and I never had a conflict, never an opposition, then we would never have opportunity to see the power of God's faithfulness to deliver us. Furthermore, we would miss the blessing that God makes come to us out of such tribulation.

The Scriptures clearly show that God will use your problems, tribulations, and enemies to promote you to fulfill His purposes for you. This principle is clearly revealed in the cycles of tribulation Joseph experienced from the time his brothers put him into a pit, until he was promoted the ruler of Egypt, 2nd only in command to Pharaoh. Thus, during a period of thirteen years (from teen-age to adulthood) he went from the Pit, to Potiphar's house, to Prison and finally to Pharaoh's Palace (Genesis 38-50). All this tribulation was a **school of preparation** God allowed Joseph to go through, in order to be prepared to fulfill God's greater purpose to preserve the children of Israel and the seed of Abraham.

This same principle of tribulation was to be found many years later in the life and ministry of the Apostle Paul and his companions.

With this in mind look carefully at Paul's words in Acts 14: 21, 22: *"And when they had preached the gospel to that city, and had taught many, they returned to Lystra, and to Iconium and Antioch, confirming the souls of the disciples, and exhorting them to continue in the faith, and **that we must through much tribulation** enter into the Kingdom of God"* (KJV). (My emphasis)

To understand the above underscored comment Paul made we must look at the background and context of this passage of Scripture. Paul was returning to the cities where he formerly preached and worked miracles. They had witnessed great deliverances, mighty miracles, and glorious signs and wonders. These converts were born again into the Kingdom of God and received eternal life as a result of the dramatic and dynamic workings of God through Paul's ministry.

Some time had elapsed since Paul's earlier visit and these believers were beginning to settle down into the everyday growth process in the grace and knowledge of Jesus Christ. **WE MUST NOT MISS THIS POINT!** I am not taking away from the dramatic and spectacular operations of the power of God. I whole-heartedly believe in that! However, there is a greater working yet to be done! There is that sanctifying work of molding and changing of the character of the believer into the image of the Son of God! This process of sanctification is necessary and incumbent upon every believer in Christ.

The following Scriptures clearly reveal this purpose of God in the tribulations of the believer:

Gal 4:19
"My little children, of whom I travail in birth again until Christ be formed in you" (KJV).

Gal 1:16
"To reveal his Son in me, that I might preach him among the heathen; immediately I conferred not with flesh and blood" (KJV).

Phil 2:13
" For it is God which worketh in you both to will and to do of his good pleasure"(KJV).

Col 1: 9-12
"9 For this cause we also, since the day we heard it, do not cease to pray for you, and to desire that ye might be filled with the knowledge of his will in all wisdom and spiritual understanding;
10 That ye might walk worthy of the Lord unto all pleasing, being fruitful in every good work, and increasing in the knowledge of God;
11 Strengthened with all might, according to his glorious power, unto all patience and longsuffering with joyfulness;
12 Giving thanks unto the Father, which hath made us meet to be partakers of the inheritance of the saints in light" (KJV).

Col 1: 27
"To whom God would make known what is the riches of the glory of this mystery among the Gentiles; which is Christ in you, the hope of glory" (KJV).

Notice Paul's attitude toward tribulations: *"And not only so, but we glory in tribulations also: knowing that tribulation worketh patience; And patience experience; and experience, hope: And hope maketh not ashamed; because the love of God is shed abroad in our hearts by the Holy Ghost which is given unto us"* (Rom 5: 3-5) (KJV).

The Amplified Version provides a much clearer understanding of this passage. *"Moreover [let us also be full of joy now!] let us exult and triumph in our troubles and rejoice in our sufferings, knowing that pressure and affliction and hardship produce patient and unswerving endurance.*
And endurance (fortitude) develops maturity of character (approved faith and tried integrity). And character [of this sort] produces [the habit of] joyful and confident hope of eternal salvation.

Such hope never disappoints or deludes or shames us, for God's love has been poured out in our hearts through the Holy Spirit Who has been given to us."

Would you notice, Paul said he "gloried," that is, he rejoiced or literally "shouted" in the tribulations. Either he is insane or he has a glorious revelation about the purpose of tribulations and hardships. And that's exactly what he had, a revelation from God and the indwelling power and comfort of the Holy Spirit! With that same understanding and power, we too can rejoice in our tribulations and hardships, praise God!

Look with me now, at this verse again in Acts 14:22 and see the building blocks of truth Paul lays out by putting the verse in reverse order.

1. *"Enter the Kingdom of God"*—They had been "born again" into the Kingdom of God, but now comes the process and struggle to move into Kingdom dimensions and live by Kingdom principles. (See Laws of the Kingdom in Part One) Jesus tells us in Luke 16:16, *"The Law and the Prophets were proclaimed until John. Since that time, the good news of the kingdom of God is being preached, and everyone is forcing his way into it"* (NIV).

That *kingdom dimension* could be a particular ministry God is calling you to. Or, it could be your struggle to gain control over a personal weakness. Whatever the particular dimension, there's a "Promised land" awaiting you and you must PRESS IN to conquer it! Joshua had a promise from God about a glorious new land of abundant blessings, but he had enemies to face and battles to fight before he and the children of Israel could enjoy the benefits of those blessings.

We must remember the sanctifying work of God's grace in our lives is progressive as well as instantaneous, and there will be struggles in the process of our "being" sanctified, as we advance into each new kingdom dimension in our spiritual pilgrimage.

2. *"Must Through Much Tribulation"*—Notice these three qualifying factors:

> a. The fact of tribulation—it is real!
> b. The fact that it is sizeable—"much"
> c. The fact there is no alternative—"must"

These three factors are "tough stuff" for us to confront. But they are factors absolutely essential for our victory and for what makes life a "Kingdom of glory," whether the victory comes through the instant "prayer-of-faith", or through the day to day "fight-of-faith."

3.   *"Confirming the souls"*—of these believers. **The Amplified Bible** states, *"Establishing and strengthening the souls and the hearts of the disciples, urging and warning and encouraging them to stand firm in the faith, and (telling them) that it is through many hardships and tribulations we must enter the kingdom of God."*

Notice the words **"establishing"** and **"strengthening."** Both words carry the thought of reinforcing or building up to make firm, strong and stable. As a system of wires support, strengthen, and steady a "propped-up" sapling, once blown over by the heavy wind and storm, the idea here is to "hold up," "to make steady and firm."

The whole idea behind tribulation taken from the Latin *tribulon* is "to press." Tribulation is pressure—count on it! However, for the most part we don't like pressure. We cry out to God for relief, to remove the pressure—when God is saying, "No, the pressure is what is making you!" Every servant of God in the Bible understood this. Pressure in its various forms is what made Joseph, Moses, David, and scores of others into the kind of person God wanted them to be.

I don't know of anything that doesn't get shaped by pressure. When the seed is planted into the ground it succumbs to pressure, which in turn changes the seed into what it was created to be. We speak of a press—the Bible is printed on one! My wife uses the word 'press' to iron out the wrinkles in my shirt. We cry, "Lord make your Church without spot or wrinkle," or "Lord help me to be patient," etc, but then comes pressure and we are not certain that is what we really want. This is what John Wesley called "the pain of answered prayer."

Now notice again John 16:33, *"These things have I spoken to you, that in Me you might have peace"* (KJV).

IN THE WORLD—tribulations, pressures, problems, tragedies, hardships, troubles—

IN CHRIST—peace, rest, comfort, confident assurance! He is our secret hiding place, our liberty, our source of freedom and victory!

Thus, with David we can shout with confidence, *"LORD, thou hast been our dwelling place in all generations"* (Ps. 90: 1 KJV).

Furthermore we confess Psalm 18:2, "The <u>LORD</u> <u>IS</u> **my** <u>**rock**</u>, and **my fortress**, and **my** <u>**deliverer**</u>, **my** <u>**God**</u>, **my** <u>**strength**</u>, in whom I will trust: **my** <u>**buckler**</u>, and **the** <u>**horn**</u> of my salvation, and **my** <u>**high tower**</u>." (My emphasis)

What a promise, *"He that dwelleth in the secret place of the Most High **SHALL ABIDE** under the shadow of the Almighty"* (Ps. 91: 1 KJV). Oh, it is IN CHRIST we abide! *"For in him we live, and move, and have our being"* (Acts 17:28 KJV).

And He promises, *"If ye abide in me, and my words abide in you, ye shall ask what ye will, and it shall be done unto you"* (John 15: 7 KJV).

Dear reader, this is *living union* with Him! Think of it!

a. Union—peace *WITH* God.
b. Communion—peace *OF* God, ruling our hearts. Communion in the sense of our *common-union* with Him: Therefore,

What He is, we are, *"because as he is, so are we in this world."* (1John 4:17)

Where He is, we are, *"Which he wrought in Christ, when he raised him from the dead, and set him at* <u>*his own right hand in the heavenly places*</u>*"* (Eph. 1:20).

"And hath <u>*raised us up together,*</u> *and made* <u>us sit together in heavenly</u> *places* in Christ Jesus" (Eph 2:6).

"Blessed be the God and Father of our Lord Jesus Christ, who hath <u>*blessed us*</u> *with all spiritual blessings* <u>*in heavenly places in Christ*</u>*"* (Eph. 1:3).

Who He is, we are, *"But of Him you are in Christ Jesus, who became for us wisdom from God—and* righteousness and sanctification and *redemption"* (1Cor. 1:30 NKJV). (My emphasis)

Continuing on with John 16:33, Jesus said, *"In the world you shall have tribulations, But!*

"Be of good cheer"—what an amazing statement! This phrase, "be of good cheer," is found no less than seven times in the New Testament. In each case the statement is made in connection with an impossible situation, humanly speaking. But with God all things are possible! The following is a brief survey of the seven cases:

1. *The Paralyzed Man*

   Matt. 9: 1, 2, *"And he entered into a ship, and passed over, and came into his own city. And, behold, they brought to him a man sick of the palsy, lying on a bed: and Jesus seeing their faith said unto the sick of the palsy;* **Son, be of good cheer**; *thy sins be forgiven thee."*

   This man had not only a serious physical handicap, that left him helpless and at the mercy of others, but a need for a deeper healing—the forgiveness and cleansing of his sins. What sweet words, *"thy sins be forgiven thee."* This is the greatest healing any of us could ever have. When the critics spoke against it and questioned His authority to do it, Jesus said in verse 6, *"But that ye may know that the Son of man hath power on earth to forgive sins, (then saith he to the sick of the palsy,) Arise, take up thy bed, and go unto thine house,' 7 And he arose, and departed to his house."*

2. *The Disciples see Jesus walking on the Sea*

   Matt. 14:27, 26, *"And when the disciples saw him walking on the sea, they were troubled, saying, It is a spirit; and they cried out for fear.*
   27 But straightway Jesus spake unto them, saying, **Be of good cheer**; *it is I; be not afraid.*
   28 And Peter answered him and said, Lord, if it be thou, bid me come unto thee on the water.
   29 And he said, Come. And when Peter was come down out of the ship, he walked on the water, to go to Jesus.
   30 But when he saw the wind boisterous, he was afraid; and beginning to sink, he cried, saying, Lord, save me.
   31 And immediately Jesus stretched forth his hand, and caught him, and said unto him, O thou of little faith, wherefore didst thou doubt?

3. *Mark's account of Jesus walking on the Sea.*

Mark 6:47-51, *"And when even was come, the ship was in the midst of the sea, and he alone on the land.*

48 And he saw them toiling in rowing; for the wind was contrary unto them: and about the fourth watch of the night he cometh unto them, walking upon the sea, and would have passed by them.

49 But when they saw him walking upon the sea, they supposed it had been a spirit, and cried out:

50 For they all saw him, and were troubled. And immediately he talked with them, and saith unto them, **Be of good cheer**: *it is I; be not afraid.*

51 And he went up unto them into the ship; and the wind ceased: and they were sore amazed in themselves beyond measure, and wondered."

4. *All followers of Jesus to face trouble and persecution.*

John 16:32, 33, *"Behold, the hour cometh, yea, is now come, that ye shall be scattered, every man to his own, and shall leave me alone: and yet I am not alone, because the Father is with me.*

33 These things I have spoken unto you, that in me ye might have peace. In the world ye shall have tribulation: **but be of good cheer**; *I have overcome the world."*

5. *Paul facing the Council and angry mob in Jerusalem.*

Acts 23:10, 11, *" And when there arose a great dissension, the chief captain, fearing lest Paul should have been pulled in pieces of them, commanded the soldiers to go down, and to take him by force from among them, and to bring him into the castle.*

11 And the night following the Lord stood by him, and said, **Be of good cheer,** *Paul: for as thou hast testified of me in Jerusalem, so must thou bear witness also at Rome."*

6. *Paul on board ship with "no hope" of survival.*

Acts 27: 20-22, *" And when neither sun nor stars in many days appeared, and no small tempest lay on us,* **all hope** *that we should be saved was then* **taken away.**

21 But after long abstinence Paul stood forth in the midst of them, and said, Sirs, ye should have hearkened unto me, and not have loosed from Crete, and to have gained this harm and loss.
*22 And now I exhort you to **be of good cheer:** for there shall be no loss of any man's life among you, but of the ship."*

7. *Paul's message to the 266 perishing passengers on board the ship.*

Acts 27: 23-25, *"For there stood by me this night the angel of God, whose I am, and whom I serve,*
24 Saying, Fear not, Paul; thou must be brought before Caesar: and, lo, God hath given thee all them that sail with thee.
*25 Wherefore, sirs, **be of good cheer**: for I believe God, that it shall be even as it was told me."*

A sidebar note: There are four references where the phrase, *"Be of good comfort"* is found. Two deal with persons facing a serious and impossible dilemma: the woman with an issue of blood found in Matt. 9: 20-22; and blind Bartimaeus on the highway out of Jericho, crying out to Jesus for mercy, found in Mark 10: 46-52.

In the face of it all—diseases, demons, death, conflict with the world, imprisonment, natural disasters, persecutions, famines, hunger, nakedness, and all manner of perils and dangers, God says, ***"Be Of Good Cheer"!*** But is this really possible, you ask? Yes it is! Jesus explains how this is possible in His final statement in verse 33 of John 16: *"I have overcome the world."* This is not a statement to boast about His individual accomplishment, but rather for our personal encouragement. What welcome words of cheer, **"I have overcome the world"!** We are over-comers through Christ! His victory is our victory!

The apostle Paul strikes this major chord of victory in Romans 8: 35-39, by declaring, *"Who shall separate us from the love of Christ? shall tribulation, or distress, or persecution, or famine, or nakedness, or peril, or sword?*
36 As it is written, For thy sake we are killed all the day long; we are accounted as sheep for the slaughter.
37 Nay, in all these things we are more than conquerors (we are coming off constantly with more than the victory) through him that loved us.
38 For I am persuaded, (I have come through a process of persuasion to the settled conclusion) that neither death, nor life, nor angels, nor principalities, nor powers, nor things present, nor things to come,

39 Nor height, nor depth, nor any other creature, shall be able to separate us from the love of God, which is in Christ Jesus our Lord."

Think of it! None of the seventeen things Paul lists here in verses 35-39, nor any of the seventeen "works of the flesh" listed in Galatians 5:19-21 can separate us from the love of God which is in Christ Jesus our Lord. What Victory! To God be all honor, glory, and praise!

10 REWARDS OF SUFFERING

Nothing is as clear in the Scriptures, as the fact that after this life there is the judgment. *"And as it is appointed unto men once to die, but after this the judgment"* (Heb. 9:27). There are different judgments for different classes of people and nations. However, for all believers in Christ there awaits us The *Bema* Judgment which is *The Judgment Seat of Christ.*

> *"But why dost thou judge thy brother? or why dost thou set at nought thy brother? for we shall all stand before the judgment seat of Christ"* (Rom. 14:10).

> *"For we must all appear before the judgment seat of Christ; that every one may receive the things done in his body, according to that he hath done, whether it be good or bad"* (2Cor. 5: 10).

There will be a definite reward(s) for all the righteous that have suffered for the cause of Jesus Christ and His Name's sake. The apostle Peter admonishes us: *"But rejoice, inasmuch as ye are partakers of Christ's sufferings; that, when his glory shall be revealed ye may be glad also with exceeding joy"* (1Petet 4: 13).

The apostle Paul gives us these encouraging words, *"Knowing that of the Lord ye shall receive the reward of the inheritance: for ye serve the Lord Christ"* (Col. 3:24).

The Lord Jesus Himself gives this promise, *"And, behold, I come quickly; and my reward is with me, to give every man according as his work shall be"* (Rev. 22:12) We shall be rewarded for the following:

1. **Greater glory in heaven** –

   "For our light affliction, which is but for a moment, worketh for us a far more exceeding and eternal weight of glory" (2Cor. 4:17).

2. **Eternal consolation** –

   "And our hope of you is steadfast, knowing, that as ye are partakers of the sufferings, so shall ye be also of the consolation" (2Cor. 1:7).

3. **Make Jesus Known** --

   "For we which live are always delivered unto death for Jesus' sake, that the life also of Jesus might be made manifest in our mortal flesh" (2Cor.4: 11).

4. **Life to others** –

   "So then death worketh in us, but life in you" (2Cor. 4:112).

5. **Making grace manifest** –

   "For all things are for your sakes, that the abundant grace might through the thanksgiving of many redound to the glory of God" (2Cor. 4:15).

6. **Guarantee of judgment** --

   'Which is a manifest token of the righteous judgment of God, that ye may be counted worthy of the kingdom of God, for which ye also suffer" (2Thess. 1: 5).

7. **Reign with Christ** –

   "If we suffer, we shall also reign with him" (2Tim. 2:12).

8. **Spirit upon us** –

   "If ye be reproached for the name of Christ, happy are ye; for the spirit of glory and of God resteth upon you: on their part he is evil spoken of, but on your part he is glorified" (1Peter 4:14).

9. Glory to God --

"Yet if any man suffer as a Christian, let him not be ashamed; but let him glorify God on this behalf" (1Peter 4:16).

10. Great joy 7 --

"But rejoice, inasmuch as ye are partakers of Christ's sufferings; that, when his glory shall be revealed, ye may be glad also with exceeding joy."

"If ye be reproached for the name of Christ, happy are ye; for the spirit of glory and of God resteth upon you: on their part he is evil spoken of, but on your part he is glorified" (1Peter 4:13, 14). 7

The hymn writer expresses what will be our deepest joy and greatest reward in the stanza and chorus of the hymn, *O That Will Be Glory*:

> "When, by the gift of His infinite grace, I am accorded in heaven a place, Just to be there and to look on His face, Will through the ages be glory for me—
>
> O that will be glory for me, Glory for me, glory for me; When by His grace I shall look on His face, That will be glory, be glory for me." 8

What greater reward than to hear Him say, "Well done, good and faithful servant." It will be worth it all when we see Jesus!

Chapter Fifteen

The Reality of Biblical Prosperity

"Beloved, I wish above all things that thou mayest prosper and be in health, even as thy soul prospereth" (3John 2) *(KJV).*

Perhaps no one subject has caused as much controversy, debate, division and criticism in the contemporary Church as the subject of prosperity in general, and the so-called *"prosperity gospel"* in particular. It is my prayer that I can help bridge some gaps and bring clarity and understanding to this controversial subject. We all know that Satan is a thief, continually seeking to steal, kill and destroy (John 10:10a), and nothing pleases him more than when he can cause strife, divisions and rob God's people of the blessings of God; the unity of the Spirit, and the mutual fellowship of the saints.

I am of the firm persuasion that GOD WANTS TO BLESS HIS PEOPLE. He is a GOOD GOD and wants to give good things to those who ask Him (Matthew 7:11). Did not Jesus say, *"I am come that they might have life, and that they might have it more abundantly"* (John 10:10b KJV)?

The so-called PROSPERITY GOSPEL has been so grossly misunderstood and abused until most ministers are fearful to make any mention of 'prosperity' lest they be labeled a false prophet along with all the others that seek ONLY wealth and abundance for selfish purposes.

This situation is very sad because it tends to deceive and lead people into a deeper form of slavery and legalism— subjecting them to a life of spiritual destitution, poverty and want.

As with any other subject or doctrine we MUST seek for the solution or answer from the WORD OF GOD. If we will rightly divide the Word and allow it to speak for itself, apart from all pre-conceived ideas and traditions of men, we will find our answers and discover the WILL of God.

Pertinent questions are always necessary in any quest for understanding Biblical truth. So in our pursuit for the TRUTH about PROSPERITY direct questions are in divine order. Therefore, I am proposing the following questions about prosperity, with the hope that the answers will provide a more accurate and clearer understanding of the subject and encourage the reader to receive and enjoy His inheritance in Christ without guilt or condemnation (Col. 1:19; John 1:16; 1Cor. 3:21; 2Pet. 1:3-4).

1. WHAT IS PROSPERITY?
2. IS PROSPERITY A BIBLICAL DOCTRINE?
3. IS IT THE WILL OF GOD FOR BELIEVERS TO PROSPER?
4. WHAT IS THE PURPOSE FOR PROSPERITY IN OUR LIVES?
5. ARE THERE DANGERS WITH PROSPERITY?

What is prosperity?

Often times people tend to confuse "having money" with prosperity. Having abundance of money only would be a very limited definition for prosperity. I have known people that possessed abundance of money but were poverty stricken in various other ways. It was once said by Henry Ford, the founder of the Ford Motor Company, "I would gladly give a million dollars if I could eat a hamburger and enjoy it." I don't have a million dollars but I can and I do eat and enjoy a hamburger.

The measuring rod for prosperity is not the same for all peoples. The criteria for prosperity in the USA, for instance, would be much different from one living in a remote village in an under-developed country. I have visited areas of the world where having a pair of shoes or a bicycle to ride would be considered very prosperous. I have ministered in remote villages in India, where the people live in grass huts and sleep on cow-dung floors, yet if the Indian farmer owned a small parcel of land and a water buffalo he was very prosperous!

Prosperity means different things to different people. However, I think a fair, simple, honest definition for prosperity is having ALL your NEEDS met with ABUNDANCE (2Cor. 9:8). That is the promise of God's Word, *"But my God shall supply all your need according to his riches in glory by Christ Jesus"* (Phil. 4:19).

The problem with most people is they confuse their "needs" with their "wants." God doesn't promise to give us ALL we want. To do so would be very dangerous and detrimental to us and to others. No loving, wise parent will give their child ALL the child wants. But they will provide for all the child's needs.

IS PROSPERITY A TRUE BIBLICAL DOCTRINE?

It is clearly evident that this meaning of prosperity is a sound Biblical truth. Jesus said: *"I am come that ye might have LIFE, and that ye might have it MORE ABUNDANTLY"* (John 10:10). Jesus came to "destroy (bring to nothing) the works of the devil" (1John 3:8) which include sin, sickness, diseases, poverty and every manner of evil that corrupts and weakens humanity. (My emphasis)

By the offering of Himself as 'the Lamb of God, which taketh away the sin of the world" (John 1:29) He redeemed us from the curse of the law (Galatians 3:13), thus opening the way for us to receive and enjoy HIS ABUNDANT BLESSINGS OF PEACE, LOVE, JOY, HEALTH, SUCCESS AND MATERIAL PROSPERITY (1Cor. 2:16; 1Cor. 1:30; Col.1: 19; John 1:16; 1Cor. 3:21; 2Pet. 1:3-4).

The following Scriptures are selected from a per-ponderous amount of Scriptures to support the truth that the prosperity of God's people is a sound Biblical teaching:

Josh 1:8
"This book of the law shall not depart out of thy mouth; but thou shalt meditate therein day and night, that thou mayest observe to do according to all that is written therein: for then thou shalt make thy way prosperous, and then thou shalt have good success."

Ps 36:7-8
"How excellent is thy loving kindness, O God! Therefore the children of men put their trust under the shadow of thy wings.
They shall be abundantly satisfied with the fatness of thy house; and thou shalt make them drink of the river of thy pleasures." (KJV)

Ps 37:11
"But the meek shall inherit the earth; and shall delight themselves in the abundance of peace" (KJV).

Ps 37:18
"The LORD knoweth the days of the upright: and their inheritance shall be for ever" (KJV).

Ps 75:10
"All the horns of the wicked also will I cut off; but the horns of the righteous shall be exalted" (KJV).

Ps 84:11
"No good thing will he withhold from them that walk uprightly" (KJV).

Ps 92:12-15
"The righteous shall flourish like the palm tree: he shall grow like a cedar in Lebanon.

"Those that be planted in the house of the LORD shall flourish in the courts of our God.

"They shall still bring forth fruit in old age; they shall be fat and flourishing;
"To shew that the LORD is upright: he is my rock, and there is no unrighteousness in him"

Prov 3:1-2
"My son, forget not my law; but let thine heart keep my commandments:
For length of days, and long life, and peace, shall they add to thee."

Ps 34:10
"The young lions do lack, and suffer hunger: but they that seek the LORD shall not want any good thing."

Phil 4:19
"But my God shall supply all your need according to his riches in glory by Christ Jesus."

3 John 2
"Beloved, I wish above all things that thou mayest prosper and be in health, even as thy soul prospereth"

Ps 35:27
"Let them shout for joy, and be glad, that favour my righteous cause: yea, let them say continually, Let the LORD be magnified, which hath pleasure in the prosperity of his servant."

Deut 28:11-12

"And the LORD shall make thee plenteous in goods, in the fruit of thy body, and in the fruit of thy cattle, and in the fruit of thy ground, in the land which the LORD sware unto thy fathers to give thee."

The LORD shall open unto thee his good treasure, the heaven to give the rain unto thy land in his season, and to bless all the work of thine hand: and thou shalt lend unto many nations, and thou shalt not borrow."

Prov. 10:22

"The blessing of the LORD, it maketh rich, and he addeth no sorrow with it."

Deut 28:8

"The LORD shall command the blessing upon thee in thy storehouses, and in all that thou settest thine hand unto; and he shall bless thee in the land which the LORD thy God giveth thee."

The Bible says, *"In the mouth of two witnesses, or at the mouth of three witnesses, shall the matter be established"* (Deut. 19: 5).

The afore mentioned Scriptures clearly establish the fact that prosperity is a sound Biblical teaching and it is incumbent upon us to teach this doctrine as faithfully as all other true Biblical doctrines, to enable all believers to *"walk in the light as He is in the light…"*(1John 1:7). Now let us consider,

IS IT THE WILL OF GOD FOR BELIEVERS TO PROSPER?

To determine what is the will of God regarding any subject relating to man and his relationship with God we must look FIRST and FOREMOST to the Word of God. Let us never forget, the Word of God is the Will of God! God's Word is the only reliable, dependable, and trustworthy report that provides the answer and in which we can place our whole-hearted confidence and trust.

There is an extremely important law in the Word of God that we must look to in determining what God's will is concerning any subject. It is what I refer to as the *"LAW OF FIRST MENTION"* in the Scriptures. What does this law say about the subject? For example, when the Pharisees came and asked Jesus, *"Is it lawful for a man to divorce his wife?" testing Him. And He answered and said to them, "What did*

Moses command you?" They said, "Moses permitted a man to write a certificate of divorce, and to dismiss her." And Jesus answered and said to them, "Because of the hardness of your heart he wrote you this precept. **_But from the beginning of the creation_**_, (first mention) God 'made them male and female.' For this reason a man shall leave his father and mother and be joined to his wife, and the two shall become one flesh'; so then they are no longer two, but one flesh. Therefore what God has joined together, let not man separate"_ (Mark 10: 2-10). (My emphasis)

Jesus made clear what the will of God was regarding their question about divorce by directing their attention to the beginning and referring to the law of first mention.

The same rule applies to the subject of prosperity. How was it in the beginning? Did God create man in the beginning a sickly, weak, poverty-stricken creature? ABSOLUTELY NOT! When God created Adam and Eve He made them a complete and wholesome being without one flaw and placed them in a GARDEN OF ABUNDANCE (Genesis 2:8), and He commanded the waters and the ground to "bring forth ABUNDANTLY" (Genesis 1:20).

After creating all living creatures of the land and fowls of the air and fishes of the sea, *"God blessed them, saying BE FRUITFUL AND MULTIPLY"* (Genesis 1:22). Then God saw that this creation was good (Genesis 1:25) and placed man, whom He had created, in control and management of all this WEALTH and ABUNDANCE (Genesis 1: 26-31).

This clearly is the record of God's Will in the beginning and His Will has not changed! Then why all the poverty, sickness, disease, war, terrorism, and human suffering in the world today, you ask? The answer is found in Genesis chapter three. The man and woman God placed in this garden of abundance listened to the lies of Satan and rebelled against God, and violated God's command, *"But of the tree of the knowledge of good and evil, thou shalt not eat of it: for in the day that thou eatest thereof thou shalt surely die"* (Gen. 2: 17), which resulted in their separation from God (Isaiah 59:2) and all the consequences of their action.

Consequently, the Lord drove this man and woman out of this Garden of Abundance and said to them: *"Thou shalt not eat of it: cursed is the ground for thy sake; in sorrow shalt thou eat of it all the days of thy life; Thorns also and thistles shall it bring forth to thee; and thou shalt eat the herb of the field; In the sweat of thy face shalt thou eat bread, till thou return unto the ground; for out of it wast thou taken: for dust thou art, and unto dust shalt thou return"* (Genesis 3:17-19).

Since this colossal fall mankind has labored under the curse of material poverty and want. But God has made a way of escape! Christ has redeemed us from the curse of the law (Galatians 3:13). He is "not willing that ANY should perish, but that ALL should come to repentance" (2Peter 2:9). God has made the way for us to have complete restoration and become "heirs of God and joint-heirs with Jesus Christ" (Romans 8:17; Galatians 3:29). **Having our every need met is the will of God, and that my friend is prosperity!** What a blessing!

I am confident that anyone who makes an honest study of everything the Scriptures have to say about God's will and desire to bless His children will arrive at the same conclusion—IT IS THE WILL OF GOD FOR HIS CHILDREN TO PROSPER. The Psalmist declares, "**NO GOOD THING** will He withhold from them that walk uprightly" (Psalms 84:11). (My emphasis)

Jesus said, "If ye then, being evil, know how to give good gifts unto your children, **HOW MUCH MORE** *shall your Father which is in heaven give* **GOOD THINGS** *to them that ask him"* (Matt. 7:11). Having ALL our needs met is a good thing, praise God! (My emphasis)

Jesus would never had said the previous verse, Matt. 7:11 nor John 10:10, *"I am come that ye might have life and that ye might HAVE IT MORE ABUNDANTLY"* if it was not the will of His Father, for He testified, *"I do always those things that please him" (*John 8:29). In John 17: 8 He clearly sates, *"I have given unto them the words which thou gavest me…"* How wonderful, what Jesus said is precisely what the Father wanted Him to speak. (My emphasis)

DOES GOD HAVE A PURPOSE FOR PROSPERING HIS CHILDREN?

The Lord God Jehovah of the Bible is a God of PURPOSE! HE DOES NOTHING WITHOUT HAVING DESIGN AND PURPOSE. A brief survey of the following scriptures makes this abundantly clear.

Acts 26:16
*"But rise, and stand upon thy feet: for I have appeared unto thee for this **purpose**, to make thee a minister and a witness both of these things which thou hast seen, and of those things in the which I will appear unto thee." (Emphasis mine)*

Rom 8:28
*"And we know that all things work together for good to them that love God, to them who are the called according to his **purpose**." (Emphasis mine)*

Rom 9:11
*"(For the children being not yet born, neither having done any good or evil, that the **purpose** of God according to election might stand, not of works, but of him that calleth;)" (Emphasis mine)*

Rom 9:17
*"For the scripture saith unto Pharaoh, Even for this same **purpose** have I raised thee up, that I might shew my power in thee, and that my name might be declared throughout all the earth." (Emphasis mine)*

Eph 1:11
*"In whom also we have obtained an inheritance, being predestinated according to the **purpose** of him who worketh all things after the counsel of his own will." (Emphasis mine)*

Eph 3:11
*"According to the eternal **purpose** which he **purposed** in Christ Jesus our Lord." (Emphasis mine)*

2 Tim 1:9
*"Who hath saved us, and called us with an holy calling, not according to our works, but according to his own **purpose** and grace, which was given us in Christ Jesus before the world began." (Emphasis mine)*

1 John 3:8
*"He that committeth sin is of the devil; for the devil sinneth from the beginning. For this **purpose** the Son of God was manifested, that he might destroy the works of the devil." (Emphasis mine)*

THE PURPOSE FOR PROSPERITY

God most definitely has a purpose for the prosperity of His children. Unfortunately, too many believers do not understand that purpose, and as a result live a very selfish life, and heap to themselves riches for the gratification of their fleshly desires and carnal pursuits.

> The purpose for God blessing Abraham was so **HE COULD BE A BLESSING.** "And I will make of thee a great nation, and **I WILL BLESS THEE,** and make thy name great; and **THOU SHALT BE A BLESSING:** And I will bless them that bless thee, and curse him that curseth thee: and **IN THEE SHALL ALL THE FAMILIES OF THE EARTH BE BLESSED"** (Genesis 12:2-3). (Emphasis mine)

That is still the purpose of God in our being partakers of the blessings of Abraham (Galatians 3:13, 14, 16, 26, 29), so we can bless the nations with the Gospel of the Kingdom (Matthew 24:14; 28:18-20; Acts 1:8).

Although God wants to give us abundant life, it is obvious from the teachings of Jesus we are not to simply gather wealth to heap and keep it to ourselves. Rather we are to **LIVE to GIVE!** *"Give"* Jesus said, *"and it shall be given unto you; good measure, pressed down, and shaken together, and running over, shall men give into your bosom. For with the same measure that ye mete withal it shall be measured to you again"* (Luke 6:38).

There are untold blessings waiting for all who **LIVE to GIVE** See **Isaiah 58 and Psalm 41.**

Living to give should be the lifestyle of every Christian, because it was the lifestyle of the Master! That is why Jesus issued this strong admonition, *"Lay not up for yourselves treasures upon earth, where moth and rust doth corrupt, and where thieves break through and steal: But lay up for yourselves treasures in heaven, where neither moth nor rust doth corrupt, and where thieves do not break through nor steal: For where your treasure is, there will your heart be also"* (Matthew 6: 19-21).

Let it be clearly understood, having money, wealth and prosperity is not the problem. **The problem is when money, wealth and prosperity HAVE CONTROL OF US!** It is a matter of the "tail wagging the dog" rather than the dog wagging his tail.

Jesus warns of this danger when He said, *"Take heed, and beware of covetousness: for a man's life consisteth not in the abundance of the things which he possesseth. And he spake a parable unto them, saying, The ground of a certain rich man brought forth plentifully: And he thought within himself, saying, What shall I do, because I have no room where to bestow my fruits? And he said, This will I do: I will pull down my barns, and build greater; and there will I bestow all my fruits and my goods. And I will say to my soul, Soul, thou hast much goods laid up for many years; take thine ease, eat, drink, and be merry. But God said unto him, Thou fool, this night thy soul shall be required of thee: then whose shall those things be, which thou hast provided? So is he that layeth up treasure for himself, and is not rich toward God"* (Luke 12: 15-21).

There is a mistaken notion and teaching by some that money is THE ROOT of ALL EVIL. Clearly, money is NOT the root of all evil rather it is the **LOVE of MONEY** that is the root of all evil (1Timothy 6:10). "He that **loveth** silver shall never be satisfied," said the Wisdom writer (Ecc.5: 10). (My emphasis) There is no intrinsic evil in the metal or paper used as a form of currency. Rather it is in our attitude toward it.

To love money for money's sake and hoard it is a serious snare. Like leprosy or cancer it will rob, devour and destroy the person. From time to time we read reports in the news that an elderly person was found dead having lived for years in abject poverty, but there was discovered in the mattress or other secret compartment multiplied thousands of dollars.

So *"if riches increase, set not your heart upon them"* (Ps 62:10) and *"let not the rich man glory in* **his riches**" (Jer. 9: 23). But understand and remember that God's blessing of prosperity is for you to **enjoy** and to **use** as a partner with God in the greatest **CAUSE** man will ever know—the cause of sharing the Gospel to "every creature" (Mk.16: 15). This leads to my final question to consider in this lesson about prosperity:

ARE THERE DANGERS IN HAVING PROSPERITY?

There is no danger in prosperity per se—rather the danger lies in one's inability to properly manage prosperity. This is equally true for having power, position, or authority. We see the abuse of power, position, and authority quite frequently because of people's inability to properly mange and control what has been entrusted to them.

The rich fool Jesus describes obviously could not properly mange wealth and prosperity. He was too consumed with himself. He did not take God into consideration nor did he give any consideration to his neighbor or anyone for that matter—**it was all about himself!** Please notice the 16 highlighted personal pronouns in this report in *Luke 12:15-21*:

15 *"And he said unto them, Take heed, and beware of covetousness: for a man's life consisteth not in the abundance of the things which he possesseth.*

16 *"And he spake a parable unto them, saying, The ground of a certain rich man brought forth plentifully:*

17 *"And **he** thought within **himself**, saying, What shall **I** do, because **I** have no room where to bestow **my** fruits?*

18 *"And **he** said, This will **I** do: **I** will pull down **my** barns, and build greater; and there will **I** bestow all **my** fruits and **my** goods.*

19 *"And **I** will say to **my** soul, **Soul**, thou hast much goods laid up for many years; take **thine** ease, eat, drink, and be merry.*

20 *"But God said unto him, Thou fool, this night thy soul shall be required of thee: then whose shall those things be, which thou hast provided?*

21 *"So is he that layeth up treasure for himself, and is not rich toward God (KJV).* (Emphasis mine)

For a beautiful comparison, I like also the way *The Living Bible* expresses this story:

15 *"Beware! Don't always be wishing for what you don't have. For real life and real living are not related to how rich we are."*

16 *"Then he gave an illustration: "A rich man had a fertile farm that produced fine crops. 17 In fact, his barns were full to overflowing-he couldn't get everything in. He thought about his problem, 18 and finally exclaimed, 'I know-I'll tear down my barns and build bigger ones! Then I'll have room enough. 19 And I'll sit back and say to myself, "Friend, you have enough stored away for years to come. Now take it easy! Wine, women, and song for you!"'*

20 *"But God said to him, 'Fool! Tonight you die. Then who will get it all?'*

21 *"Yes, every man is a fool who gets rich on earth but not in heaven"* (TLB). 1

The obvious point of this story is NOT that money, abundance, or prosperity is intrinsically evil, but the wrong attitude toward wealth and the inability to properly manage it to glorify and serve the purposes of God. So, there can be dangers in possessing wealth and prosperity. The following are the most prevalent:

The danger of pride and forgetting God

Perhaps the greatest danger in having wealth and prosperity is that we can get caught up in pride and forget God. This is made abundantly clear in God's warning to the children of Israel.

Deut 8:11-14
11 *"Beware that thou* **forget not the LORD thy God,** *in not keeping his commandments, and his judgments, and his statutes, which I command thee this day:*
12 *"Lest when thou hast eaten and art full, and hast built goodly houses, and dwelt therein;*
13 *"And when thy herds and thy flocks multiply, and thy silver and thy gold is multiplied, and all that thou hast is multiplied;*
14 **"Then thine heart be lifted up, and thou forget the LORD thy God,** *which brought thee forth out of the land of Egypt, from the house of bondage."* (Emphasis mine)

The sin of **pride is listed first** among the seven deadly sins of abominations God hates *(Pro. 6; 16-19).*

16 "These six things doth the LORD hate: yea, seven are an abomination unto him:
*17 "**A proud look**, a lying tongue, and hands that shed innocent blood,*
18 "An heart that deviseth wicked imaginations, feet that be swift in running to mischief,
19 "A false witness that speaketh lies, and he that soweth discord among brethren (KJV). (My emphasis)

Please read carefully some other Scriptures about the sin of pride:

Prov 16:18
18 "Pride goeth before destruction, and an haughty spirit before a fall."

Prov 29:23
23 "A man's pride shall bring him low: but honour shall uphold the humble in spirit" (KJV).

Obad 3
3 "The pride of thine heart hath deceived thee, thou that dwellest in the clefts of the rock, whose habitation is high; that saith in his heart, Who shall bring me down to the ground" (KJV)?

1 John 2:16
16 "For all that is in the world, the lust of the flesh, and the lust of the eyes, and the pride of life, is not of the Father, but is of the world" (KJV).

The danger of selfishness

The sin of selfishness is very subtle and dangerous. Lurking behind every form of evil—wars, crimes, violence, terrorism, divorce, strife, divisions, etc., is the SIN OF SELFISHNESS! We are born with this innate propensity to want for ourselves. It came with the curse!

Wealth creates power and power and wealth in the hands of untamed and uncontrollable selfishness results in all manner of evil and human tragedies.

Dealing with "self" and selfishness is the first and primary requiset Jesus requires and demands of us to be able to become His disciple. *"And he said to them all, 'If any man will come after me,* **let him deny himself***, and take up his cross daily, and follow me'"* (Luke 9:23). (My emphasis)

During His ministry with His disciples He was continually teaching and demonstrating this "lifestyle" of self-denial and living for the benefit of others. He demonstrated that living this lifestyle they would never live to be in WANT for anything. There are many examples of this truth demonstrated in His life and ministry.

> When He needed a boat, one was provided (Mk. 8:13). When He needed a donkey, one was waiting (Matt.21: 2). When He needed to pay the taxes, the fish was carrying the money (Matt. 17: 24-27). When the multitude needed to be fed, a few loaves of bread and fishes were available for Jesus to bless and multiply (John 6: 9). Jesus clearly taught this golden truth, when we live to "seek first the kingdom of God and His righteousness, then ALL these THINGS shall be added unto us" (Matt. 6: 33). (My emphasis)

"The earth is the **LORD's,** *and the* **fulness thereof***; the world, and they that dwell therein* (Ps. 24: 1). From the beginning of creation God demonstrates His ownership of everything He created. He created this planet and all its vast wealth and resources. Did He create it to be monopolized by the unconverted? Absolutely not! He created it for the prosperity of His children who do His Will. (My emphasis)

This fact is well established when He created Adam and Eve and gave them the privilege to manage and enjoy the Garden of Abundance He had created for them. It was only through deception and disobedience they forfeited this blessing. BUT GOD provided the way of restoration to His FAMILY, His FELLOWSHIP and His divine FAVOR.

The danger of a greedy spirit (heart)

Webster defines "greedy" as "an insatiable desire to possess or acquire something to an amount inordinately beyond what one needs or deserves." Such a greedy insatiable passion for wealth, takes the victim one step deeper from its twin selfishness into the insane pit of debauchery and abomination.

When one is controlled by a greedy spirit one's conscience becomes seared and hardened to the point where the person will use any form of manipulation, malice, and madness to gain what one desires. Truly it is an insatiable drive and desire. It is wicked, to say the least!

World history bears evidence and record of such greedy people like the evil Pharaoh's, Roman tyrants, King Herod, Hitler, Stalin, Mào, Saddam Hussein, etc, etc. This is why I caution people about wealth, power and prosperity—if you cannot handle it, then pray God you never get it, for *"what is a man profited, if he shall gain the whole world, and lose his own soul? Or what shall a man give in exchange for his soul?"* (Matthew 16: 26). (My emphasis)

The danger of a lonely life

The subtle danger of wealth and riches is that it can lead one into a state of fear and insecurity. There is a haunting fear of losing all one has and so the victim clings tenuously to his possessions and becomes highly suspicious that everyone wants a piece of his wealth. The grip of this sense of distrust builds a barrier of separation with others until the victim, like the rich fool Jesus describes, lives a very lonely obscure life.

Some of the happiest and most contented people I've known had very little in terms of worldly possession, but were surrounded by a host of family members and friends. They were not lonely but lively, not poor but rich in qualities and blessings that no amount of money can buy. On the other hand, some of the world's wealthiest people have been the most paranoid, fearful and lonely people who ever lived.

Although there are serious dangers associated with wealth and prosperity, the fact remains, God's desire and will is to bless His children with Life Abundantly!

The FAVOR of His ABUNDANT BLESSINGS has been provided through the Lord Jesus Christ, the "Captain of our SALVATION" (Heb. 2: 10). *"Salvation"* is the all-inclusive word that embraces **everything that Jesus accomplished for us in His death on the Cross:** " *SOZO"* is the word, meaning, "Forgiveness, deliverance, rescue, safety, freedom, liberty, protection, preservation, health, wholeness, soundness, peace, righteousness, victory." By it we are saved, recreated, healed, restored, made strong—and all of this applies to the whole person, **spiritually, physically, mentally and materially** (3John v.2; 1Thess. 5:23).

We read in 2 Corinthians 9:8, *"And God is able to make all grace abound toward you; that ye, always having all sufficiency in all things, may abound to every good work:"*

THINK OF IT! ALL GRACE—ALL SUFFICIENCY—ALL THINGS—THAT DEAR ONE, IS PROSPERITY!

Allow me to encourage you to do some serious meditation on the following scriptures:

Prov 10:22
"The blessing of the LORD, it maketh rich, and he addeth no sorrow with it" (KJV).

2 Cor 8:9
"For ye know the grace of our Lord Jesus Christ, that, though he was rich, yet for your sakes he became poor, that ye through his poverty might be rich" (KJV).

Eph 2:4
"But God, who is rich in mercy, for his great love wherewith he loved us" (KJV).

Ps 112:1-3
" Praise ye the LORD. Blessed is the man that feareth the LORD, that delighteth greatly in his commandments.
His seed shall be mighty upon earth: the generation of the upright shall be blessed.
Wealth and riches shall be in his house: and his righteousness endureth for ever" (KJV).

Prov 22:4
"By humility and the fear of the LORD are riches, and honour, and life" (KJV).

Rom 11:33
" O the depth of the riches both of the wisdom and knowledge of God! how unsearchable are his judgments, and his ways past finding out" (KJV)!

2 Cor 8:2
" How that in a great trial of affliction the abundance of their joy and their deep poverty abounded unto the riches of their liberality" (KJV).

Eph 1:7

" In whom we have redemption through his blood, the forgiveness of sins, according to the riches of his grace" (KJV).

Eph 1:18
" The eyes of your understanding being enlightened; that ye may know what is the hope of his calling, and what the riches of the glory of his inheritance in the saints" (KJV).

Eph 2:7
"That in the ages to come he might shew the exceeding riches of his grace in his kindness toward us through Christ Jesus" (KJV).

Eph 3:8
"Unto me, who am less than the least of all saints, is this grace given, that I should preach among the Gentiles the unsearchable riches of Christ" (KJV).

Eph 3:16
" That he would grant you, according to the riches of his glory, to be strengthened with might by his Spirit in the inner man" (KJV).

Phil 4:19
" But my God shall supply all your need according to his riches in glory by Christ Jesus" (KJV).

Col 1:27
" To whom God would make known what is the riches of the glory of this mystery among the Gentiles; which is Christ in you, the hope of glory" (KJV).

Col 2:2
"That their hearts might be comforted, being knit together in love, and unto all riches of the full assurance of understanding, to the acknowledgement of the mystery of God, and of the Father, and of Christ" (KJV).

1 Tim 6:17
" Charge them that are rich in this world, that they be not highminded, nor trust in uncertain riches, but in the living God, who giveth us richly all things to enjoy" (KJV).

Ps 37:11
" But the meek shall inherit the earth; and shall delight themselves in the abundance of peace"(KJV).

Ps 72:7
" *In his days shall the righteous flourish; and abundance of peace so long as the moon endureth"* (KJV).

Rom 5:17
" *For if by one man's offence death reigned by one; much more they which receive abundance of grace and of the gift of righteousness shall reign in life by one, Jesus Christ"* (KJV).

2 Cor 8:2
"How that in a great trial of affliction the abundance of their joy and their deep poverty abounded unto the riches of their liberality" (KJV).

Prov 28:20
"A faithful man shall abound with blessings: but he that maketh haste to be rich shall not be innocent" (KJV).

Rom 15:13
"Now the God of hope fill you with all joy and peace in believing, that ye may abound in hope, through the power of the Holy Ghost" (KJV)

2 Cor 8:7
"Therefore, as ye abound in every thing, in faith, and utterance, and knowledge, and in all diligence, and in your love to us, see that ye abound in this grace also" (KJV).

2 Cor 9:8
"And God is able to make all grace abound toward you; that ye, always having all sufficiency in all things, may abound to every good work:" KJV

Phil 1:9
"And this I pray, that your love may abound yet more and more in knowledge and in all judgment" KJV

Phil 4:12
"I know both how to be abased, and I know how to abound: every where and in all things I am instructed both to be full and to be hungry, both to abound and to suffer need" (KJV),

Phil 4:17-18
" *Not because I desire a gift: but I desire fruit that may abound to your account."*

"But I have all, and abound: I am full, having received of Epaphroditus the things which were sent from you, an odour of a sweet smell, a sacrifice acceptable, wellpleasing to God" (KJV).

1 Thess. 3:12
"And the Lord make you to increase and abound in love one toward another, and toward all men, even as we do toward you" (KJV).

2 Peter 1:8
"For if these things be in you, and abound, they make you that ye shall neither be barren nor unfruitful in the knowledge of our Lord Jesus Christ" (KJV).

Ps 91:16
" With long life will I satisfy him, and shew him my salvation" (KJV).

Isa 58:11
"And the LORD shall guide thee continually, and satisfy thy soul in drought, and make fat thy bones: and thou shalt be like a watered garden, and like a spring of water, whose waters fail not" (KJV).

Ps 36:5-10
"Thy mercy, O LORD, is in the heavens; and thy faithfulness reacheth unto the clouds.
"Thy righteousness is like the great mountains; thy judgments are a great deep: O LORD, thou preservest man and beast.
"How excellent is thy lovingkindness, O God! therefore the children of men put their trust under the shadow of thy wings.
"They shall be abundantly satisfied with the fatness of thy house; and thou shalt make them drink of the river of thy pleasures.
"For with thee is the fountain of life: in thy light shall we see light.
"O continue thy lovingkindness unto them that know thee; and thy
righteousness to the upright in heart" (KJV).

Ps 23:1
"The LORD is my shepherd; I shall not want" (KJV).

Ps 34:9-10
"O fear the LORD, ye his saints: for there is no want to them that fear him.
"The young lions do lack, and suffer hunger: but they that seek the LORD shall not want any good thing" (KJV).

2 Cor 8:14-15

"But by an equality, that now at this time your abundance may be a supply for their want, that their abundance also may be a supply for your want: that there may be equality:

" As it is written, He that had gathered much had nothing over; and he that had gathered little had no lack" (KJV).

2 Cor 9:8-12

"And God is able to make all grace abound toward you; that ye, always having all sufficiency in all things, may abound to every good work:

"(As it is written, He hath dispersed abroad; he hath given to the poor: his righteousness remaineth for ever.

"Now he that ministereth seed to the sower both minister bread for your food, and multiply your seed sown, and increase the fruits of your righteousness;)

"Being enriched in every thing to all bountifulness, which causeth through us thanksgiving to God.

"For the administration of this service not only supplieth the want of the saints, but is abundant also by many thanksgivings unto God" (KJV).

Prov 22:9

"He that hath a bountiful eye shall be blessed; for he giveth of his bread to the poor" (KJV).

Ps 41:1-3

Blessed is he that considereth the poor: the LORD will deliver him in time of trouble.

"The LORD will preserve him, and keep him alive; and he shall be blessed upon the earth: and thou wilt not deliver him unto the will of his enemies.

"The LORD will strengthen him upon the bed of languishing: thou wilt make all his bed in his sickness" (KJV).

Ps 41:1-3

"Blessed is he that considereth the poor: the LORD will deliver him in time of trouble.

"The LORD will preserve him, and keep him alive; and he shall be blessed upon the earth: and thou wilt not deliver him unto the will of his enemies.

"The LORD will strengthen him upon the bed of languishing: thou wilt make all his bed in his sickness" (KJV).

Prov 28:27

"He that giveth unto the poor shall not lack: but he that hideth his eyes shall have many a curse" (KJV).

You will recall from the lessons in part two the vital importance of understanding the laws of God's Kingdom and the necessity of observing those laws. The same is equally important for the believer to remember about prosperity and how to make it a reality in ones life. There are certain laws or principles one must observe and put into practice if one is to enjoy the abundant life of God's prosperity. These laws are summarized from the writings of Finis Dake in his excellent work, *God's Plan for Man,* under the heading, *Laws of Prosperity.*

1. *Believe that it is God's will for YOU to prosper and that YOU are in His Will (Luke 12:32).*

2. *Make God your partner in life (Gal. 2:20).*

3. *Get into the lifework that you feel God would have you in or that for which you are best suited.*

4. *Have faith in God.*

5. *Do not fear launching out into new ventures and make the best of your opportunities that come.*

6. *Faithfully follow certain business principles taught in scripture (Rom. 12:9-21).*

7. *Obey the golden rule.*

8. *Always "seek first the Kingdom of God and His righteousness" (Matt. 6:33).*

9. *Cultivate the practice of giving to others (Luke 6:38).*

10. *"Honour the Lord with thy substance and with the first fruits of all thine increase" (Prov.3: 8-9). 2*

You might call these the Ten Commandments for prosperity. As you diligently practice these principles of living you will discover the joy of living in the reality of His prosperity and all the benefits provided for us in the glorious redemption Christ purchased for us.

Epilogue

It would not be fitting to share this information on the Kingdom without closing with our attention focused on the main key and business of the Kingdom which is summed up in Matt. 24:14, *"And this gospel of the kingdom shall be preached in all the world for a witness unto all nations; and then shall the end come."*

The supreme business of the Church is the Great Commission of Jesus Christ! The vital importance of the Commission is seen in the fact that each of the gospel writers, plus the book of Acts make record of it. The heart of this Commission is the good-news of reconciliation—God made the way for lost mankind to be redeemed and brought back into His divine favor, family and fellowship! Paul clearly shows in his Corinthian letter that ever "born-again, new creature in Christ" (2Cor.5:17) is under the same mandate as the early disciples and New Testament Church.

It is interesting how Luke brings out this point in Acts 1: 1; *"...all that Jesus began both to do and teach"*, we are to continue, then he records twenty-eight chapters of the glorious work of the Holy Spirit through the believers to accomplish it. The point becomes very obvious in the twenty-eight chapter of the book of Acts. Notice, Paul was maximizing his final days in a Roman prison, by having the Jews and all others who would visit him, sharing the things (realities) of the Kingdom of God with them. When we come to the last several verses there is no hint to a conclusion, benediction, or ending of the book Acts. What was started in Chapter 1: 1 **WAS TO BE CONTINUED**—thus, the Church today is under the same assignment! The plan has not changed! *"Go ye into all the world and preach the gospel to every creature."* That is our assignment and we dare not slack up or drop the divine orders! Each generation must witness to and reach its generation.

Any unbiased student of the life and ministry of the Lord Jesus Christ would agree Jesus was on a mission and the harvest was what He was all about (Jn. 3:16; 4: 34-38; Luke 19:10). We too must be about our Father's business. The harvest is what we are all about.

I'm convinced if the reader carefully studies and practices the laws and realities of the Kingdom, heretofore mentioned, like the Master, he too will be passionate about the harvest.

Make no mistake about it! The harvest is very real! Jesus said, *"Say not ye, There are yet four month, and then cometh harvest? Behold, I say unto you, lift up your eyes, and look on the fields; for they are white already to harvest."* (Jn. 4: 35) This harvest is sizeable—of the earth's seven billions of people more than two billion remain unreached with the gospel. Despite all our wonderful technology and advancements that have been made in travel, education, and communication, thousands of 'people-groups' remain living in spiritual darkness and destitution without the gospel.

We must continue what He began both "to do" and "to teach"! As Dr. Oswald J. Smith would often say, "we are just one generation away from the extension of the gospel". We dare not fail our generation! In closing, let me remind us of several very important facts: The *opportunities* to preach the gospel and win this harvest have never been greater! The *opposition* to the preaching of the gospel has never been stronger! The *coming of Christ* has never been nearer!

This is our finest hour for the harvest! We are witnessing the fulfillment of a prophecy given by two prophets: Habakkuk 2: 14 and Isaiah 11:9, *"The earth shall be filled with the knowledge of the glory of the Lord, as the waters cover the sea."*

This is what Paul said in 2Cor. 2: 14, *"Now thanks be to God who always leads us in triumph in Christ, and through us diffuses the fragrance of his knowledge in every place."*

> "Great God, the nations of the earth
>   Are by creation thine;
> And in thy works, by all beheld,
>   Thy radiant glories shine.
> But, Lord, thy greater love has sent
>   Thy gospel to mankind,
> Unveiling what rich stores of grace
>   Are treasured in thy mind.
> Lord, when shall these glad tidings spread
>   The spacious earth around,

Till every tribe and every soul
    Shall hear the joyful sound?
Smile, Lord, on each divine attempt
    To spread the gospel's rays,
And build on sin's demolished throne
    The temples of thy praise." **1**
Thomas Gibbons.

NOTES

PART I

Introduction

1.   Finis Jennings Dake, *God's Plan For Man* (Lawrenceville, GA, Dake Bible Sales, Inc. 1949), p. 42

2.   Ibid: p. 558, 559

3.   Ibid: p. 559

4.   Finis Jennings Dake, *Dake's Annotated Reference Bible* (Lawrenceville, GA, Seventh Printing, May 2004), NT page 37

5.   Finis Jennings Dake, *God's Plan For Man* (Lawrenceville, GA, Dake Bible Sales, Inc. 1949) p. 560

Understanding Life In The Kingdom Of God

1.   *Life Application Bible*, 1988, Tyndale House Publishers, Inc, Wheaton, Ill. p. 1894

2.   Ibid: p. 1897

3.   Kenneth S. Wuest, *Wuest's Word Studies In The Greek New Testament*, 1953, Wm. B. Eerdmans Publishing Company, Grand Rapids, Michigan, Volume I, The Exegesis of Ephesians, p. 49

4.   The Methodist Hymnal, 1932, 1935, 1939, Whitmore & Smith, Nashville, Tenn. Page 169

PART II

Chapter One

1.   Spiros Zodhiates, The *Hebrew-Greek Key Study Bible,* AMG Publishers, Chattanooga, Tn. 37422, p. 1681

Chapter Four

1.   Lester Sumrall, *Living Faith*, LeSea Publishers, South Bend, Indiana, p.4

2.   W.G. Ketcheson, *Gems of Truth*, Economy Printing Concern, Inc. Berne, Indiana, p.242

3.   Kenneth Hagin, *New Thresholds of Faith*, RHEMA Bible Church, Tulsa, Oklahoma, 1982, p. 8

Chapter Five

1. Source Unknown
2. Spiros Zodhiates, *The Hebrew-Greek Key Study Bible*, AMG Publishers, Chattanooga, TN 37422, Strong's No. 2347, p. 1697
3. Finis Jennings Dake, *Dake's Annotated Reference Bible*, Dake Publishing, Inc, Post Office Box 1050, Lawrenceville, Georgia 30046, p. 336 New Testament.
4. Ibid: p. 993
5. Ibid: p. 1079
6. Albert Orsborn, Tom Jones, *"Let The Beauty Of Jesus Be Seen In Me"* Lillenas Publishing Company, *Lillenas.Com* –Song Finder Summary, 10/1988.

Chapter Six

1. Rev. W. G. Ketcheson, *Gems of Truth*, Economy Printing Concern, Inc. Berne, Indiana,

Chapter Seven

1. Finis Dake, *Dake's Annotated Reference Bible,* Dake Publishing, Inc, P.O. Box 1050, Lawrenceville, Georgia 30046, p. 935
2. James Strong, *Exhaustive Concordance of the Bible*; A Concise Dictionary of the words in The Greek Testament, Abington Press, New York-Nashville, No. 5484, p. 77

PART III

Introduction-- *Kingdom Realities*

1. Spiros Zodhiates, Hebrew-Greek Study Bible, *Greek Dictionary of the New Testament*, AGM Publishers, Chattanooga, TN 37422, U.S.A., No 5046, p. 1733
2. Finis Dake, *Dake's Annotated Reference Bible,* Dake Publishing, Inc. P.O Box 1050, Lawrenceville, Georgia 30046, New Testament, p. 374
3. Ibid: p. 374
4. Spiros Zodhites, Hebrew-Greek Study Bible, *Greek Dictionary of the New Testament*, AGM Publishers, Chattanooga, TN 37422, U.S.A., No 5046, p. 1733

5. Finis Dake, *Dake's Annotated Reference Bible*, Dake Publishing, Inc. P.O Box 1050, Lawrenceville, Georgia 30046, New Testament, p. 380

6. Ibid: p. 9

Chapter Eight

1. E.M. Bounds, *Power Through Prayer*, Zondervan Publishing House, Grand Rapids, Michigan, 1964, p. 35

2. Ibid: pp. 36,37

3. Ibid: p. 36

4. W.G. Ketcheson, *Gem of Truth*, Published by Author, Economy Printing Concern, Inc., Berne, Indiana, p. 64

5. T. M. Anderson, *Prevailing Prayer,* Wilmore Press, Wilmore, Kentucky, p. 7

6. Ibid: p. 10

7. Finis Jennings Dake, *Dake's Annotated Reference Bible*, Dake Publishing, Inc., P.O. Box 1050, Lawrenceville, Georgia 30046, p. 159

Chapter Nine

1. Kenneth Hagin, *Bible Prayer Study Course,* P.O. Box 50126, Tulsa, Oklahoma, 74150, pp. 1-8

Chapter Ten

1. The Herald, *The Lord is in His Holy Temple,* Wilmore Press, Wilmore, Kentucky, May 1976, p. 3

2. *The Methodist Hymnal,* The Methodist Book Concern, Whitmore & Smith, Nashville, Tenn. 1932, 1935, 1939, Hymn No. 4

Chapter Eleven

1. Adapted from *The Power Of His Presence,* "Where Should We Praise God?" Graham Truscott, World Map Press, Burbank, California, 1969, pp. 230-235.

2. Ibid: pp. 238-252.

Chapter Twelve

1. C. S. Lovett, *Dealing With The Devil,* Personal Christianity Chapel, 1981, p. 6

2. W. E. Vine, *An Expository Dictionary Of New Testament* Words, PC Study Bible, Version 5, BIBLESOFT, Seattle, WA

3. H. Orton Wiley, *Christian Theology*, II, p. 73

4. Finis Jennings Dake, *God's Plan for Man,* Dake Bible Sales, Inc. Lawrenceville, Georgia, 1949, p.88

5. Hugh B. Skelton, *Power Encounter (Spiritual Warfare)* Syllabus, pp. 4, 5

6. Spiros Zodhiates, *The Hebrew-Greek Key Study Bible,* AMG Publishers. Chattanooga, TN, 1984, 1985, *Greek Dictionary Of The New Testament* p 9, 32

7. Charles Wesley, *The Methodist Hymnal,* The Methodist Publishing House, Whitmore & Smith, Nashville, Tenn. 1932, 1935, 1939, Page 282

Chapter Thirteen

1. Kenneth Hagin, *A Commonsense Guide to Fasting*, Rhema Bible Church, Tulsa, Oklahoma, 1981, p. 1

2. Finis Jennings Dake, *Dake's Annotated Reference Bible*, Dake Publishing, Inc. P.O. Box 1050, Lawrenceville, Georgia 30046, 1999, p. 1043

3. R.D. Foley, *Biblical Fasting and Prayer*, P.O. Box 328, Waynesboro, Pennsylvania 17268, pp. 12-17

4. Finis Jennings Dake, *Dake's Annotated Reference Bible*, Dake Publishing, Inc. P.O. Box 1050, Lawrenceville, Georgia 30046, 1999, p. 1208

5. Ibid: p. 1208

6. Ibid: p. 1209

7. Ibid: p. 1043

Chapter Fourteen

1. Finis Jennings Dake, *Dakes Annotated Reference Bible*, Dake Publishing, Inc. P.O. Box 1050, Lawrenceville, Georgia, 1999, p. 472 New Testament

2. Ibid: p. 473 New Testament

3. Ibid: p. 473 New Testament

4. Ibid: p. 897 Old Testament

5. Ibid: p. 897 Old Testament

6. Ibid: p. 468 New Testament

7. Ibid: p. 473 New Testament

8. Chas. H. Gabriel, *Melodies of Praise*, No. 94, The Gospel Publishing House, Springfield, Missouri, 1957

- For further information on Christian Persecution--Google U.S. Center for World Missions and Brother Andrew Ministries.

Chapter Fifteen

1. TLB
2. Finnis Jennings Dake, *Gods' Plan for Man*, *The Laws of Prosperity*, Dake publisher, Lawrenceville, Georgia 1949 pp. 217-23

Epilogue

1. *Hymnal of the Methodist Episcopal Church*, Walden & Stowe, Cincinnati, Ohio Copyright 1878 by Nelson & Phillips, New York p. 559.

www.ingramcontent.com/pod-product-compliance
Lightning Source LLC
Chambersburg PA
CBHW080458110426
42742CB00017B/2927